Laurence Turnbull

The advantages and accidents of artificial anæsthesia.

Being a manual of anæsthetic agents, and their modes of administration, considering their relative risk, tests of purity, treatment of asphyxia, spasm of the glottis, syncope, etc

Laurence Turnbull

The advantages and accidents of artificial anæsthesia.
Being a manual of anæsthetic agents, and their modes of administration, considering their relative risk, tests of purity, treatment of asphyxia, spasm of the glottis, syncope, etc

ISBN/EAN: 9783337730260

Printed in Europe, USA, Canada, Australia, Japan

Cover: Foto ©ninafisch / pixelio.de

More available books at **www.hansebooks.com**

THE

ADVANTAGES AND ACCIDENTS

OF

ARTIFICIAL ANÆSTHESIA.

BEING

A MANUAL OF ANÆSTHETIC AGENTS,

AND THEIR

MODES OF ADMINISTRATION,

CONSIDERING

THEIR RELATIVE RISK, TESTS OF PURITY, TREATMENT OF ASPHYXIA, SPASM OF THE GLOTTIS, SYNCOPE, ETC.

BY

LAURENCE TURNBULL, M.D., Ph.G.,

FELLOW OF THE AMERICAN ASSOCIATION FOR THE ADVANCEMENT OF SCIENCE; FORMERLY LECTURER ON CHEMISTRY APPLIED TO THE ARTS, FRANKLIN INSTITUTE; AURAL SURGEON TO JEFFERSON COLLEGE HOSPITAL; VICE-PRESIDENT OF THE MEDICAL SOCIETY OF THE STATE OF PENNSYLVANIA.

WITH TWENTY-FIVE ILLUSTRATIONS.

PHILADELPHIA:
LINDSAY AND BLAKISTON.
1878.

PREFACE.

This little work was originally written by the Author as a Report for a Medical Society, and was subsequently extended to its present form to supply a want that evidently exists at the present day, for a convenient handbook, on the administration of the various anæsthetics, that the practitioner of Medicine or Dentistry can consult to enable him to decide which one he can best employ. Many valuable books have, unquestionably, been written on the subject of anæsthetics, but, as far as the writer's observation extends, none of a practical character have appeared within the last few years. Much useful matter in relation to sulphuric ether, nitrous oxide, and chloroform, employed as anæsthetics, has accumulated within this period, but this valuable information is contained in various monographs, journals, etc., where, associated with what is extraneous, it is unprofitable to the busy practitioner.

The object of this work may be stated to be:—

First. To give in as concise a manner as possible a description of the most available agents that may be successfully and safely employed as anæsthetics.

Second. To present the chief chemical tests of the

purity of each substance considered, with its composition, physical characters, and medical properties.

Third. To exhibit the best methods of administering the various anæsthetics, to give careful directions, and to state the precautions to be taken to avoid risk to the life of the patient.

Fourth. To note the personal experience of the author, his assistants and friends, with the various forms of anæsthetics and inhalers in use, with a selection of the most approved of them; not withholding, however, the objections and experiments of other reliable investigators.

Fifth. To compare the relative mortality from all the anæsthetics now employed, endeavoring to assist the reader in forming a fair and candid opinion on this most important subject, which is now and has for so long a period occupied the attention of the public as well as of the medical profession.

To conclude are added practical hints on Local Anæsthesia, the use of the various Anæsthetics in the practice of medicine; the Medico-Legal Nature and Importance of Anæsthetics; with a brief History of the discovery of Artificial Anæsthesia.

1502 Walnut Street,
March, 1878.

CONTENTS.

INTRODUCTION.

ANÆSTHETICS OF THE ANCIENTS . . . . . . *Page* 13
List of the Principal agents that will produce anæsthetic sleep 16

CHAPTER I.

General anæsthetics—Alcohol—Ether. Mixtures of alcohol and ether. Methylic alcohol for inhalation; mode of action the lightest and least injurious; its resemblance to chloroform. Varieties of ether, chemical tests, and mode of preserving in hot climates. The ordinary method of administering ether: towel, cone, sponge, or bag. Test when the patient is fully under its influence, with cautions in regard to solid food before etherization. The three stages of etherization. Peculiar effects of ether in the first stage; observations by Dr. J. F. B. Flagg. Use of ether in ophthalmic surgery; views of Dr. Carter of London. Ether inhalers—Hawksley, Cheatham, Lente, Allis—Experiments with Dr. Allis' inhaler. Experiments of Dr. D. Webster in Manhattan Eye and Ear Hospital, New York, with the cone of newspaper. Experiments with ether by the late Dr. J. Morgan, of Dublin, with his ether inhaler. Experiments of Mr. Morgan, of London, and Surgeon-Major J. H. Porter with the same form of inhaler. Ether inhalers of Dr. B. W. Richardson, of Dublin, Dr. Angrove and J. T. Clover, of London
Page 17–39

CHAPTER II.

Sulphuric Ether, not altogether free from danger, always gives warning. What to do in case of alarming symptoms when employing ether as an anæsthetic. Use of air, artery forceps, artificial respiration in fainting, inversion of the body and head, application of stimulants, in case of blood, food or ether entering the trachea or bronchi. Statistics in reference to death from ether, Dr. Andrews, of Chicago, Dr. Richardson, of London. Recent cases of reported deaths collected by the writer. Mr. Lawson Tait on the advantages of boiling anhydrous ether. Examination of the Royal Medical Chirurgical Society, of London, into the comparative merits of ether and chloroform.

Experiments with ether, with illustrations, by the sphygmograph, and conclusions by the late Dr. Morgan, of Dublin. Case of apparent failure of the heart's action, during the inhaling of ether, with recovery. Primary and secondary effects of ether. Reports of deaths from ether, by Drs. Holmes, A. Matthewson, G. M. Lowe, Shreve, T. G. Morton, and Saundly. Abstract of the report of the Boston Committee on the alleged dangers from ether. Inflammability of ether. Conclusions of the author in regard to ether . . *Page* 40–64

CHAPTER III.

Mixtures of Ether and Chloroform; Dr. Washington L Atlee on. Death of a lady in Boston under Dr. Eastham, a dental surgeon of that city. Coroner's jury under charge of Dr. Ainsworth. Autopsy by Dr. Fitz, pathologist to the Massachusetts General Hospital. Methylic ether, its safety and best method of employment, by Dr. B. W. Richardson, of London; also Dr. Carter's opinion, and Dr. Jones's, of Cork. Use of bichloride of methylene, by Dr. Spencer Wells, at Samaritan Free Hospital; his doubts about its composition. Dr. Taylor's statement that it is a mixture. Report of five cases of death from this compound. Amylene; introduction and use by Dr. Snow. Bromide of ethyl or hydrobromic ether, chemical composition and properties; experiments with frogs, rabbits, dogs, etc., by "Rabuleau." Mode of preparation Experiments of the writer on frogs and man. Its use in the ear, etc. . . . . *Page* 65–80

CHAPTER IV.

Chloroform, chemical composition, impurities, tests. Recent investigations, by Bowditch, of Boston. Deaths from chloroform in England. Aid of the legislature to stop the employment of chloroform in France. Mode of use in Scotland, by Professor Macleod, with form of apparatus, and all the necessary precautions in case of impending death. Report of twenty-one cases of chloroform administration. Dr. Allis' Chloroform Inhaler. Employment of anæsthetics in labor. M. Pichard. Congress at Geneva. Drs. Lusk, Wilson, and Smith. Statistics of death from chloroform, by the late Dr. Morgan, of Dublin. Dr. Sims on Nélaton's method. Nitrite of amyl as an antidote to chloroform. Observations and cases, by Drs. Richardson, Burrall, Lane, and Mundé. Dr. Clover's inhaler. Mixed narcosis, use of morphia before inhalation of chloroform. Dr. Richardson's experimentation upon reported deaths from chloroform, etc. Conclusions in reference to the use and safety of chloroform, by Drs. Chisholm, Erichsen, and Gross . . . . *Page* 80–111

CHAPTER V.

Original observations and experiments with Hydrate of Chloral. Liebreich on the impurities of chloral in cakes, test of purity, etc. Experiments of Dr. John A. Campbell at Garland Asylum, Carlisle. On chloral as an anæsthetic in children, by Dr. Bouchut, of Paris. M. Couty, of Paris, on death from chloral. Prof. Ore, of Bordeaux, venous injections of chloral. Dr. J. M. Fothergill, of London, on the great utility of strychnia in chloral poisoning. Case of death from the use of chloral, and post-mortem appearances. Drs. Taylor and Tuke's opinions upon the effects of the long-continued use of chloral. The use of chloral for a long period with no serious results. . . *Page* 112–129

CHAPTER VI.

Nitrous oxide gas as an anæsthetic. Practical observations and experiments of Dr. J. D. Thomas. The Thomas inhaler, description and mode of use. Mode of manufacturing nitrous oxide for inhalation. Impurities and mode of purification. Mode of administration Use of *prop* in extracting teeth, while under its influence. Risks, and treatment of accidents. Coxeter's form of cylinder for liquid nitrous oxide. . . . . . *Page* 129–138

CHAPTER VII.

Physiological action of nitrous oxide gas. Resemblance between the effects produced by nitrous oxide and asphyxia. Summary of the facts bearing on this subject. Not merely a passive agent. Dr. Evans' (of Paris) experiments with nitrous oxide and other gases, and his conclusions Dr. J. H. McQuillen's experiments in 1868, and his repeating them in conjunction with the writer. Personal experiments of Dr. Jeannel in 1869; he dwells upon the non-fatal character of nitrous oxide, and the rapidity with which its effects pass away. Also the corroborative experiments of M. Limouzin. Original experiments of Dr. Robert Amory in 1870, with his conclusions, and opinions of Dr. Johnston. Mode of action of anæsthetics. Experiments of Professors Heinrich Ranke and D. C. Binz on morphia, chloral, ether, chloroform, amylene, bromoform, and bromohydrate. Physiological action of nitrous oxide gas, by the editor of "Binz's Therapeutics." List of authorities on the nature and action of chloroform, ether, and nitrous oxide. Deaths from the inhalation of nitrous oxide. Post-mortem changes, etc. . . . . *Page* 139–160

CHAPTER VIII.

J. F. Clover's improved apparatus for the combined use of nitrous oxide gas and ether. On the prevention of accidents from their use, and how to treat them successfully. Dr. F. N. Otis, of New York; his opinion of this inhaler. Death under the administration of nitrous oxide and ether. Sir Henry Thompson, of London; successful use of these agents combined. Inhaler of Codman and Shurtleff, of Boston, for the use of nitrous oxide or ether combined or for each. Dr. J. D. Thomas's experiments with this inhaler. Letter of defence of Codman and Shurtleff. Bonwill's method of anæsthesia produced by rapid breathing of atmospheric air . . . *Page* 161–172

CHAPTER IX.

Ether, its local application in the form of spray. Rhigolene. Dr. Latamendi's new method of utilizing the anæsthetic effects of ether spray. Anæsthetic mixture of ether and camphor. Excision of cancer of the breast by scissor-cutting under ether spray. Extract of eucalyptus as a local anæsthesia in dental operations. Snow, ice, and salt. Carbolic acid. Sulphate of morphia applied to sound skin, also when the epidermis has been removed . . . . *Page* 172–183

CHAPTER X.

An abstract of the therapeutic employment of chloroform and ether, alone and in combination, of chloral hydras, and of butylchloral in practical medicine . . . . . . *Page* 183–195

CHAPTER XI.

Medico-legal relations of anæsthetics. Case in Philadelphia of a surgeon dentist. The important question, whether chloroform can be administered for criminal purposes; cases in France, England, and the United States. Dr. N. L. Folsom, R. M. Denig. Ethers as poisons. Experiments of A. Martin Ewald, Hitzig, C. Bernard and Binz. Ether intoxication. *Chloroform; its action as a poison*, with the treatment . . . . *Page* 195–207

APPENDIX.

DISCOVERY OF THE ART OF ARTIFICIAL ANÆSTHESIA . *Page* 208

ARTIFICIAL ANÆSTHESIA.

INTRODUCTION.

ANÆSTHETICS OF THE ANCIENTS.

THE ancient Greeks, it is stated, possessed a plant called mandrake. It belonged to the same family of plants as the belladonna, or deadly nightshade. From the root of this plant was extracted, by means of wine, a narcotic which was employed by them as an anæsthetic. Lucius Apuleius, who lived about 160 A. D., and of whose works eleven editions were republished in the fourteenth and fifteenth centuries, says "that if a man has to have a limb mutilated, sawn, or burnt, he may take half an ounce of mandragora wine, and whilst he sleeps the member may be cut off without pain or sense." To prove that this was true, Dr. B. W. Richardson, of London, after a lapse of five centuries, obtained a fine specimen of mandragora root, and made mandragora wine, and tested it, and found it was a narcotic, having precisely the properties that were anciently ascribed to it. He found that in animals it would produce even the sleep of Juliet, not for thirty or forty hours, a term that must be accepted as a poetical license, but easily for the four hours named by Dioscorides, and, on awakening, there was an excitement which tallied with the same phenomenon that was observed by the older physicians. Another fact was noticed by the ancients, that many volatile substances acted more promptly by inhalation than by the stomach, and this form of medication was employed in Greece, Rome, and Arabia. By their published works, the knowledge of these facts was extended to other parts of the world.

In China, in ancient times, the word *ma-yo* meant not

only Indian hemp, but anæsthetic medicine; other substances besides hemp entered into these benumbing recipes, such as the datura, a solanaceous plant, probably identical with the atropia mandragora; also aconite, hyoscyamus, etc. Some of these drugs form constituents of the formula said to be employed by kidnappers of children, and robbers, and are therefore naturally forbidden in China, at the present, to be sold or employed.

The Indian hemp, under the name *bhang*, was extensively used by the Mohammedans and others in Central Asia. The most wonderful properties are ascribed to it. "Taken in excess, the spirits and demons may be seen; it confers prophetic powers; it is sometimes taken by persons wishing to indulge in spiritualism, and it is used as an antidote to forgetfulness." (Dudgeon).

A strong impulse was given to the study and application of the "different kinds of airs and gases" by the discovery of oxygen by Priestley and Scheele, in the middle of the last century, and numerous experiments were made by physicians with it. Another still more practical result was obtained by Sir Humphry Davy, and published in 1800. "That nitrous oxide appears capable of destroying physical pain, and may be used with advantage during surgical operations." This valuable and practical suggestion remained without fruit for a long time, and the surgeons, physicians, and accoucheurs still employed alcohol, in some form, or opium and its salts, to deaden as far as possible the sensibility to pain during their various operations. It was not until 1844 that an effort was made in the United States to make Davy's discovery useful. But the crowning result was obtained in 1846 by Dr. Morton in the Massachusetts General Hospital, where it was demonstrated successfully that the inhalation of "ether" was capable of so deadening the sensibility of the nervous system, that any operation, no matter how painful, could be performed, and the patient not suffer from its effects. It was also proven that ether was safe, and not at all like the wine of that insane root which, says Macbeth,

"Takes the reason prisoner.
And in this borrow'd likeness of shrunk death
Thou shalt remain full two and forty hours."

This most valuable agent required but to be inhaled for a few minutes, when the patient, being in a pleasant frame of mind, would thus remain asleep, and after a more or less prolonged operation, " would awake and inquire if the diseased limb were still there, and could be told that the offending member was gone without his knowledge."

No one can form, even at the present day, a just estimate of the true value of the various anæsthetics, or express in words their wonderful and extended application to the relief of human suffering.

To the general surgeon it gives the opportunity of operating on grave cases of disease and injury, without which the death of the patient would be inevitable. It also affords, by the immediate relief from pain, the power to manipulate the broken or injured parts with facility, and thus obtain a correct diagnosis in the most obscure diseases and painful accidents.

To the obstetrician and gynæcologist it is useful in assuaging the terrific pain of labor, and makes the dreaded instruments a blessing in disguise. In the diagnoses and treatment of abdominal diseases, it gives precision and almost marvellous results, and in the removal of large masses or tumors great freedom from the dreadful effects of shock to the nervous system. For the ophthalmic surgeon the anæsthetic reduces the sensibility of the eye so that it can be touched with impunity, and severe and dangerous operations can be performed upon this delicate and sensitive organ without pain and with much less risk.

Again, in the removal of foreign bodies from the eye or ear, particularly in children, by the use of the anæsthetic all spasm is relieved, and the act is accomplished without injury. The profound sleep gives a most favorable opportunity to the aural surgeon to perforate the membrana tympani, cut the minute tendon of the tensor tympani muscle, or perforate the mastoid cells.

There are some thirty substances which are of so volatile a character, that they can be employed in producing anæsthesia.

The following is a

List of the principal agents that will produce anæsthetic sleep:—

Nitrous oxide gas.
Carbonic oxide gas.*
Carbonic acid gas.
Bisulphide of carbon.
Light carburetted hydrogen
  (Hydride of methyl, or marsh gas.)
Methylic alcohol.
Methylic ether gas.
Chloride of methyl gas.
Bichloride of methylene.
Terchloride of formyl, or chloroform.
Tetrachloride of carbon.
Heavy carburetted hydrogen gas.
  (Olefiant gas or ethylene.)
Ethylic. or absolute ether.
  (Sulphuric ether.)
Chloride of ethyl.
Bichloride of ethylene.
  (Dutch liquid.)
Bromide of ethyl, or hydrobromic ether.
Hydride of amyl.
Amylene.
Benzol.
Turpentine spirit.

Those anæsthetics which are employed in the practice of medicine may be reduced in number at the present day to about four or five, namely—alcohol, ether, chloroform, and nitrous oxide. These can be employed alone or mixed in various proportions. They can be reduced to a still smaller number, viz., nitrous oxide gas, and alcohol of various grades of power, as each of the eleven alcohols will by the chemical action of an acid produce its ether or chloroform.

---

* Carbonic oxide has been used as a local anæsthetic to cancerous or raw surfaces; but, when inhaled, it is a powerful narcotic poison. Owing to its superior affinity, it displaces the oxygen in the red blood-corpuscles, and unfits them for the functions of respiration.

CHAPTER I.

General anæsthetics—Alcohol—Ether. Mixtures of alcohol and ether. Methylic alcohol for inhalation; mode of action the lightest and least injurious; its resemblance to chloroform. Varieties of ether, chemical tests, and mode of preserving in hot climates. The ordinary method of administering ether: towel, cone, sponge, or bag. Test of the patient when fully under its influence, with cautions in regard to solid food before etherization. The three stages of etherization. Peculiar effects of ether in the first stage; observations by Dr. J. F. B. Flagg. Use of ether in ophthalmic surgery; views of Dr. Carter of London. Ether inhalers—Hawksley, Cheatham, Lente, Allis—Experiments with Dr. Allis' inhaler. Experiments of Dr. D. Webster in Manhattan Eye and Ear Hospital, New York, with the cone of newspaper. Experiments with ether by the late Dr. J. Morgan, of Dublin, with his ether inhaler. Experiments of Mr. Morgan, of London, and Surgeon-Major J. H. Porter with the same form of inhaler. Ether inhalers of Dr. B. W. Richardson, of Dublin, Dr. Angrove and J. T. Clover, of London.

IT has long been recognized as a fact, that, when persons are under the controlling influence of alcohol, either in the form of wine, gin, whiskey, or brandy, they may be cut, bruised, or even have their bones broken, without expressing, or experiencing, much, if any, pain. Alcohol was very early employed by surgeons to produce immunity from the pain of the knife, long before any true anæsthetic was discovered. Indeed we find that a small portion of brandy or whiskey given prior to the administration of any anæsthetic agent is found to facilitate the action of the agent employed.

Dr. John Lynk* predicts that alcohol will, by the close of the next decade, rank first as an anæsthetic. He states that he has long employed it in this capacity, and he is gradually learning to appreciate it more and more, until he now depends upon it almost entirely in his surgical operations. He has not as yet tried it in a capital operation,

---
* Cincinnati Lancet and Observer, May, 1876.

but has employed it, in the proportion of about one pint, for a strong adult, in tablespoonful doses every twenty minutes in an amputation of the finger, extraction of teeth, in a case of severance of the posterior tibial nerve, with the use of chloroform; also ligation of radial and ulnar artery, in which he only used two drachms of chloroform, and one pint of whiskey. This latter operation he thinks served to demonstrate the value of the whiskey as an anæsthetic, leaving the other functions, especially the heart, in a more normal condition than by the chloroform alone, which, he states, was proven by the strong pulsations of the heart after the chloroform had been withdrawn.

A mixture of chloroform and alcohol, known as the compound spirit of chloroform of the London Pharmacopœia, has been employed by many other surgeons with more or less success. Another mixture is employed at Guy's Hospital, when chloroform is not well borne, by first bringing the patient under the influence of the chloroform and then keeping up the anæsthetic effects by inhaling the following mixture:—

  R. Alcohol,   f ʒj.
    Chloroform, f ℥ij.
    Sulphuric ether, f ℥iij.—M.

The late Dr. E. Sansom preferred a mixture of—

  R Chloroform,   f ℥ij.
   (Absolute alcohol), f ℥ij.—M.

By careful experimenting with these and various combinations of chloroform and alcohol, I have always found, that, when such mixture was poured upon an inhaler, the most volatile spirit will arise first, then the next, and so on, leaving the least easily evaporated upon the inhaler; this fact should always be borne in mind: that in all these compounds we must employ all the precautions to be observed in the use of chloroform alone.

Methylic Alcohol.

Ordinary alcohol is an organic radical called ethyl, which is obtained by the distillation of rye, barley, or wheat whiskey. Thus obtained it is a clear liquid containing more or less water, which, by redistillation in conjunction with lime, becomes what is known as absolute alcohol. There are two other alcohols which are found in commerce, one called methylic, and the second amylic alcohol. The methylic alcohol is obtained by the dry distillation of *wood*, and the amylic by the distillation of *potatoes*. They are both used for adulteration and for commercial purposes. Methylic alcohol, pyroxic spirit, or wood spirit, as this has been differently called, has been known for about sixty-two years, and when analyzed by Messrs. Dumas and Peligot, it was found to contain 37.5 per cent. of carbon, 12.5 per cent. of hydrogen, and 50 per cent. of oxygen. When pure it remains clear in the atmosphere. It has an aromatic smell and taste, with slight acidity, and boils at 140° Fahr. According to the experiments of Dr. B. W. Richardson, of London, this alcohol, owing to its volatile nature, may be exhibited freely by inhalation, in the same manner that chloroform is administered. It then enters the blood by being carried with the air that is inspired into the pulmonary tract, and thus into the air vesicles. Here it is absorbed into the circulation by the minute bloodvessels which make their way from the heart through the lungs, and which ramify upon the vesicles. By administrating the vapor of methylic alcohol in this way, its effects are rapidly developed, for it condenses quickly in the blood, is carried rapidly into the left side of the heart, and thence is distributed by the arteries over the whole body, as quickly as can be condensed and absorbed.

This alcohol is recommended by Dr. Richardson, and he has obtained better results from its use than from the heavier or ethylic spirit. It is much more rapid in its action, and much less prolonged in its effects than common alcohol, and, what is of more importance, it demands the least possible ultimate expenditure of animal force for its elimination from the body. According to the same authority the lighter the alcohol therefore, *cæteris paribus*, the less injurious its action. When inhaled, its effects are developed in four distinct stages.

First stage, there is excitement, flushing of the body,

and dilatation of the pupils, after a time there follows languor, and the muscular movements become irregular.

Second stage, muscular prostration, and labored breathing, attended by deep sighing movements and rolling over of the body.

Third stage, complete insensibility to pain, with unconsciousness to all external objects, with inability to exert any voluntary muscular power. The breathing now becomes embarrassed and blowing, with bronchial râles, due to the passage of air through fluid that has accumulated in the finer bronchial passages. The heart and lungs, however, even in this stage, retain their functions, and therefore recovery will take place if the conditions for it be favorable. Also, if the body be touched or irritated in parts, there will be a response of motion, not from any knowledge or consciousness, but from reflex action. During all these stages there is no violent convulsive action, but step by step a reduction of temperature, so at last the loss of heat will become dangerous, for the cool body cannot throw off the water freely, and therefore fluid collects in the lungs and there is a risk of suffocation, as from drowning. If the administration of the methylic spirit be continued when the third degree has been reached, there is a last stage, which is that of death. The two remaining nervous centres which feed the heart and respiration cease simultaneously to act, and all motion is over. If, however, after the third stage of insensibility, the administration of methylic spirit be stopped, recovery from the insensibility and prostration will invariably take place *on one condition*, that the body be kept warm for seven hours.*

There is but little doubt that this sudden reduction of temperature is one cause of death after the administration of ether and chloroform. The patient is apparently all right, and is transferred to the ward from the warm operating room, no special means are employed to keep up the temperature, and gradually the patient sinks into an unconscious state, from the fluid which collects, and dies from congestion of the lungs, the result of neglect.

* On Alcohol. A course of six Canton Lectures, delivered before the Society of Arts (London, 1875, by Benj. W. Richardson, M.A., M.D., F.R.S).

By the action of acids upon the alcohols, causing the dehydration or removal of the water which they contain, various ethers are formed.

ETHER—ETHYL OXIDE (C_4H_5O—$C_4H_{10}O$). PURITY AND CHEMICAL TESTS.

The ordinary ether sold has a specific gravity of 0.750; when shaken with an equal quantity of water it loses $\frac{1}{6}$ of its volume. *Ether fortior* should have a sp. gr. of 0.728, and will not, when shaken with an equal bulk of water, lose more than $\frac{1}{8}$ of its volume. If pure, ether will not redden litmus paper.

The specific gravity of chemically pure ether is 0.713 —0.725, and its boiling point 95° F. A test tube filled with it and held in the warm hand, should boil on the addition of fragments of broken glass. In hot countries, like India and our own, or in the close wards of a hospital, if preserved in imperfectly stoppered bottles, ether will absorb oxygen, and forms acetic acid, and becomes impure, mixing with water in large proportions; unsuitable for inhalation.

Ether does not mix with water, but is slightly soluble in it; it mixes readily with alcohol.*

The ordinary method in use of administration of the first discovered anæsthetic, namely, washed sulphuric ether, is as follows:—

An inhaler is made by folding a towel into a large cone or bag, and then placing a coarse sponge in its apex. Ether is then poured upon it with a free hand— half an ounce or more at a time—and repeated as necessary by removing the cone from the patient's mouth to

---

* The ether which is most generally employed in Philadelphia, and, indeed, throughout the United States, is that manufactured by the reliable firm of Powers & Weightman, and it is uniformly of most excellent quality. Occasionally the ether of Dr. Squibb, of Brooklyn, N. Y., is resorted to; it is of higher price and is freer from water, and, we think, is more apt to produce irritation if used too freely; this can be obviated by moistening with warm water the sponge cone, or inhaling apparatus. If in doubt about the purity of your ether, agitate it with lime-water and then decant it before using.

renew the supply of ether. The lower part of the face, mouth, and nose is covered with the cone so as to exclude most of the air, and allow the patient to fill his lungs with more or less diluted ether vapor, depending on the care with which the cone is applied. There will be, at the beginning of the inhalation, attempts to struggle, on account of the irritating nature of the ether, which are to be gently, but firmly restrained, using as little force as possible, and only one or two inspirations of pure air allowed; subsequently complete quiescence usually follows, and the patient passes into a profound state of insensibility. If, however, the face become livid or very pale, the cone is lifted entirely away for a time until this condition disappears. In delicate persons, it is well to notice any unusual slowness or intermittence in the condition of the pulse. One of the best tests of the patient being fully under the influence of the ether, is when the conjunctival surface of the eye can be touched with impunity, and the arm can be raised and will fall as if paralyzed. Dr. Snow states that he found the eye sensible to light in all stages of etherization.

Ether should not be inhaled immediately after a full meal, indeed it is better to take only a biscuit or cracker and a glass of wine or a teaspoonful of brandy and water, or a scruple of bromide of potassium in water, half an hour before, always avoiding the risk and annoyance of a full stomach for several hours previously. Nothing like hard boiled eggs, ham, or beef should ever be allowed a feeble patient before inhalation for twenty-four hours. If nourishment is necessary, let it be of a liquid character, as solid food, not digested, has been the cause of death in more than one person.

Perfect quiet should be enjoined on all around the patient, as noises, or even loud talking, interfere with the perfect and rapid action of the anæsthetic. Nothing like a tight band or garment should prevent the free action of the throat, chest, or interfere with the muscles of respiration. False teeth should always be laid aside until after the inhalation is over.

It is always well to bear in mind that there are three well-marked stages of etherization: 1. That of muscular relaxation; 2, tetanic or slight convulsive action; 3, complete loss of sensibility, with snoring, and muscular motion; unless this latter stage is reached there is not full insensibility to pain.

A peculiar effect of etherization, which has been early noticed and published* by a careful writer and experimenter of this city, Dr. J. F. B. Flagg, and which result has been confirmed by us and by others, is stated as follows:—

"There is a particular point of etherization, which, if improved at the moment (slight operations can be performed) will leave the patient in full possession of all his faculties with the single exception of the *sense of pain*, and particularly the consciousness of *touch* is as acute as under ordinary circumstances, if not quickened."

In our own experiments the sense of sound was always very active, and Dr. Thomas takes advantage of this by having a musical box playing during the action of nitrous oxide, so as to make a pleasant impression on the patient. If, however, the patient is roused from his first anæsthetic sleep by the pain of the knife, or a sudden noise, or a rough touch, we have always found it more difficult to cause such a patient to pass into a profound state of insensibility by means of the ether. Yet, if a patient will not breathe the ether properly when it is required for an operation, it will sometimes do good to prick or scratch the surface with a knife and then insist upon the patient breathing the ether so as to get rid of the pain. Some patients suffer at the time from tinnitus aurium, or buzzing noises in the ear, and some have these symptoms some days after etherization.

Almost all American surgeons employ ether in the various operations, even for the most delicate, viz., on the eye and ear. In Great Britain and Ireland, the surgeons for a time employed chloroform to the almost entire exclusion of ether, but within the last few years the subject of the greater danger in the use of chloroform has excited much attention, and many of them have changed their views since the visit of Dr. B. J. Jeffries, of

---

* Ether and Chloroform. Their employment in surgery, dentistry, midwifery, therapeutics, etc. By J. F. B. Flagg, M.D., Surgeon Dentist. Philadelphia, Lindsay & Blakiston, 1851, p. 89.

Boston, during the International Ophthalmological Congress in London, 1872.* Dr. Carter, the distinguished ophthalmic surgeon of St. George's Hospital, London, has, he states, since that time employed ether with perfectly satisfactory results as regards the (spasm) of the muscles, and without the appearance of any symptoms to indicate a possibly prejudicial action. In lieu of the folded napkin, he has substituted for some time a cone of thick felt covered with water-proof tissue.

He also states that he has employed with success the "*Hawksley Inhaler.*" It consists of "a glass vessel capable of holding ten ounces of ether, with an inlet valve for air, and its sliding tube is graduated in ounces for the purpose of measuring the quantity of ether consumed. A pipe conveys the vapor to the face-piece, the edge of which is surrounded by a water cushion to secure exact adaptation. There is also a shutter valve for regulating the admission of air, either at the beginning of an operation or during its course. It has also an additional pipe, furnished with a valve, which conveys the expired vapor to the floor." This latter is a useful addition, when employed in a hospital where a large number of patients are to be etherized in succession, so that the ether is not diffused in the air around the operator. When in use, the vessel in which the ether is contained is immersed in water, heated to 100°, which promotes a more rapid and equable evaporation of the ether. "Ether boils at about 90°; but before the quantity contained in the vessel has reached that point, the temperature of the surrounding water will have fallen." This is a valuable inhaler; it is too complicated for every-day use by the physician or surgeon, but will be found very useful in large hospitals, and cause a great saving in the amount of ether employed.

* Re-introduction of Ether into England. By B. Joy Jeffries, M. D. Reprinted from "Boston Medical Journal" of October 3d, 1872.

Cheatham's Ether Inhaler.

This operates by Lente's method of replenishing the evaporating surface without removing it from the face. A patient cannot be etherized as quickly with it as with the common cone, but with much less ether, and by it you avoid the disagreeable effects of having the ether permeating every part of the office or house in which it is used. Its convenience of application is also quite obvious. The ease with which the face-piece (being paper) can be removed immediately after use and thrown away is, I think, a strong recommendation in its favor.

The apparatus consists of a tin cup (Fig. 1, A) holding

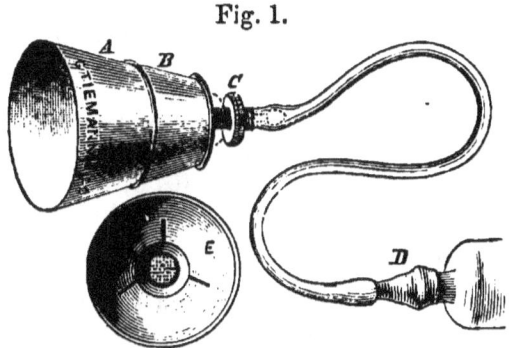

Fig. 1.

in the inside a sponge as an evaporating surface, and connected from the top by rubber tubing with the bottle that contains the anæsthetic. This tube has attached to its distal end a cap, D, that will fit over the neck of almost any bottle, thus doing away with Lente's graduated bottle.

Mode of using the Inhaler.—Make a cone of paper, cut the top off, so, when the tin cup, A, is slipped inside the top of the cup, it will protrude a line or two from the top of cone. Place tin cup, B, over both cup and cone, screw it down tightly by means of nut, C, and you have the cone held tightly. Attach tube to top of cup, and the apparatus is complete. The smaller the cone, the more quickly you can get the patient under the influence of the anæsthetic. I would suggest after the cone is in position, the bottom should be trimmed, leaving a part of it (we shall call it the back part) that is intended to go over the chin, three inches longer than the cup, and sloping forwards and upwards, leaving the front part, intended to go over the nose, about an inch longer than cup. E gives an inside view of cup, A.

These various forms of Inhalers are made by George Tiemann & Co. of New York; also Gemrig, Snowden, or Kolbe, instrument makers, of this city, and by Codman & Shurtliff, of Boston.

Dr. Lente's Ether Inhaler.

As early as 1866, Dr. Lente invented a form of inhaler, but which has recently been modified (see Fig. 2). The present improved instrument resembles very much the face piece of "Waldenburg's" apparatus for the inhalation of condensed and rarefied air. The idea of using sheet brass and the india-rubber air-cushion was taken from it. The air-cushion, however, proved a failure, and the inventor substituted hair for stuffing the cushion, which he states retains sufficient of its rotundity to fit the face airtight.

Fig. 2.

Mode of employing this form of Inhaler.—A piece of sheet lint is stuffed into the cone, a piece of wire or whalebone is slipped in, so as to keep the lint in place and prevent its touching the face. The lint is saturated with ether and placed over the face. There is an opening, fitted with a cork stopper at the apex, large enough to admit air. This is usually closed, but, if it is found necessary, the stopper can be removed. The ether can be poured in at this opening without removing the apparatus from the patient's face. Its cleanliness is perfect, as a different piece of lint ought to be employed each time. My assistant at Howard Hospital has experimented with this form of apparatus, and found it satisfactory in administering ether as an anæsthetic.

Dr. Allis' Ether Inhaler.

In operations upon the eye and ear in the same institution, the inhaler we have chiefly employed is that designed by our colleague, Dr. O. H. Allis, of this city, whose experience in this department, both in the use of ether and chloroform, has made him an authority on the subject. The apparatus has been described and exhibited before our various medical societies (see Fig. 3). It consists of a wire frame work sufficiently large to cover the lower part of the face; these wires are parallel and about one-quarter of an inch apart. Between the wires, and from side to side, a strip of muslin bandage, two and a half inches wide and three yards long, is passed (see Fig. 5). The wire frame is five inches long and three inches at its greatest width. Outside of the wire frame there is a covering of sheet brass, and over this a patent leather cover, with a cushioned edge to fit, over the face, covering both the nose and mouth.

Fig. 3.

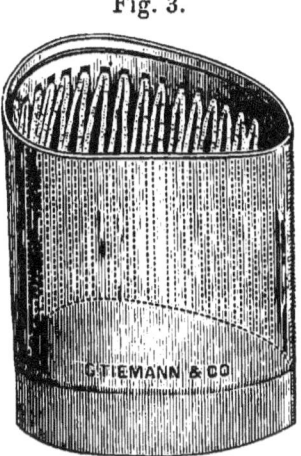

When ready for use the top is left open for the free entrance of air and for supplying the ether from without.

Each section of the bandage is separated from the adjoining one, thus permitting the air and ether to pass freely on both sides of it. The ether is supplied from a bottle with a glass dropper.

Placing the apparatus over the face, a small portion of ether is gradually dropped at a time until deep inspirations are noticed, when it is poured in, and, in doing so, we should be careful to watch it so as not to irritate the larynx.

The objections to this form of apparatus are: 1st. That the exhaled vapor is not conveyed to the floor, but is diffused in the air, to be breathed by the operator and his assistants. For a single operation, this is not of much importance, but where there are a number of cases the arrangement is not conducive to the comfort of the operator.

2d. The bandage of muslin across the bottom becomes clogged with saliva, and at times by discharges from the stomach, and cannot be readily removed.

3d. Owing to the peculiar arrangement of the muslin strips, it is tedious and difficult to remove or replace them.

In a conversation with Dr. Allis, he stated that he considered the chief merit of his instrument was, that it thoroughly and instantaneously liberated the ether, and that while there was not the least impediment to respiration, yet all the air was impregnated with the anæsthetic.

Neither ether nor chloroform can be inhaled in the pure state.

It is always atmospheric air, impregnated with the anæsthetic, that sustains life and produces anæsthesia.

The expressions "give him nothing but ether, exclude the air," are only relative terms; they simply mean *saturate the air as much as possible with the ether. Permit* the patient to have *no fresh air*, but *compel* him to breathe *air charged with ether.*

Now, in Allis' apparatus there is no chance for the ether to remain in its fluid state, but exposed as it is on a thin stratum of muslin, it yields its anæsthetic principle promptly.

When he first employed his instrument, bystanders would suggest that it be closed at the top, so as to permit no escape of ether.

This will show that the true laws of ether were overlooked; ether-vapor, while it will diffuse itself throughout an entire room, is of greater specific gravity than atmospheric air and tends to the floor.

To close this apparatus at the top, would necessitate ingress of air at the part surrounding the mouth, for air *must* be admitted.

If it be excluded at the bottom and left open at the

top, the advantage of having a constant supply of ether dropping upon the folds is very great.

Some suggested that the frozen moist vapor that is seen at the top of the instrument indicates a waste of ether, but the small quantity used and the rapidity with which anæsthesia can be effected, are complete refutations of this.

The untidiness can be entirely avoided with a little care.

The instruments are now completed with a little drawslip, the suggestion of Dr. W. W. Keen.

This can be easily withdrawn, and a clean one substituted.

Dr. Allis' mode of using it is, first, to apply directly to the mouth and nose, but as soon as the first indications of anæsthesia present themselves, he places a single fold of a coarse towel directly over the mouth and nose, and over this reapplies the apparatus.

Ether and chloroform cause vomiting, hence both necessitate the precaution of a basin and a towel, and if these are provided at the outset there will be less confusion, delay, and annoyance from troublesome emesis, at the critical moment of the operation.

In regard to the trouble of removing and replacing the bandage, this certainly can be said, the operator can do it all himself, and does not require skilled labor to do it for him, by sewing the end of the bandage to a card and slipping it through in a few moments.

Improvements have been made in this apparatus, by Mr. Snowden, of this city, which will be seen by the new illustrations even without a more minute description. Fig. 4 shows the frame-work of metal, before applying the bandage, Fig. 5 exhibits the mode of passing in the strip of muslin so as to give the large surface, yet not permitting the bandage to come together when wet with the ether. Fig. 6 shows the completed inhaler with its covering of patent leather arranged for use, and the drawing strings to draw it together if necessary. Fig. 7 shows the mode of using the completed apparatus, its application to the patient's mouth being protected by a towel or napkin placed across the chest in case of sickness of stomach, the mode of holding the inhaler and the use of the dropper, so that the inhaler is not removed from the patient's mouth when once placed there,

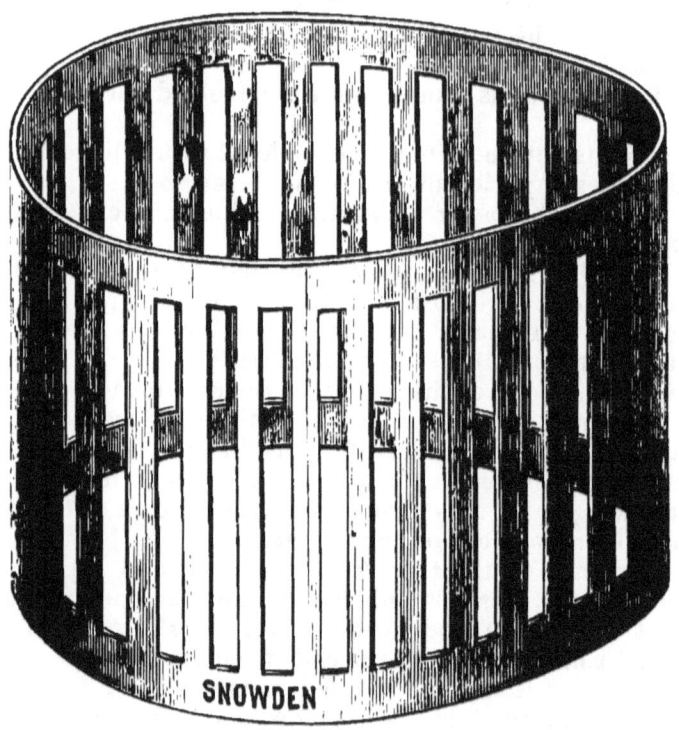

and yet the large evaporating surface is kept moist all the time until the patient is fully under its influence.

Dr. G. H. Coburn, late resident physician of Howard Hospital, carefully recorded all the cases at my request occurring during the years 1875-6, in which this form of Allis' inhaler was employed in the various surgical operations performed in the institution. It was found by him that the shortest time required to produce complete anæsthesia in a young female patient was three minutes, and the amount of ether employed was only one fluidounce. The longest period required in an adult female was seven minutes, and the amount of ether used two ounces and a half. The doctor did not notice in any of the cases but slight redness of the eyes. In a few instan-

Fig. 5.

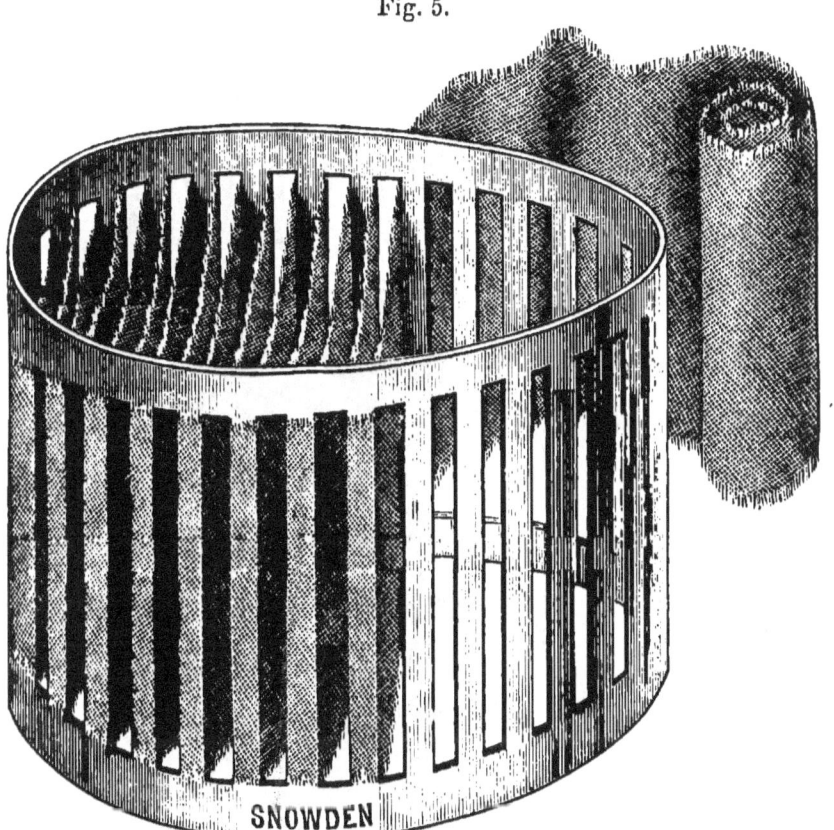

ces there was a hysterical tendency among the females. If solid food had been taken, occasional vomiting would follow, but after liquid or light forms of nourishment, vomiting was very rare, not more than one in fifty cases. In *temperate* males the time for full anæsthesia was from five and a half to eight minutes; ether consumed, minimum quantity, two ounces, maximum, three ounces. In one hundred cases of the administration of ether by

Dr. David Webster,[*] in the Manhattan Eye and Ear Hospital, New York, the average length of time occu-

Fig. 6.

pied in producing anæsthesia (with a newspaper cone lined with a towel) was 5.84 minutes. The shortest

[*] New York Medical Journal, August, 1872, p. 153.

time recorded, one and a half minutes, which was in the case of a child; the longest was twenty minutes, in

Fig. 7.

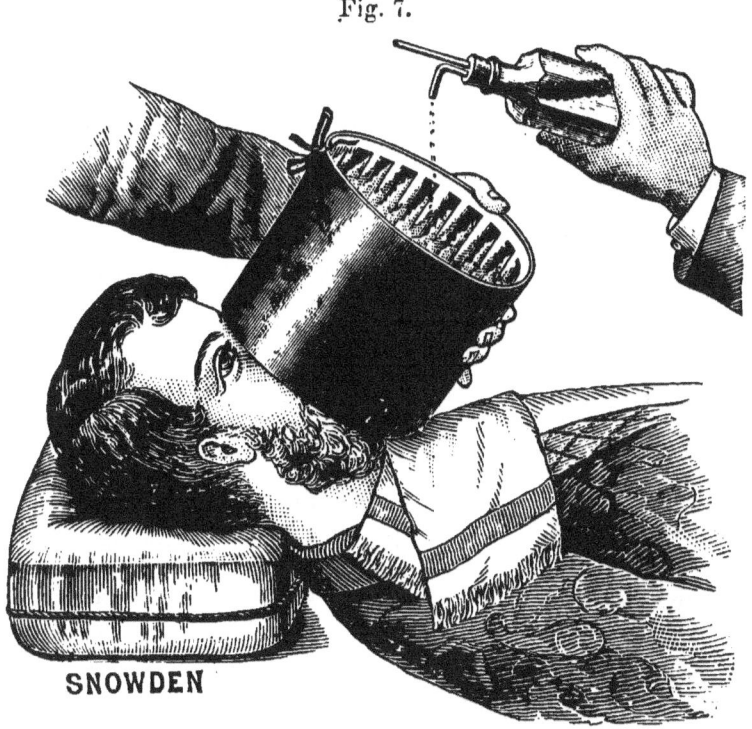

which case the patient acted badly, the ether having to be "let up" from time to time, in consequence of his becoming asphyxiated. Vomiting occurred in forty-two per cent. of the cases. The quantity of ether consumed was not noted. The doctor observes, "That the cone of newspaper should be *short*, so as to be as little as possible in the way and in the light. It should be *thick*, so as not to be easily saturated with ether; for when the paper is wet through it cannot be made to retain its proper shape, but has an *unpleasant tendency to collapse* and *asphyxiate the patient by direct contact with his nose.*"

Of thirty patients, the last which the late Dr. J. Morgan, of Dublin, etherized by means of his inhaler, sickness of the stomach occurred only in *two*, and in these instances food had been taken one hour and a half before operating. The inhaler invented by this distinguished advocate of the use of ether, was a round box, filled with cotton, with a glass cover and an india rubber diaphragm at the top of the instrument moving at each respiration. The ether was inhaled through a flexible tube, to which is attached a mouthpiece to fit over the face. When about being used, pour in gradually two fluidounces of sulphuric ether, of s. g. 0.720 for an adult, but proportionately less for a child, and apply the mouthpiece so as to include the mouth and nose. Should the patient not yield in four or five minutes, pour in gradually another two ounces, as more will seldom be required.

Dr. Morgan has comparatively tested the cone and sponge with the inhaler, and finds that the time is not only much longer in the first form of apparatus, but the effects also far less satisfactory both as to the temporary and after condition of the patient.

Mr. Morgan, Surgical Registrar at St. George's Hospital, London, has suggested a modification of the felt cone ordinarily in use in this and other hospitals in England.

"The instrument consists of a cone of felt, in the apex of which a piece of sponge is fixed, on which the ether is poured. This is fitted into a case of metal surrounded by an outer one of similar shape, but sufficiently large to leave a space between them through which the expired air can freely circulate before it escapes. There are two valves, acting in opposite directions: one admitting the air, which passes through the sponge moistened with ether; the other, through which it escapes into the chamber between the two metal cones. The close application of the instrument to the face is secured by means of the india-rubber cushion, which is filled with air by the tap, so that all the air inspired must pass through the valve. The warmth produced by the air which circulates between the two cones prevents the ether on the sponge from freezing, and the vapor which escapes is carried off by a tube to any distance which may be desired. The quantity of ether required in this apparatus is much smaller than in the ordinary cone; and the advantage it thus possesses, as well as the safety and freedom from ether-vapor obtained by the administrator, render it superior to other similar apparatus. Several American surgeons, whose knowledge and experience of ether are generally recognised, have expressed considerable approbation of this invention. It is manufactured and sold by Messrs. Blaise & Co., 67 St. James's Street."

The following results* were obtained by the use of Morgan's inhaler.

Report of Experiments with Ether in 21 and 26 Cases.†

	Minutes.	Seconds.
Shortest time taken to place a patient under the anæsthetic influence	3	30
Longest time	24	0
Average time	8	10
Average time under influence	19	6
Smallest quantity of ether used in one case	2 ounces	4 drachms.
Largest	9 "	
Average	5 "	1 "

Vomiting occurred in 11 cases during or after the administration of the drug. Excitement occurred in 7 cases to a marked degree during or after administration of the drug. (Does our experimenter mean resistance as excitement, or, if in a female, hysterical excitement?) The anæsthetic was invariably given on an empty stomach. The ether was given by Morgan's inhaler. Ether analyzed and found to be perfectly pure, s. g. 720.2 at 64° Fah.

Ether Inhaler of Dr. Richardson.

In 1873 Dr. B. Willis Richardson,‡ of Dublin, designed and employed a simple form of ether inhaler for use in

---

* Those who have used both the English and American ethers state that the former gives less favorable results than our washed ether, æther fortior, U. S. P.

† By Surgeon-Major Porter, Assistant Professor of Military Surgery. London: 1875.

‡ Description and Illustration of an Ether Inhaler, etc. By B. W. Richardson, F.R.C.S.I. John Falconer, Dublin, 1873.

hospital practice. The ether box, of metal, has a capacity of three ounces, with an oval air-opening half an inch long, and about an eighth of an inch from its upper margin. By rotating the lid, which has a similar shaped opening in its side, the admission of air can be easily regulated. At the beginning of the inhalation, the inner opening may be fully exposed and gradually covered. The ether box communicates with the face-piece by means of a tube an inch in length and one inch and a half in diameter, the ether-box opening of the tube being two-thirds closed by a fixed diaphragm. This prevents the fluid ether from passing into the tube when the patient is in the horizontal position. The face-piece opening of the tube has a diameter of one inch. The tube itself, in order to increase the evaporating surface, should be nearly filled with soft cotton candlewick, having, when in use, one end submerged in the fluid ether. The inhaler may be made of silvered copper or of block-tin, but the margin of face-piece should be formed of flexible metal and covered with morocco leather.

"This inhaler the inventor states to be simple in form and moderate in price, and designed as a substitute for the towel and sponge, in the use of which there is much waste of ether, a matter in hospital economy that may be of some importance."

Dr. Richardson has employed and prefers anhydrous sulphuric ether, because it was found to produce the most rapid anæsthesia.

Dr. Angrove's Handy Ether Inhaler.*

This gentleman states that in England there is a great want felt just at present for an effective, handy and cheap inhaler. He has endeavored to supply this want. His inhaler "consists of a cylinder, on which fits, by a bayonet joint, a cap, around the rim of which are attached several stout wires. The top of the cap is perforated with holes, and through the middle is inserted a long metal tube reaching nearly to the bottom of the cylinder.

---

* The Description of a Handy Ether Inhaler. By W. T. Angrove, House Surgeon to the Yarmouth Hospital. "London Lancet," March, 1877, p. 123.

One end of an air-tight silk reservoir is fastened to the cap, and the other to the flexible tube, which is also attached to the mouth-piece. The flexible tube runs through the reservoir, and is directly connected with the metal tube. The inside of the cylinder is lined with felt, and a couple of turns of the same material are wound round the wires, thus presenting three surfaces for the evaporation of the ether. Having filled the reservoir with air, an ounce of ether is poured into the cylinder through the nozzle; this suffuses itself all over the felt. The mouth-piece is then applied to a patient; he is told to 'draw in his breath;' the vapor he inspires comes from the reservoir, passes through the holes in the cap, over the evaporating surfaces of felt, and up through the whole length of tube; he expires the same vapor, which passes back to the reservoir, and becomes recharged with ether during the next inspiration. The inventor further states he has completely anæsthetized several individual patients in a little over one minute, one in forty seconds. An ounce of ether is sufficient to keep a patient about ten minutes."

The cylinder is five inches high and three in diameter. The reservoir holds about a pint and a half. The length of the tube can be made according to taste. To show that they are still at sea in England in regard to ether inhalers, I will conclude this part of my subject by giving a description of one of the latest invented, from the *British Medical Journal.*

The Portable Regulating Ether Inhaler of J. T. Clover, F.R.C.S.

" In the *British Medical Journal*, of July 15th, 1876, I described an apparatus for giving laughing gas and ether, separately or combined. Experience in more than three thousand cases in which I have used it convinces me that the administration of ether may be made far less unpleasant to the patient, and equally effective and safe, by first giving enough gas to render the patient unconscious of its taste.

"The arrangement of the apparatus enables one to cause the patient to breathe directly into and out of a
4

bag, or partly, or entirely, through a vessel containing liquid ether; and, even without gas, it is very efficient, inasmuch as it gives the power of varying and of sustaining the strength of the vapor. I have used it a great many times without gas, and find it as safe as any other way of giving ether, whilst the risk of coughing and sickness is much lessened.

"The plan of excluding fresh air until insensibility has been induced, and admitting it very sparingly afterwards, has now been extensively tried in various ways, and, so far as I know, it is practically free from the danger of causing serious obstruction to the pulmonary circulation and overdistension of the right cavities of the heart. Of course, air cannot be indefinitely excluded, but the pulse and respiration give timely notice when air is required. A single artificial respiration of fresh air in these cases affords more relief than several such respirations when the apnœa has resulted from an overdose of ether or chloroform. The reason for this is, that in the former case the symptoms depend chiefly on the want of oxygen, and in the latter upon the presence of a substance which has not only entered the blood, but has penetrated the tissues of the body. If the apparatus be overheated, or if the ether be turned on too quickly, the ordinary coughing and struggling would, of course, be produced. The apparatus, however, requires a little more attention to temperature and other details, and is rather too complicated for general use. I have made several attempts to avoid the necessity of warming it. This can be effected by having the ether-vessel surrounded by a larger quantity of water at the ordinary temperature; but then the size and weight of the inhaler become objectionable. Better success attended modifications of the instrument having the ether-vessel placed close against the face-piece, so as to receive more warmth from the patient's breath and from the hand of the administrator.

"I am greatly indebted to Messrs. Mayer and Meltzer for their patience and ingenuity in carrying out my ideas, and my present object is to call attention to a portable regulating inhaler made by them. Its advantages are these: 1. It has no valves; 2. It supplies the vapor so gradually that patients breathe quietly; 3.

It produces sleep in two minutes; 4. It does not require fresh ether during the continuance of an operation; 5. The recovery from a short operation is more speedy than with most other inhalers; 6. It does not need to be warmed before it is used; 7. No sponge or felt is required; 8. Ether left in the inhaler can be saved for another time.

"The face-piece is edged with an air-cushion. The ether-vessel and water-chamber rotate upon the mouth of the face-piece. When the instrument is first applied, the stopper should be towards the patient's forehead, and now he breathes in and out of the bag directly. As the ether-vessel is turned round, the air is obliged to enter the ether-chamber and pass through it before it reaches the bag; and, when the vessel is turned half round, so that the stopper is opposite the patient's chin, all the air going in and out of the bag must pass through the ether-vessel. Two ounces of ether (specific gravity 735) are enough for a long operation. Usually an ounce and a half is the proper charge. The opening for supplying the ether is arranged to prevent an excessive quantity being supplied; but, to guard against the possibility of a few drops escaping through the inner openings, there are two recesses made to catch them, and prevent the liquid ether from reaching the patient's lips.

"The ether-vessel is spherical in shape, and one-half is surrounded by a closed water-compartment, to prevent the ether from becoming too cold. The bag need not be much distended when in use, and can be kept on one side so as not to obstruct the light in operations on the eye. The instrument is intended for giving ether without gas; but, by connecting the bag with a supply of nitrous oxide, it forms a tolerably efficient substitute for the gas and ether-inhaler above mentioned."

CHAPTER II.

Sulphuric ether, not altogether free from danger, always gives warning. What to do in case of alarming symptoms when employing ether as an anæsthetic. Use of air, artery forceps, artificial respiration in fainting, inversion of the body and head, application of stimulants, in case of blood, food or ether entering the trachea or bronchi. Statistics in reference to death from ether, I r. Andrews, of Chicago, Dr. Richardson, of London. Recent cases of reported deaths collected by the writer. Mr. Lawson Tait on the advantages of boiling anhydrous ether. Examination of the Royal Medical Chirurgical Society, of London, into the comparative merits of ether and chloroform. Experiments with ether, with illustrations, by the sphygmograph, by the late Dr. Morgan, of Dublin, and his conclusions. Case of apparent failure of the heart's action, during the inhaling of ether, with recovery. Primary and secondary effects of ether. Reports of deaths from ether, by Drs. Holmes, A. Matthewson, G. M. Lowe, Shreve, T. G. Morton, and Saundly. Abstract of the report of the Boston Committee on the alleged dangers from ether. Conclusions of the author in regard to ether.

SULPHURIC ETHER is not altogether free from danger, but it always gives warning before it causes the death of the patient. The countenance should be watched and the difficulty in breathing promptly attended to the moment the face assumes a purple, dusky, or extremely pale hue. The first thing to be done is to remove the inhaling apparatus, and admit fresh air; if this is not sufficient, draw forward the tongue by means of a pair of artery forceps, or a napkin or handkerchief wrapped around it, also draw forward and support the jaw. If these means should fail to reëstablish a healthy action of the lungs and cause due oxygenation of the blood, resort at once to artificial respiration, by means of Marshall Hall's method, or mouth of the physician to that of the patient, or by the use of a small pair of hand-bellows, or air bag and nozzle having its valve on the side or base.

In the condition of depression or fainting, position—the inversion of the head and body—will be found of importance, with careful administration of stimulants and nitrite of amyl to the patient's nostrils, using a tube with air bulb to force it into the lungs. Use heat by means of bottles of hot water or hot iron, wrapped in flannel and applied to the pit of stomach, frictions with mustard or pepper in hot water or oil of turpentine. If they should fail resort to a galvanic or faradic current; one pole to chest and the other to nape of the neck. If blood, food, or ether should have gotten into the trachea or bronchi, compression of the stomach and chest should be resorted to, also turn the head downwards, drawing at the same time the tongue around, and keeping the mouth open. Expose the face and chest of the patient to pure air, but do not chill the body if moist, cold, or clammy.

By combining the statistics collected in the United States by Dr. Andrews, of Chicago, and those of England by Dr. Richardson, of London, we obtain the mortality caused by ether (up to 1872), such as four deaths in 92,815, or one to 23,204. Since that period several more deaths have been reported (up to 1877) from ether in New York, Boston, Chicago, Philadelphia, and England. The fourth in Chicago, of which we have a published account; it being the first fatal result in an operation on the eye in this country. We republish this latter case, feeling almost sure that ether entered the trachea on account of the use of the wet cone and sponge. "The patient being in the horizontal position, and in her 74th year, having suffered from cough, had râles in her chest, etc. The details of the first operation have also been given; it having been successful under the ether, but giving such warning that the other eye should not have been operated upon at the time or under the same anæsthetic." Dr. Holmes states:* "In the latter part of December the eyes were in so favorable a condition that I considered it safe to perform a preliminary iridectomy.

---

* Death following the administration of ether at the Illinois Charitable Eye and Ear Infirmary, by E. L. Holmes, M.D., Chicago Medical Journal and Examiner, May, 1876.

The patient took no food after breakfast. Squibb's ether (stronger) turned upon a large porous towel, folded several times and covered with paper, was given to the patient while lying on her back with her head slightly elevated. The patient breathed very quietly until she seemed to be unconscious, when coughing commenced. This was no more violent than is often observed when this anæsthetic is administered. Scarcely any mucus or saliva collected in the throat. Soon after this the breathing ceased, and the face became remarkably livid, while the pulse continued regular and strong. Pressure on the chest aroused the respiration, when more ether was given, and the operation on each eye completed without further unpleasant symptoms.

"There was no vomiting. The wounds in the corneal border healed readily, although, from a repeated recurrence of slight conjunctivitis, I did not consider the eyes to be in a condition fit for the extraction of cataract for about three months. Meanwhile, the general health had continued as good in every respect as it had been.

"Dr. T. N. Danforth had given the patient simple remedies to relieve a trifling cough and *asthma*, and to overcome the undue perspiration.

"The asthma never prevented sleep in the recumbent position.

"At half past three, on the twenty-seventh of March, Squibb's ether was again administered under precisely the same circumstances as at the previous operation. I must confess that nothing in the patient's condition excited the least suspicion, either in Dr. Danforth or myself, that a fatal result should follow. The thought never entered my mind, although I had some solicitude regarding the success of an extraction of cataract in an eye which might be considered predisposed to inflammation.

"The patient was in a cheerful state of mind, and inhaled the ether quietly till about *half a pound* had been consumed, when quite violent coughing commenced.

"This was soon followed by an extremely livid appearance of the face, and then by a cessation of breathing. I placed my finger on the pulse, found it failing in strength, and directed my assistant to remove the towel, and others in the room to raise the foot of the bed as high as possible. Meantime I raised the tongue, and, with the other hand, made very forcible pressure every few seconds on the side of the chest. Respiration was at once re-established, as also full action of the heart, when I directed the foot of the bed to be let down. The lividity in a great measure disappeared. Even at this moment I did not think of danger, but, without giving more ether, rapidly commenced and completed the section, and, as iridectomy had already been performed, as rapidly removed the lens. This passed through the wound at once with only the least possible manipulation. The bandage was speedily adjusted. I cannot think two minutes elapsed from the commencement of the section to the final adjustment of the bandage.

"I made the steps as rapidly as was consistent with care, being not quite certain that the patient had taken ether enough to keep her unconscious sufficiently long for the possible delay in 'delivering' the lens, which occasionally happens.

"My usual method of applying the compressive bandage reduces the time to a minimum, since I place an elastic band around the forehead, ready in any emergency to be slipped over the eyes. I am confident, therefore, that all this required less than two minutes, when I observed that the patient did not breathe, that the face was more livid and the pulse very weak. The same course was pursued as before the operation as regards drawing up the tongue, raising the foot of the bed, and inducing artificial respiration, and, in addition, by forcing air into the lung(?) by the breath. At the end of a minute or more I could feel no pulse nor hear the heart; the face had become exceedingly livid.

"The efforts I have described, except raising the foot of the bed, and forcing the breath into the mouth, were continued an hour and a quarter.

"There were present my assistant, the matron, the resident pupil, and one of the nurses. Galvanism was not employed. No autopsy was obtained.

"In neither case was the towel held so close to the face as to prevent the entrance of sufficient air into the lungs."

Mr. Lawson Tait* has stated that he had a case of severe bronchitis in an aged person following the administration of ether, and he therefore advises the administration of the vapor of boiling anhydrous ether, pure and free from any admixture of air. His apparatus consists of a reservoir, which holds about ten ounces of ether, free from water, furnished with a spring pump, which drives over into the glass boiler about a drachm of ether at each stroke. This boiler is suspended in a hot-water tank beneath which is a spirit lamp; from the boiler there is an exit tube, four or five feet long, which passes to a "Junker's" mouth-piece. In the writer's experience he has never known bronchitis to result from the inhalation of ether, except in persons who were already suffering at the time from some pulmonary difficulty. In a recent case in which the writer administered ether, by means of the inhaler, to a young person suffering from a bronchial attack, with a most irritable cough, the patient was found to be better after the full influence of the anæsthetic than before its use. In the dyspnœa dependent upon chronic bronchitis Prof. G. B. Wood, of Philadelphia, considers the inhalation of ether doubly useful, if carefully managed, both by relieving the distressing sensation and favoring mucous secretion.†

Dr. W. Y. Gadberry,‡ of Yazoo City, Mississippi, records some cases of capillary bronchitis treated effectually with inhalations of ether.

A careful examination was conducted by the Royal Medical Chirurgical Society of London into the comparative merits of ether and chloroform, by means of the hemadynamometer in testing the effects on the heart's action and the influence of these agents upon it. The report states: "The essential difference between the action of chloroform and ether is to be found in the effect produced upon the heart. The first operation of both agents is to stimulate the heart and augment the force of its contractions; but, after this, chloroform *depresses* the heart's action, whereas ether appears to exert but little influence upon the muscular movements of that organ."

* The Practitioner, March, 1876, p. 206.
† Wood's Therapeutics, second edition, vol. ii. p. 697.
‡ Nashville Journal of Medicine and Surgery, Oct. 1866.

The general accuracy of these experiments and results, although tested by so comparatively coarse an instrument, is borne out by observations and experiments with the sphygmograph by the late Dr. Morgan,* of Dublin, who, with this delicate instrument, made numerous observations and experiments which are here given, and concludes, "I have taken all but one of these examples (eight cases) as the most unpropitious, occurring in patients of diminished health and vitality, yet it is evident that the most perfect anæsthesia could be invoked under the influence of ether, with an absolute stimulating effect on the circulation; and that the condition of insensibility could be maintained for a considerable time, yet there was no material alteration of the 'pulse writing,' and the most perfect sense of security was established. *It is, therefore, established that while chloroform exerts a depressing influence on the heart, ether exerts a stimulating one, and that chloroform is the most dangerous.*"

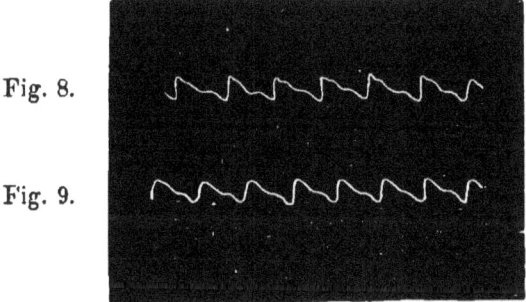

Fig. 8.

Fig. 9.

Fig. 8 represents the pulse of a female patient, aged twenty-five, who had been confined to bed for five months; pulse writing taken before etherization.

Fig. 9 represents it during its full influence. It will

* The Dangers of Chloroform and the Safety and Efficiency of Ether, etc., by J. Morgan, M.D., F.R.C.S., Professor of Surgical and Descriptive Anatomy, Royal College of Surgeons, Ireland, etc. London, 1872, p. 28.

Fig. 10.

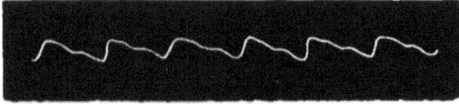

be seen that the heart power indication was rather stronger during etherization than before.

Another instance of a female, aged seventeen, also long

Fig. 11.

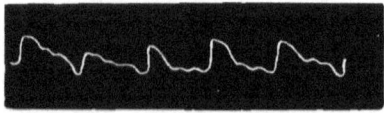

confined in bed. The contrast of Fig. No. 10, taken before etherization, and of Fig. No. 11, during profound etherization, is notable; the elevation of the pulse line

Fig. 12.

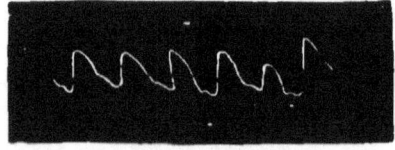

showing the stimulating property of the ethereal influence.

Fig. 12 represents the excited pulse writing of a small

Fig. 13.

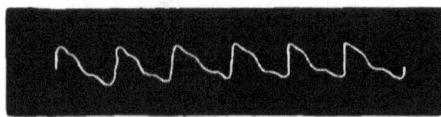

and nervous female, previous to etherization and operation.

Fig. 13 represents the pulse writing of the same patient

when steadied by etherization. The contrast is remarkably favorable.

Fig. 14 represents the pulse writing of a healthy young man, of twenty-two, previous to operation for artificial

Fig. 14.

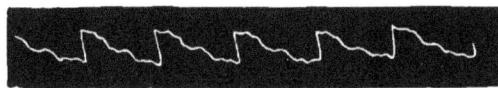

pupil; an affection which had not interfered with his general health.

Fig. 15 represents the same when taken under full etherization, and after the completion of the operation.

Fig. 15.

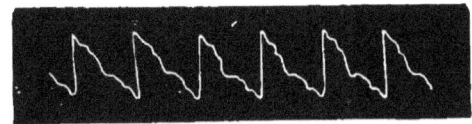

A comparison of this pulse writing with that of the natural soft pulse, will be ample evidence of the safety of etherization in its action on the heart.

Apparent Failure of Heart's Action during Inhalation of Ether.

This interesting case is reported by Mr. Morton, M.B.,* senior house-surgeon Royal London Ophthalmic Hospital. " George S., shipwright, aged forty-four, a strong, healthy-looking man, came to the hospital on the 25th Sept. 1876, with his left eye lost by an injury sustained some time since. He consented to have the eyeball removed, for which purpose anhydrous ether, as prepared by Messrs. Robbins & Co. for general anæsthesia, was administered by Mr. Morton, after the method always employed at this hospital, namely, a conical sponge hollowed in the middle, and lined with flannel. There was

* London Lancet, January, 1877. Am. ed. p. 12.

not nearly so much struggling as there is frequently, though there was some unwillingness to respire freely, and a tendency to dropping of the lower jaw, with a falling back of the tongue; but by forcibly holding forwards the lower jaw by means of his beard, the patient was fully anæsthetized in about seven minutes, after inhaling about five ounces of ether. All went well to the completion of the excision, when, having removed the inhaler, though still holding forward the man's lower jaw, Mr. Morton was proceeding to compress the bleeding tissues when he observed that there was no hemorrhage. The man's lips were then noticed to be very pale, as was also his whole face; and his respiration had ceased. Artificial respiration was at once commenced, and one of the assistants, who was raising and lowering the arms, felt that the pulse was extremely feeble. *The tongue was also forcibly drawn forwards, as it had fallen far back in the mouth, although the lower jaw was being held forwards.*

"After the artificial respiration had been continued some eight or ten minutes the patient made one or two feeble efforts to breathe, and the conjunctivæ were becoming sensitive, when one of the clinical assistants suggested the use of *nitrite* of *amyl*, four minims of which were accordingly given on a piece of lint, and artificial respiration continued; but the patient soon began to breathe for himself, and speedily recovered consciousness, walking out of the theatre a few minutes afterwards.

"This case, according to Mr. Morton's impression, seems to have been one of cardiac failure, as indicated by the pallor of the face and lips and the feebleness of the pulse, though it may be thought by some to have been due to an obstruction to the respiration from his tongue having fallen back. This is scarcely likely, for he had breathed to within a very few seconds of the time that the absence of respiration and the extreme pallor were noticed. Further, Mr. Morton remarks that in all cases, now more than 500, in which he has administered ether, if there has been any obstruction to the respiration it has always been accompanied by intense congestion of the face and blueness of the lips; yet in some cases, where vomiting is about to occur, this is preceded by pallor and profuse sweating, but that does not apply to the present case, for there was no vomiting, nor any tendency to it. It would be interesting to know whether others have seen cases in which there has been cardiac failure during the inhalation of ether, and it is important to note the fact that holding forward the lower jaw did not prevent the tongue falling back, as it is commonly alleged to do. In conclusion, it may be stated, that the patient has a slight mitral regurgitant murmur, and occasionally suffers from difficulty in breathing, after a hard day's work."

Secondary Results of the Use of Ether.

Death under the care of Dr. A. Matthewson, of Brooklyn.*—" The ether was taken rapidly (time not given). The operation of iridectomy was performed, and recovery so far advanced (not complete) that the patient was left with an attendant (not a medical man). A quarter of an hour later the house surgeon was called, and told that, after some efforts to vomit, the patient had a fit (either from food in the larynx or the falling back of the tongue, causing asphyxia, followed by convulsions), and so the patient died.

" At the autopsy a large hemorrhage was found under the arachnoid, on the upper surface of the left hemisphere. The vessels on the side were full, and there were numerous capilliform extravasations. There was a large clot in the right ventricle, a smaller one in the left; the corpus striatum and optic thalamus were softened and broken down, and the vessels of the base of the brain were atheromatous."

* Boston Medical and Surgical Journal, Oct. 1876.

Primary Results following Death from Inhalation of Ether.

"We regret to have to record a case in which the administration of ether terminated fatally, and which occurred in the practice of Dr. G. M. Lowe, of Lincoln. The patient was a lady forty-eight years of age, who had discharged the duties of a governess in the family of Dr. Lowe, and had for some time past been suffering from cancer of the breast. A consultation was held, and the removal of the tumor determined upon. The administration of the ether was confided to Dr. Mitchinson, who had large experience in its employment. All proper precautions appear to have been taken. Dr. Mitchinson examined the heart, and, finding it rather feeble, directed the patient to take a little brandy and water. She was quite cheerful, though somewhat nervous. Half an ounce of ether was poured on the inhaler, which was placed over the mouth in the usual way. The valves were open, and gave free ingress and egress to the air. After a few inhalations the patient's face suddenly became turgid and the hands white. The inhaler was at once removed, the tongue brought forward, cold water dashed over the face, and the chest rubbed with brandy; but the breathing became stertorous, the face more and more congested, the pulse failed, there was an effort at vomiting, and death took place within a few seconds. A post-mortem was made by Mr. T. Sympson, the Senior Surgeon of the Lincoln County Hospital, assisted by Mr. T. Brook. On examining the heart, they found that it was feeble and flabby, and some of the tissue, being afterwards examined, was found to have undergone fatty degeneration. The liver was firm, but the whole of its upper surface was attached by old adhesions to the under surface of the diaphragm—the muscular partition between the chest and the abdomen. There was a little effusion of serum on the brain. The air-cells of the lungs were dilated. The valves of the heart were in a perfectly healthy condition. They also carefully examined the throat, and found nothing there to throw light on the cause of death. The stomach was perfectly healthy; the deceased had not partaken of any food for some time before the ether was administered, which is a point of great importance. Mr. Sympson attributed the fatal result to failure of the heart's action, and the impairment of the functions of the diaphragm in consequence of its attachment to the liver. The fibres of the heart were so feeble as to be unable to bear any extra strain, and the efforts at resuscitation proved abortive, owing to the failure of the functions of the diaphragm. Mr. Brook's evidence was to the same effect. They noted, in addition, that the right side of the heart was gorged with blood, that the walls of the right ventricle were very thin, and that there were some nodules of cancer in the liver and lungs."*

"Some cases in which ether has been followed by alarming symptoms have lately been recorded. They have been termed syncope, but the word is not appropriate, as the heart continued to beat after respiration ceased. This is what should have been anticipated. When death is produced by ether, the animal's heart continues to beat long after the arrest of respiration. The pulse is quickened by ether, and maintains its force through a long state of anæthesia. In these facts lies the safety of ether. But it should never be forgotten that there is danger at a certain stage, and the danger is from the side of the respiration, which at length ceases.

"Stertorous breathing proceeds from paresis of the muscles of the palate, and should lead to the ether being suspended. So respiration, growing more and more shallow and less frequent, is a warning, and should not be overlooked. It is very rare that the heart fails—perhaps never. Pallor is rare, too, and should excite attention if it occurs. But, we repeat, the danger of ether is from the side of respiration, that of chloroform from the heart, and this fact goes far to explain their relative safety. In chloroform narcosis the danger is much more sudden. Ether gives warning."†

* Lancet, Nov. 17. † The Doctor, London.

Fatal and Dangerous Effects from Ether.

The following cases are given in the "Practitioner," August, 1877, by Dr. Shreve:—

"CASE 1.—Was seen in consultation. The patient was a young man, sixteen years of age, of dark complexion, and of good muscular development. His previous habits good, and also his general health. One month previously he had received a pistol-shot wound. The bullet entered just above the knee, and emerged on the posterior part of the limb, just below the popliteal space. *His condition when seen was that of anæmia, consequent on loss of blood at the time of the injury, and the pain and inflammation that succeeded.* The pulse was regular and *weak*, the *face was extremely pale*, and respiration regular; he complained of pain in the region of the knee, which was very much swollen and tense. Ether was administered, and he passed under its influence very pleasantly; there was no excited period during its inhalation. An incision was made into the most dependent part of the swelling, and a *large quantity of old clots* escaped. This was followed by quite *a smart hemorrhage* from the direction of the *popliteal artery*. The hemorrhage was controlled by the immediate application of pressure. The respiration, which up to this time had been perfectly regular and quiet in its character, suddenly stopped. He had inhaled only three ounces of ether, and the sponge had been removed from his nose for a minute or two. The face and lips were extremely pale, and arrest of respiration took place with such insidiousness that it seemed as if the patient had suddenly omitted a breath. The pulse was regular and feeble at the wrist, and for a moment it seemed like the slight arrest of respiration seen in the administration of ether, where a shake arouses the patient, and he makes a deep inspiration, and goes on breathing regularly. Artificial respiration was resorted to, ammonia injected hypodermically, stimulating enema administered; all without avail, as the patient never breathed again, although the pulse continued perceptible at the wrist for some time after the stoppage of the respiration."

Remarks on the first case:—Here there was sufficient cause of death without the *ether;* there was evidently air admitted into the circulation, or death occurred from loss of the small quantity of blood remaining in the system, or the sudden formation of a heart clot. No stimulant was given before this severe operation upon an anæmic subject, nor is it stated in what position he was in, which was surely indicated by his feeble pulse. No post-mortem was made, which increased the uncertainty of the case.

"CASE 2.—Was a case of abortion, in a lady aged about forty, married, and of dark complexion. She was fleshy and sallow, and had been flowing forty-eight hours when I was called to see her, in consultation. Ether was administered to relieve the pain of removing the placenta, as the uterus was situated high up in the pelvis. The pulse before the operation was moderately strong and slightly accelerated. The patient passed under the effects of the anæsthetic without a struggle. The placenta was removed in pieces, it being adherent to the walls of the uterus; its removal was accompanied by no undue amount of hemorrhage, *and the etherization was discontinued. Having examined the pulse, and found it somewhat fuller than before the operation, and the respiration regular,* I left the attending physician in care of the patient, and went to another part of the room to wash my hands, where I was joined by the doctor, and while engaged in conversation with him, and the same time looking at the patient, her respiration suddenly ceased. Our efforts for her relief were directed entirely to artificial respiration. After about two minutes she began to respire again, at first feebly and at intervals, but soon after with strength and regularity. The pulse was regular and weak at the wrist during the whole period of stoppage of the respiration."

Remarks on the second case.—Here again the etherization had ceased, and the gentleman had left the patient all right, and we feel satisfied the ether had little or nothing to do with this feeling of fainting, which is almost certain to follow a detached placenta. It is always proper to administer under such circumstances some stimulant, either brandy or whiskey, with some preparation of ergot. We have frequently had the pulse to cease almost at the wrist, and no apparent respiratory movement, from filling up of the uterus with a soft clot, when rough handling of the patient or kneading of the uterus will cause expulsion of the clots, and with it relief to all the symptoms. The italics are ours in each of the cases.

"CASE 3.—Was seen in consultation. The patient was a lady of about forty years of age, married, and had had several children. *She had been ill with menorrhagia for eleven years, and presented a degree of anæmia that was most ghastly. Her complexion was perfectly waxy, and almost transparent in its whiteness.* On digital examination of the vagina the cervix admitted the tip of the index finger, and was full of granulations. A sponge-tent was introduced, and left until the next day, when it was decided to etherize sufficiently to relieve the pain of the examination of the uterine cavity. The immediate effects of the etherization was all that could be wished. The whole lining membrane of the uterus, like the cervix, was lined with granulations and fungosities. While the attending physician was confirming my diagnosis the respiration suddenly ceased. The head, which had been low, was placed still lower, and artificial respiration was immediately resorted to. After persistent efforts for about three minutes, that seemed an eternity, I discovered a slight superficial respiration, which we continued to supplement and assist until respiration became normal. The pulse remained about what it was before the etherization, both as to its regularity and strength, during this whole period. I might add that the action of the sponge-tent proved entirely remedial, although originally used only as a means of diagnosis."

Secondary Results of the Use of Ether.*

"David D. P., aged nineteen, single, a telegraphic operator, consulted me in May, 1876, in regard to his right

* Am. Jour. Med. Sciences. "Details of a case in which death is supposed to have resulted from ether used as an anæsthetic;

limb, which was quite useless from general atrophy, and an angular partial anchylosis of the knee, evidently a result of old scrofulous inflammation. I advised division of the flexor hamstring tendons, which were very much contracted, and immediate straightening of the limb, and directed an appropriate brace to be made, with a high heel and sole to the shoe for after-use. On the 2d of June the patient was admitted into the hospital, when the following notes were made by Dr. W. B. Hopkins, the resident in charge: 'Until the patient was two years old, when he began to walk, he had been considered a perfectly healthy child; soon after this a posterior spinal curvature developed; when four years old, inflammation of the knee set in, with subsequent contraction of the flexor thigh muscles, with general arrest of development in the limb, and subsequent partial anchylosis of the knee-joint, the angle of deformity being slightly obtuse; there had been apparently no suppuration of the joint, at least to the extent of an abscess.'

"The spinal and limb troubles combined prevented the patient from walking until he was six years old, when, with crutches, he began to get about; there is no history of winter cough or previous chest trouble, and his general health, although not being vigorous, seems not to have been markedly impaired, and no evidence of any hereditary disease can be traced out. The patient is rather pale, but his appetite is good, and he expresses himself as in excellent health; there is marked posterior curvature, which has produced the usual deformity, with great sternal prominence. The right limb is much atrophied and shortened, and presents angular deformity, with a partial luxation backward of the tibia, the anchylosis not being complete. June 3d, after a consultation with Drs. Hewson and Hunt, the tendons were divided, and the limb was straightened, and the apparatus, made especially for the case, was adjusted by Mr. Kolbé.

"The etherization was conducted by Dr. Wharton, one

with a Brief Account of all the Fatal Results which have been ascribed to the use of Anæsthetics at the Pennsylvania Hospital; with remarks." By Thomas G. Morton, M.D., Surgeon to the Pennsylvania Hospital.

of the resident physicians; at the close of the operation I saw that the patient was pale, somewhat depressed, but as comfortable apparently as we generally observe after the use of an anæsthetic. The patient was left in charge of Dr. Hopkins, whose subsequent notes are as follows: 'At 12.30 P. M., patient, having been removed fifteen minutes ago to his room, was seized with symptoms of asphyxia; pulse moderately full, 160; respirations nearly ceased; general cyanotic condition more marked in the face and tips of the fingers; his tongue was at once depressed, cold water dashed on his chest, which produced only violent respiratory efforts. At 1 P. M. condition remains much about the same, and there being evidences of pulmonary engorgement, with frothy blood-stained mucus constantly collecting in the throat, while the heart's action was active and labored, the radial artery was opened, and about eight ounces of blood were drawn; dry cups were applied to the chest; for a time the respiration seemed slightly improved; the volume of the pulse increased somewhat, and fell from 160 to 152 per minute. At 1.45 rapidly sinking; hypodermics of whiskey and carbonate of ammonia were used without avail.' Dr. H. sent me the following note: 'P. died at 2 P. M.; about ten minutes after the operation he was removed to his room, being perfectly conscious, and I having seen to it that he had perfectly recovered from the ether, he suddenly became asphyxiated; the ordinary remedies proved of no avail.'

"Dr. Morris Longstreth, the hospital pathologist, made the post-mortem twenty-one hours after death. 'The rigor mortis was well marked; there was considerable deformity of the chest; the lumbar portion of the spinal column was at its lower part bowed backwards, so that the last two vertebræ were nearly in a right line with the upper portion of the sacrum, thereby making the cavity of the pelvis very capacious. The abdominal viscera were normal, although somewhat out of position. Thorax—the pleural cavities contained a considerable amount of serum, included in the meshes of an abundant firm network of inflammatory adhesions (old). The serum contained no recent lymph, and it was impossible to determine its quantity, on account of the very great amount of similar serum pressed out from the lungs in the process of their removal; the lower part of the right pleural cavity was, to a considerable extent, obliterated by very firm adhesions existing between the diaphragm and the costal pleura. The amount of serum was not very great at any one portion of the pleural sac, but rather diffusely infiltrating the adhesions present. Both lungs were moderately well crepitant throughout, pitted deeply on pressure everywhere; on section, serum, frothy and a little bloody, exuded with great freedom and in large amount, as though from a saturated sponge; their cut surface was grayish, showing some blood points; there was no solidification or even deep congestion of their tissues. Divided portions, as well as the whole, floated well in water, and there was no evidence of plugging of their vessels, and the blood in them was entirely fluid. Pericardium contained a considerable amount of clear, very pale serum; the heart was only moderately in a state of muscular contraction, a slight amount of fat covered its surface along the grooves; the blood within the cavities was quite fluid; the muscular tissue, the valves, and the large vessels were all normal. There was no foreign substance of solid nature discovered in the larger bronchi or in the trachea. The other parts of the body were not examined.'

"The unfortunate result in this case, apparently caused by ether, naturally produced, not only upon myself, but upon those who had a knowledge of it, a profound impression, as it was seemingly a proper one for the use of the anæsthetic. Ether or 'washed ether' as an anæsthetic agent has been uniformly looked upon as perfectly safe; personally, I have administered it on all occasions, at all periods of life, from infancy to extreme old age, with the feeble as well as in the strong. In giving ether I have never used any 'inhaler,' so called, but have invariably made use of a napkin or coarse towel, on which the ether is poured, when the cloth is then simply folded in a conical shape, and held over the patient's mouth and nose; so soon as the napkin becomes the least soiled or 'ether-logged,' a fresh one is substituted. Dr. Wharton, the resident who gave the ether in this case, says: 'I am satisfied that not over two and a half or three ounces were administered in P.'s case; he seemed to be readily affected, and was not under its influence over twenty minutes. There was no vomiting, and the respirations were not labored; on removal of the napkin he rapidly regained consciousness.' Although this patient had a marked spinal curvature, with chest capacity below the average, anæsthesia on this account was not contraindicated, for I have frequently used ether in cases where the deformity of the chest was much more marked without the least difficulty. The autopsy demonstrated that the lungs were seriously restricted in their natural movements by the adhesions which bound them down in all directions, and consequently the secretions which formed were not expelled; at the close of the etherization there was no evidence of any mucous collection, at least when I last saw the patient at 12 M.; fifteen minutes later, when Dr. Hopkins was called, the change was very marked, and it was during this short interval that the serious symptoms were manifested. Mucous secretion, which often rapidly forms, is one of the most annoying symptoms in the course of etherization; in many cases it is not observed at all, but when it occurs to any extent, it is much safer to suspend anæsthesia until the throat is thoroughly cleansed, or the patient is relieved by his own efforts. I have often observed that those patients who have been the most difficult to manage while being etherized, are the easiest to keep anæsthetized after the first excitement of the ether has passed over, and seldom suffer from any mucous secretions. Gross (Surgery, vol. i., 569, 5th ed.), when on the subject of death from ether, says: 'How the inhalation of ether proves fatal has not been decided; when death occurs promptly, as during, or very soon after, the administration, the probability is that it is caused by asphyxia, whereas, when it occurs at a later period, as after the lapse of hours or days, there is reason to believe that it is due to the effects of congestion of the brain and lungs, either alone, or in conjunction with gastric irritability, which often exists in a most distressing degree.'

"In P.'s case death was the result of the mucous secretion and serous effusion which invaded every available space, thus suffocating the patient; there was not the least evidence of any intra-cranial difficulty; the patient was quite rational to the close.

"There is seldom any danger from ether when properly administered, and there is abundant evidence to show that fatal results are less likely to follow its use than any other anæsthetic agent. The fact of ether having uniformly been looked upon as a perfectly safe agent on every occasion may, I am inclined to think, have induced great carelessness in its use; the occasional deaths from or at all associated with ether should in the future be sufficient to serve as cautionary signals, a constant watchfulness should be observed by the etherizer, and every symptom carefully noted, especially all complications arising from bronchial secretion, pulse failure, or vomiting, and I am satisfied that not only should the patient be watched by a medical man during anæsthesia, but until reaction has been thoroughly established, and the ether effects entirely passed over; I have seen, as probably all surgeons have, ether poured upon the inhaler or napkin in great excess, so as to flow down on the patient's face and neck; the cloth thus becomes saturated, is not pervious to air, and the patient almost suffocates; such practice cannot but be severely condemned.

"The assistant should devote his attention exclusively to the patient, while a few drachms at a time, with care, poured on the napkin will generally induce anæsthesia promptly; when the napkin becomes the least soiled, another should be substituted, and when complete anæsthesia has been induced, occasional inspirations of pure air should be allowed. Ether has been most successfully employed in the Pennsylvania Hospital for more than twenty-five years; it was introduced about 1850, and first used in a case of luxation of the femur, which resisted repeated attempts at reduction with the pulleys; it is needless to say that after etherization no diffiulty was experienced, and from that time to the present this agent has been in daily use, and with the few exceptions herein noted has been the only anæsthetic employed."—*American Journal of the Medical Sciences*, October.

A death from ether has been lately recorded. Mr. Robert Saundly, of Birmingham, gives the following typical instance in the London *Medical Press and Circular:* "M. C., aged 35, was admitted for contracted knees. On October 4th, at 12.45 P.M., I administered ether with Ormsby's apparatus; it appeared to me a very favorable case; very little of the anæsthetic was used; there were no alarming incidents; very little stertor or cyanosis; no vomiting; no obstruction to respiration, which was throughout regular and full. After Mr. Bartleft had straightened the limbs, some time was consumed in adjusting splints, during which time no ether was given; and, as there appeared to be absolutely nothing to call for any notice at the time, I watched her with the utmost satisfaction, and allowed her to be carried out of the theatre without arousing her from the sleep into which she had fallen. She was removed on a stretcher, and was well wrapped up, but, to reach her ward, was carried about fifty yards across to the open court, the day being fine. After being placed in bed, she roused and spoke to the nurse, who noticed nothing unusual about her. At 2.45, about one hour and a half after her return to the ward, she became suddenly alarmingly ill, and when seen by the house physician (in the absence of the house surgeon) she was cyanotic and pulseless, with *râles* all over the thorax. All attempts to rally her were fruitless, and she died at 4.15 the same afternoon.

"The post-mortem examination made the following day showed some œdema of the membranes of the brain; no thrombosis of the pulmonary artery; heart healthy, containing little blood in the right auricle; ventricles contracted; lungs pale and œdematous; other organs healthy.

"There seems to be no doubt that the deceased completely recovered from the ether narcosis, but died from œdema of the lungs, which supervened one hour and a half after her removal from the theatre."

Alleged Dangers which accompany the Inhalation of the Vapor of Sulphuric Ether.*

Had we space, we should be very glad to copy the whole of this able pamphlet, but we must be content to give the conclusions which accompany it. We had before receiving it copied from Dr. Taylor on Poisons all the cases reported by him; but we found, on carefully reading it, that his cases were included in the appendix to the report of the Boston Society. In justification of the conclusions arrived at by the committee there are presented in this report forty-one cases gathered from every available source up to the year 1861, the date of publication.

"The general conclusions which have been arrived at by your committee may be summed up as follows:—

"1st. The ultimate effects of all anæsthetics show that they are depressing agents. This is indicated both by their symptoms and by the results of experiments. No anæsthetic should, therefore, be used carelessly, nor can it be administered without risk by an incompetent person.

"2d. It is now widely conceded, both in this country and in Europe, that sulphuric ether is safer than any other anæsthetic, and this conviction is gradually gaining ground.

"3d. Proper precautions being taken, sulphuric ether will produce entire insensibility in all cases, and no anæsthetic requires so few precautions in its use.

"4th. There is no recorded case of death, known to the committee, attributed to sulphuric ether, which cannot be explained on some other ground equally plausible, or in which, if it were possible to repeat the experiment, insensibility could not have been produced and death avoided. This cannot be said of chloroform.

"5th. In view of all these facts, the use of ether in armies, to the extent which its bulk will permit, ought to be obligatory, at least in a moral point of view.

"6th. The advantages of chloroform are exclusively

---

* Report of a Committee of the Boston Society for Medical Improvement on the Alleged Dangers which accompany the Inhalation of Sulphuric Ether, pp. 36. Boston: David Clapp, 334 Washington Street. 1861.

those of convenience. Its dangers are not averted by its admixture with sulphuric ether in any proportions. The combination of these two agents cannot be too strongly denounced as a treacherous and dangerous compound. Chloric ether, being a solution of chloroform in alcohol, merits the same condemnation."

Inflammability of Ether.

Two accidents have come to our knowledge in which the ether was ignited, and, although causing no actual injury, produced much fear and confusion. The first was where a bottle of ether was accidentally broken and ignited while Dr. Wm. Hunt was operating, during the night, at the Pennsylvania Hospital. The second occurred while Dr. Wm. H. Pancoast was applying the actual cautery to a patient at the Jefferson College Hospital clinic during the day. Dr. Bigelow, of Boston,[*] in commenting upon the inflammability of the vapor of ether, observes, "Its practical safety is doubtless partly owing to the fact that the air, cooled by its evaporation, establishes a downward current,[†] so that a match placed a few inches above an ether sponge at the edge of a table will not ignite it; while below, the vapor readily takes fire." It would, therefore, be much safer, when operating at night with ether, to have the flame of the lamp covered with a shade, and have the light always placed several inches above the ether.

General Conclusions.

The great safety of this anæsthetic agent depends upon the warning which it always gives in regard to its influence upon the life of the patient. The number of cases of death from its direct effects have been very few compared with the immense number of cases of prolonged application. It will also be noticed that, in our city, where ether has been employed from the first discovery of its valuable qualities, the only death re-

[*] Boston Medical and Surgical Journal.
[†] This is due to the greater density of ether *vapor*, for whilst the ether itself has a sp. gr. of .728, its vapor has 2.568 for its sp. gr., and this fact may be readily noted by observing the downward currents of vapor when pouring from one bottle to another.

ported has been from its secondary effects upon the lungs of the patient (see Morton's case), and some time after the case had been removed from the operating room to the ward, and, as I am now convinced, from a reduction of temperature of the skin, causing congestion of the lungs and brain, the avoidance of which will prevent such results. I have not failed to collect from every source within my reach every case of injury or death which has been ascribed to ether. That ether is not entirely free from danger, in the hands of careless or incompetent persons, no one would dare or attempt to deny, for we at times find the most simple article of the *materia medica*, when improperly employed, become a fatal agent. Ether has proven by experience to be the safest anæsthetic agent that has yet been discovered, with the exception of nitrous oxide gas, and this latter, from its naturally restricted character, cannot be employed in all operations. According to Dr. H. M. Jones,[*] "within the last three or four years the advantages of ether over chloroform or methylene have been forced on the notice of the profession in the United Kingdom, and it has been adopted exclusively in some and partially in many of the large hospitals." This is strong evidence in its favor from a source for which we must all have a very high respect. The surgeons of Great Britian had a natural pride in employing chloroform, its practical usefulness as an anæsthetic having been discovered and applied in that country. Still they were forced by medical public opinion to these very conclusions from the constantly recurring deaths from chloroform. This condition of things was well expressed by the editor, Dr. Hart, of the *British Medical Journal.* "Collecting," he says, "from every source, information as to the administration of ether as an anæsthetic, we have invited from all quarters comment and communication, calculated to completely inform the professional mind. The papers by Clover, Hayward, Norton, Bowditch, Fifield, Hutchinson, the late John Murray, and a host of others, appeared to *us to establish the superior safety of ether*

---

[*] See Dr. Jones's valuable pamphlet on the Medical Responsibility in the Choice of Anæsthetics, pp. 37. H. K. Lewis, London, 1876, 3.

over chloroform, and this led to a very large and general substitution of ether for chloroform as a surgical anæsthetic."

There are a few cases in which ether should not be employed as an anæsthetic; these we shall endeavor to enumerate. The first class is in very aged persons with emphysema, hypertrophy of the heart, fatty heart, or valvular lesion. The second class are those who are known to faint from very slight causes. The third class are habitual drunkards, or persons who drink in small quantities frequently each day. The fourth class is from limited action of the lungs from old pleurisy, or pneumonia or irritation of the mucous membrane with excessive secretion.

In anæsthesia by ether the real danger to be avoided is over-inebriation. It may be divided into three stages.

First stage, of exhilaration; second stage, that of stupor with snoring, or complete insensibility, which, with care, can be gradually increased or diminished with safety; third, dangerous state, that of *coma* with stertor, or the patient becomes livid with true asphyxia, or may alternate between lividity, with a falling pulse, with apparently alarming indications.

There are a certain class of patients that pass into an almost profound state of unconsciousness without these distinct stages, while others require two or three assistants to hold them while inhaling, and have a wild excited stage, then pass, after a longer or shorter time, into the stage of stupor; these latter are termed by those who are familiar with the administration of anæsthetics "bad etherizers," and here comes the importance of experience. Indeed, no one should be trusted with the inhalation unless he has passed through a course of instruction; for, unless great discretion is shown in giving or withdrawing the agent, the result may be fatal, while, with proper care, even in these bad cases, you may ultimately reach a stage of stupefaction, and all go well. The following case illustrates another class:—

Oct. 4, 1877, Jefferson College Hospital. In a case of mastoid disease, in which I perforated the bone and opened the cells, my friend, Dr. Allis, administered the ether, the patient made but little effort at respiration, and, after consuming from six to eight ounces of ether for a full half hour without producing the true anæsthetic result, he had to resort to the use of chloroform, pure and alone. This is not the first case in which, in the hands of even the most careful administrators, the ether has not produced the result desired, and we are under the necessity of resorting to the use of the more dangerous agent, but this must not be done until a full and free trial of the milder and safer agent, always in careful hands, and only in the most important and very painful operations.

CHAPTER III.

Mixtures of ether and chloroform; Dr. Washington L. Atlee. Death of a lady in Boston under Dr. Eastham, a dental surgeon of that city. Coroner's jury under charge of Dr. Ainsworth. Autopsy by Dr. Fitz, pathologist to the Massachusetts General Hospital. Methylic ether, its safety and best method of employment, by Dr. B. W. Richardson, of London; Dr. Carter's opinion, also Dr. Jones, of Cork. Use of bichloride of methylene, by Dr. Spencer Wells, at Samaritan Free Hospital; his doubts about its composition. Dr. Taylor's statement that it is a mixture. Report of five cases of death from this compound. Amylen; introduction and use by Dr. Snow. Bromide of ethyl or hydrobromic ether, chemical composition and properties; experiments with frogs, rabbits, dogs, etc., by "Rabuleau." Mode of preparation. Experiments of the writer on frogs and man. Its use in the ear, etc.

A MIXTURE of two parts of ether with one of chloroform has been employed with success by so careful an operator as Dr. Washington L. Atlee.

I have had the charge of the anæsthetic mixture (one part by measure of chloroform and two of washed sulphuric ether) in an operation by Dr. Washington L. Atlee, during the successful removal of an ovarian tumor weighing forty pounds, and have also assisted him in three cases in which others gave this same mixture, with good results, and with no apparent risk to the safety of the patients.

Dr. Atlee always administers the anæsthetic after the patient is upon the operating table, and one individual has charge of and is responsible for it. In his three hundred ovariotomies he informed me he had never lost a patient by the anæsthetic.

The mixture is given in almost every instance by means of the starched towel.

Dr. B. Willis Richardson,* of Dublin, writes: "I confess that I am myself in favor of a mixture of equal parts of chloroform and spirits of wine for producing anæsthesia, and, therefore, it is the comparative safety of this fluid I propose testing against the ether" (but he gives no results). The mortality caused by a mixture of chloroform and ether given by inhalations is 2 to 11.176, or 1 to 5.588. With this mixture of chloroform and alcohol, when administered from a handkerchief or sponge, according to "Snow," very little of the spirit is inhaled, as the greater part remains behind after the chloroform has evaporated; but it acts by lowering the amount of vapor which is given off, just as diluting a strong solution of ammonia with additional water diminishes the amount of the volatile alkali which escapes as gas. One hundred cubic inches of air are capable of taking up fourteen cubic inches of vapor, at 60°, from pure chloroform, and becoming expanded to 114 cubic inches; but, when the chloroform is diluted with an equal volume of alcohol, it will only yield eight cubic inches of vapor to 100 of air. In passing over a sponge or handkerchief the air would take up less than this, usually four or five per cent., which is a quantity sufficient to cause insensibility without the risk of sudden accident, in four or five minutes. The same result is produced in the mixture of ether and chloroform. Dr. Atlee is of the opinion that there is a chemical union of the ether and chloroform; and Professor Maisch, of this city, found that, if this mixture was exposed to the light, a change took place which rendered the mixture not fit for the purposes of inhalation; it therefore should

* Op. cit. 25.

be kept from the light, and mixed just before being employed. Dr. Atlee keeps his mixture in a bottle and in a tin case. In less careful hands than those of Dr. Atlee the chloroform is apt to result fatally, as is shown in the records of the following case:—

A death of a lady had occurred in the practice of Dr. Eastham, a dentist of Boston, causing much excitement in professional circles. The death had taken place about noon, but very few, except those particularly interested, were aware of it till the next day. The coroner, Dr. Ainsworth, who was called in directly after the accident, formed a jury of physicians and apothecaries, and ordered an autopsy. This was made the next morning by Dr. R. H. Fitz, pathologist to the Massachusetts General Hospital; and on the same day the jury met, and, having viewed the body, adjourned until the 14th. The anæsthetic was either chloroform or a mixture of chloroform and ether. The latter proves to be the one used. The jury met again on the 14th, and, having heard a part of the evidence, readjourned till the evening of Wednesday the 19th. We present the following account of the proceedings :* On November 14th, the first witness was Dr. Edson, who testified that he had twice attended Mrs. Crie, the deceased, during her confinements, but had never given her an anæsthetic, though she had desired it. This was owing to his disapproval of anæsthetics during labor, except in rare cases. He would have given one to the deceased as readily as to any patient in her case.

Dr. Fitz was next called, and read the following account of the autopsy :—

Examination made twenty-one hours after death. Body preserved in ice ; rigidity well marked ; no discoloration of face or anterior portions of the body ; skullcap and dura mater normal ; longitudinal veins empty ; moderate amount of blood in the veins of the arachnoid ; nothing abnormal observed at the base of the brain. The bloodvessels in this region contained but little blood ; cerebral substance firm, containing much less blood than usual, not particularly moist ; absence of any anatomical changes ; ventricles apparently nor-

---

* Boston Medical and Surgical Journal, November 20, 1873.

mal. Pericardium healthy. Heart moderately contracted, unusually small, and of usual color; aorta of less than the normal calibre, walls unusually thin and elastic; cavities of the heart contained dark fluid blood, of no unusual odor or color; right side of the heart contained more blood than the left; valves healthy, muscular substance apparently normal. Pleural cavities healthy, containing a small amount of reddish fluid. Lungs of a bluish-red color, the posterior dependent portions quite dark; tissue contained air and a somewhat increased amount of blood; absence of any special degree of œdema; in upper lobes of both lungs a rare, small, cheesy nodule. The larynx, trachea, bronchial tubes, and the larger vessels at the root of the lungs free from changes. Spleen of normal size and firmness, the color dark blue. Kidneys unusually firm, capsule rather more adherent than usual; in sections, the organ was of a grayish-slate color; bloodvessels, including the Malpighian organs, unusually distinct from the presence of blood; tubular structure apparently healthy. Bladder healthy. Uterus and ovaries well developed; an old *corpus luteum* present; the lining membrane of the body of the uterus unusually injected, covered with a viscid, bloody fluid. Liver of normal size, dark color, containing rather more blood than usual, otherwise healthy; stomach and intestines presented no unusual appearances.

The anatomical examination gave no evidence of recent disease of any of the organs, or of chronic alterations sufficient to account for death; the fluid conditions of the blood, the diminished amount in the brain and the increased amount in the thoracic and abdominal organs, were abnormal, and might have been the result of various causes; the diminished size of the heart and of the aorta were probably of congenital origin.

Question. Do you consider the absence of blood in the brain and cerebral cavities as abnormal? *Answer.* Yes, sir.

Q. Do you ever find the blood liquid so long after death, except where chloroform is used? *A.* Yes, sir; it is so in any case of death from asphyxia, in cases of poison from certain gases, and in cases of some very malignant forms of disease where decomposition is very rapid.

Q. I suppose a perfectly healthy woman would not be likely to have this sudden change take place in her without some cause similar to those you have mentioned? *A.* Very unlikely.

Dr. Eastham then testified that he graduated in medicine in 1841, had practised dentistry nearly all the time since, and had used anæsthetics from their introduction. The deceased had been his patient for twelve or fourteen years, during which he had on several occasions given her anæsthetics—chloroform, ether, and gas—both severally and in combination. The deceased came to his office in the forenoon of the 10th, and there met Mrs. Sawyer, whose tooth he extracted after giving nitrous oxide. Mrs. Sawyer urged the deceased to take gas, but she insisted upon ether. He made a mixture of a little *chloroform and ether.*

Question. You made a mixture at the time? *Answer.* Yes, sir; I usually do that way.

Q. Please tell me whether or not on this occasion you measured the quantity? *A.* No. I have been so familiar with it that I usually guess at the proportion. I never measure it. I always calculate to have more ether than chloroform.

Q. How much of this mixture did you make? *A.* Not more than an ounce or an ounce and a half.

Q. How did you administer it? *A.* I always administer it on a sponge. I always drop the window at the top, so as to have fresh air. I pour on to this sponge (it is a hollow one about the bigness of my two hands) about a big teaspoonful, as near as I can judge.

Q. That would have been about a third of the mixture? *A.* No, not so much as that. I always begin gradually in applying it, first holding the sponge a little distance from the nose and then moving it nearer. As she began to breathe it, she said, "Give me enough this time, sure." This she repeated three times. I did not fully etherize her, nor did I intend to. After she had breathed two or three minutes, I said to her, "I am going to take this tooth out." She shook her head, as much as to say she was not ready, but I took hold of the tooth. She straightened back, groaned and screamed a little as if in pain. After I had pulled the tooth, she went back into a sort of hysterics, and became rigid, as if in spasms.

Q. At this point in the case, did you notice her lips, whether they were pale? *A.* Not much.

Q. Any change in her countenance? *A.* Not much.

Q. Did you notice her eyes? *A.* They were set, wide open, like one in a spasm.

Q. You did not notice whether there was anything particular about the lips? *A.* No.

Q. Did you try the pulse at that time? *A.* No. I seized a napkin, moistened with water, and gave her a splash on the forehead. She seemed to revive, and I saw a flush of color come over her face. I set her up and took my ammonia water and applied that to her nose; then I spoke to Mrs. Sawyer. Mrs. Crie was sitting up in the chair, inclined a little forward at that time, and I was applying ammonia and water to the face. Mrs. Sawyer came in, and I asked her to loosen her dress, which she did. Then I saw a change again, back to paleness, and I said, "Call the other doctors." Dr. Osgood arrived first. We unloosed Mrs. Crie's corsets. Dr. Osgood rubbed her spine, and I sent the porter after another physician. We continued to rub her and apply very strong ammonia, and, finally, after Dr. Lamson came in, we removed her to the large room, and, raising her arms, tried in every way to set up respiration. We sent for a battery and used that. We worked over her till we all came to the conclusion that she was past all restoration.

Q. Can you tell us how long after she fell back into this spasm it was before respiration ceased? *A.* I should say about fifteen minutes.

Q. How long did the flush continue? *A.* It might have been two minutes.

Q. Then, as I understand, she fell back at once? *A.* As soon as the shade went back, I called for help. After administering these anæsthetics, there are two peculiar shades. There is the shade for faintness, and a shade from sickness at the stomach, and they are perfectly distinct.

Q. What was your opinion of this peculiar shade then? *A.* I thought it was a pallor from faintness.

Q. From the time she had this spasm, and during the time you were administering the ammonia, was she sitting up in the chair? *A.* Yes, sir; but after the doctors came in they removed her to the waiting-room and laid her down.

Q. Was she breathing then? *A.* She was dead.

Q. How long had you begun the administration of ether before you extracted the tooth? *A.* About a minute or a minute and a half.

Q. During that time did you feel no pulse? *A.* Never do that. Always watch the side of the head, the temporal artery.

Q. Do you think there is any danger of death occurring from giving ether alone? *A.* I never had anything that appeared like it myself; nor in chloroform.

Q. You have not considered then that there was any danger? *A.* No, I do not—that is, unless you administer it as they do in England. I should think they would kill every other one, by using a napkin as they do. But if chloroform be given as I give it, on a sponge, with plenty of fresh air, I don't consider it any more dangerous than ether; but a person must discriminate between individuals, whether he would give ether, or gas, or chloroform, or anything, and these things must be learned by practice.

Q. You considered her to be a person lacking somewhat in vitality, and therefore you didn't choose to put her fully under the influence of it (the anæsthetic)? *A.* Yes, sir.

Q. Do you consider either of these anæsthetics more dangerous than the others? *A.* I suppose chloroform would decompose blood quicker than ether.

Q. Do you know of any difference in chloroform? *A.* I have never used but one kind, Squibb's.

Q. In what way do you keep it? *A.* Always in a dark closet and corked as tight as I can.

Q. Do you know of any difference in the quality of ether? *A.* No, only from the seller's opinion of it. I use Powers & Weightman's concentrated.

Q. How much of this mixture did you generally make

at a time? *A.* Not more than a couple of ounces at once.

Q. What was the proportion of chloroform that you generally intended to have in? *A.* Less than half, by volume.

Q. Did you keep that mixture a long time? *A.* No, but I would most always add more ether if it had been standing a little while.

Q. Did you state that you made this mixture you administered to Mrs. Crie that day? *A.* I had a little in a bottle, and I added more to it before I gave it to her. I had used it a week before.

Q. What is your reason for adding chloroform to the ether? *A.* Well, I think it is safer. Ether is a great stimulant, and when you have a little chloroform, the patients are not so noisy or excited as they are under pure ether. That is my reason, not that I feared one or the other.

Q. You would not hesitate to give any quantity of chloroform? *A.* No, sir. If amputation was to be performed I would as soon use chloroform as ether.

Q. On the whole, which anæsthetic do you consider the most safe? *A.* I think I should use ether for safety. Ether and chloroform combined, in my idea, is much better than either of them alone.

Q. Do you feel any anxiety when about to administer chloroform or ether or the mixture? *A.* No.

In the above case, instead of death resulting from ether, it was, as was proven by analysis, due to *chloroform*, and the coroner's jury presented the following verdict, " death was caused by the inhalation of chloroform, administered in a mixture of chloroform and ether."*

Methylic Ether.

Are there any other ethers which can be employed with safety, and what is the best method of employing them? Dr. Richardson, of London, has used methylic ether, which he regards as one of the best (after sulphuric). This conclusion, it is stated, he reached after experimenting with eight or ten of the best known anæs-

---

* Boston Medical and Surgical Journal, Nov. 27, 1873.

thetics. He prefers a solution of methylic ether in ethylic ether, which latter will take up more than one hundred volumes of the methylic-ether gas. This mixture he then styles methylic ether. In Dr. Carter's work, before quoted, he states, "In Dr. Richardson's own hands, I have seen the various (new) ethers act perfectly well, producing complete unconsciousness and relaxation of muscle without either struggling or sickness, and without unpleasant symptoms of any kind; but I cannot judge how far such results may have been due to the qualities of the agents employed, how far due to specially skilful or careful administration, or how far to the state of the patients themselves." Bichloride of methylene was introduced by Dr. B. W. Richardson in 1867, and it has been employed not only in short operations, but also in such operations as ovariotomy. "Of this agent, Dr. Jones,* of Cork, has had considerable experience, having used it constantly for all minor operations in hospital and private practice for over seven years. Hard drinkers or old tipplers bore this form of anæsthetic badly, and on some occasions he has been alarmed and compelled to desist from its administration. He also found it to be dangerous in old cases of chest affection. His mode of administration was in a conical gauze bag lined with flannel, and containing a small sponge."

Bichloride of Methylene.

For some years, the bichloride of methylene has received the fullest trials at Moorfields Ophthalmic Hospital, London, where they now (1876) use almost exclusively sulphuric ether. Within the two years' trial of the bichloride of methylene in the hospital above referred to, two deaths occurred without any indication of danger from the state of the pulse or heart. In the last instance of death it occurred from the exhibition of one drachm and a half of methylene to a healthy sailor, aged twenty-seven years. Bichloride of methylene is employed in the

* Medical Responsibility in the Choice of Anæsthetics. By H. M. Jones, M.D., Surgeon of Cork Ophthalmic Hospital. Cork, 1876.

7

Samaritan Free Hospital of London, and the officer in charge of the anæsthetic states it to be very satisfactory. Junker's form of apparatus is used for its administration.

The mortality from this agent is 2 in 10,000 or 1 to 5000. . . . .

As I have stated above, the strongest advocate for the bichloride of methylene or chloromethyl is Mr. J. Spencer Wells, who believes that with this agent he has had all the advantages of complete anæsthesia with fewer drawbacks than any other. This is his experience of five years, and of three hundred and fifty serious operations. He gives it diluted with air by Junker's apparatus, and, from his doubts of its composition, we suspect what he employs to be a mixture of methylic alcohol and chloroform; these are his own words. But whatever may be its chemical composition, whether it is chloroform mixed with some spirit or ether, or whether it is really bichloride of methylene, I am still content with the effects of the liquid sold under that name.—*Meeting British Medical Association*, 1877.

Dr. Taylor* also states, that " a mixture of chloroform and ether has been sold as bichloride of methylene. On shaking this mixture with water, the chloroform is separated and sinks." He reports three deaths from this agent, and the allegation, therefore, that the vapor possesses any greater degree of safety than chloroform in surgical practice, is not supported by facts.

Death from the Bichloride of Methylene.

CASE 1.—A death from bichloride of methylene took place at the Ipswich Hospital, England, which affords a remarkable illustration of the relative safety of that drug and of ether. The patient was 56 years of age, and was to have had a necrosed bone removed from his leg. He was first given the methylene, which was changed for ether for some cause which is not stated, but which may have been some alarming symptom produced by the methylene. Having taken the ether with safety until anæsthesia was obtained, the operation was

* On Poisons, op. cit. p. 629.

proceeded with, but, the patient being allowed to wake too soon, the methylene was again resorted to. In fifteen seconds he was dead. No *post-mortem* examination was made, but some ingenious person hazarded a guess that there had been unobserved apoplexy, and the jury, happy at any alternative except condemnation, adopted the hint, and voted the death accidental, and the medical officers free of all blame. A most unsatisfactory case in all its aspects, and one which should please the medical officers inculpated less than any one else. Such a fatality may be hidden away by such a verdict, but no one can be satisfied, without evidence, that the case was not one of anæsthetic manslaughter.—*Medical Press, London.*

CASE 2. *Pharmaceutical Journal*, 1871, p. 875. Male, æt. 40. Given during an operation on the eye. Result, death in five minutes. *Post-mortem*, congestion of the lungs.

CASE 3. *Pharmaceutical Journal*, 1871, p. 875. Male. Inhaled ʒiss. Result, death rapid. *Post-mortem*, no special post-mortem appearances.

CASE 4. *Lancet*, Oct. 23, 1869, p. 532. Mr. Marshall. Male, æt. 39, ʒiss. The man was sitting in a chair during the time of administration, and preparing for an operation. Symptoms, pupils slightly dilated; no stertor or lividity of countenance. Result, death.

CASE 5. One of the most painful cases of death from the vapor of methylated ether occurred in the Birmingham Hospital, England, under Mr. Tait. A patient was about to undergo the operation of ovariotomy. Five drachms of methylated ether in vapor were administered to her on a fold of a towel, by the resident medical officer. The pulse suddenly stopped, the pupils became dilated, and respiration ceased. All efforts at restoration were fruitless. On inspection of the heart and all the other organs they were healthy except the ovary.— *Lancet*, July 5, 1873, p. 23.

Amylen.

The vapor of this liquid was introduced by the late Dr. Snow as a substitute for the vapor of chloroform. It produces a loss of sensibility without causing complete coma or stupor. Its use has already led to at least two deaths, and is, according to Dr. Taylor,* not so safe an agent as chloroform vapor for surgical purposes. The only appearance met with in one fatal case was an emphysematous state of the lungs, or excessive dilatation of the air-cells (*Med. Times and Gaz.*, April 4 and 18, 1857, pp. 332, 381), and in the other a distension of the right cavities of the heart with dark fluid blood. There was no congestion of the brain, and no smell of amylen perceptible in the body.—*Med. Times and Gaz.*, Aug. 8, 1857, p. 133.

Bromide of Ethyl or Hydrobromic Ether.

Bromide of ethyl (C_2H_5B), or "hydrobromic ether," is a colorless liquid with an agreeable odor; it boils at about 40° C., has a density of 1.43, and burns with difficulty. The boiling point and density are, therefore, intermediate between those of chloroform and sulphuric ether. Bromide of ethyl absorbed by the respiratory passages produces, according to M. Rabuleau, of Paris,† absolute anæsthesia as rapidly, or even more rapidly, than chloroform. This result has been established with frogs, rabbits, dogs, etc. After five minutes' (sometimes after two minutes') inhalation by means of a sponge saturated in bromide of ethyl, dogs were completely anæsthetized. The animals recovered more rapidly than when chloroform was used.

Bromide of ethyl is not caustic, nor even irritant, when compared to chloroform. It can be ingested without difficulty, and applied without danger, not only subcutaneously, but to the external auditory meatus, and to the mucous membranes. In this respect it is preferable to chloroform, which is very caustic, and to sulphuric ether, of which the ingestion is nearly impossible. Introduced into the human stomach in doses of from one to two grammes, bromide of ethyl does not produce anæsthesia as when absorbed in sufficient quantity by the

---

* On Poisons, op. cit. p. 627.

† Comptes Rendus, vol. lxxxiii. p. 1294; Pharm. Journ. and Trans.

respiratory passages. It soothes pain and does not disturb the appetite.

This hydrobromic ether is nearly insoluble in water; nevertheless, water shaken with it acquires a pleasant taste and odor. Frogs placed in water so saturated undergo anæsthesia in ten or fifteen minutes. It is eliminated nearly entirely, if not completely, by the respiratory passages, whatever may have been the mode of absorption. At most, only traces of it are found in the urine when it has been introduced into the stomach, and an extremely small quantity can be detected in that secretion when it has been inhaled. Bromide of ethyl does not decompose in the organism to form an alkaline bromide. Bromide of ethyl is an anæsthetic agent possessing properties intermediate between those of chloroform, bromoform, and ether. I have experimented with this ether, prepared for me by Prof. Jos. P. Remington, of this city.

This ether was discovered by Serullas in 1827. It is produced by the action of bromine, hydrobromic acid, or bromide of phosphorus on alcohol.

The method which Mr. Remington employed was that of the celebrated chemist De Vrij, by distilling 4 parts pulverized bromide of potassium, with 5 parts of a mixture, of 2 parts strong sulphuric acid and 1 part alcohol of 96 per cent.

Properties.—Transparent and colorless liquid, heavier than water (Serullas); specific gravity 1.40 (Löwig), 1.4733 at 0° (Pierre); vapor density 3.754 (R. Marchand J. per cm. 188); very volatile; boiling point 40.7° C. when the barometer stands at 757 mm. (Pierre); has a strong ethereal odor and pungent taste (Serullas). According to Löwig, its taste is strongly and disagreeably sweetish, with a somewhat burning after-taste. The vapor, when inhaled, exerts an anæsthetic action, like chloroform (Robin, *Compt. Rend.* xxxii. 669). It is sparingly soluble in water, but mixes in all proportions with *alcohol* and *ether*.

Decompositions.—1. Vapor of hydrobromic ether passed through a glass tube at a low red heat is resolved into ethylene and hydrobomic acid gas. 2. It burns with difficulty, but with a beautiful green flame, which does not smoke, a strong odor of hydrobromic acid being at the same time evolved. 3. It is not decomposed by nitric acid, oil of vitriol, or potassium. 4. With ammonia it yields hydrobromate of ethylamine.

The first experiment was upon a small quantity, and subsequently upon four ounces. I found it to contain all the physical qualities as described by M. Rabuleau. It was colorless, with an agreeable odor and pleasant taste. The boiling point, 40.9° C., and its density heavier than water. When inhaled, it produced more of the agreeable effects of chloroform, and did not increase the pulse over its normal beat, whilst its action was very rapid, and in the second state it caused an intermission of the pulse every second beat. Three teaspoonfuls were added to a pint of water, and they sank to the bottom in globules, and upon being shaken it was in part diffused in the water without producing any change in the color. A large-sized lively frog was then placed in this pint of water thus charged, and he made numerous endeavors to get out of it, and it required twenty minutes before he was fully under its influence. The anæsthetic effect was most profound; even his heart could just be felt making a most feeble effort, and his respirations entirely ceased, as far as I could judge. He was perfectly relaxed; the extremities became a livid-red color, and apparently lifeless, and no pinching or pricking was felt by him. After the frog had been removed he remained in this state for fifty-eight minutes, and then began to make some slight movements, and, when the hour was up, was able to move about in a languid manner.

Owing to the peculiar action on the pulse, I feared the hydrobromic ether might not be perfectly free from some toxic agent, so I took the specimen back to Mr. Joseph P. Remington, and he carefully redistilled it over lime, and he stated in a note to me that it was now perfectly pure. The boiling point is 40.9° C., or about 104° Fahr. This very nearly corresponds with Pierre's observation, i. e., 40.7° C., density 7.43; burns with difficulty, producing a greenish flame.

I made the following experiment with it in the ear: A teaspoonful was mixed with one of glycerine, and was placed in the ear of a patient who was suffering from otalgia. The patient stated it gave her some pain, with a feeling of heat; but these sensations soon passed away, and her pain was relieved. No inflammation or caustic effects resulted from its use in the auditory canal, which was very irritable. I attempted to use a small quantity of chloroform on cotton in the same ear, but it could not be borne in contact even for a few seconds, it caused so much distress and irritation of the parts.

When hydrobromic ether is administered by the mouth, it should be triturated with glycerine, gum-arabic in powder, or a small portion of spermaceti, as it is so much heavier than water, and its effect upon the mucous membrane is slightly irritating if not given properly (mixed), as it produces a feeling of warmth, and, as usual, eructation of gaseous ether. A third use of it, by inhalation, on a patient about to undergo a painful operation, induced a slight feeling of nausea, and she was very rapidly brought under its influence, and it did not produce the intermission in the pulse as in the first case. In two cases in which the ear was inflamed this preparation of ether could not be borne by the patient even on cotton.

Mr. Remington made me a second specimen of hydrobromic ether by the use of phosphorus, which I inhaled myself, and also administered to a patient, and found it was free from the irritating effects upon my lungs and heart. In certain cases where ordinary sulphuric ether was objectionable, this ether might be substituted. It evidently holds an intermediate place between chloroform and ether, and is worthy of a more extended trial.

One of the common impurities of hydrobromic ether is bromoform, CHB^3, produced by the simultaneous action of bromine and caustic potash on wood spirit, alcohol, or acetone; also by action of bromine on acetous, citric, or malic acid; and by decomposing bromal with alkalies. It is a limpid liquid of sp. grav. 2.13, having an agreeable odor and saccharine taste. It is less volatile than chloroform, very little soluble in water, to which, however, it imparts its taste and odor;

soluble in alcohol, ether, and essential oils. It burns with difficulty.—*Watts's Dictionary of Chemistry*, London, 1872.

CHAPTER IV.

Chloroform, chemical composition, impurities, tests. Recent investigations, by Bowditch, of Boston. Deaths from chloroform in England. Aid of the legislature to stop the employment of chloroform in France. Mode of use in Scotland, by Professor Macleod, with form of apparatus, and all the necessary precautions in case of impending death. Report of twenty-one cases of chloroform administration. Dr. Allis' Chloroform Inhaler. Employment of anæsthetics in labor. M. Pichard. Congress at Geneva. Drs. Lusk, Wilson, and Smith. Statistics of death from chloroform, by the late Dr. Morgan, of Dublin. Dr. Sims on Nélaton's method. Nitrite of amyl as an antidote to chloroform. Observations and cases, by Drs. Richardson, Burrall, Lane, and Mundé. Dr. Clover's inhaler. Mixed narcosis, use of morphia before inhalation of chloroform. Dr. Richardson's experimentation upon reported deaths from chloroform, etc. Conclusions in reference to the use and safety of chloroform, by Drs. Chisholm, Erichsen, and Gross.

Chloroform.

CHLOROFORM; dichlorinated chloride of methyl; terchloride of formyl, $CHCl^3$. Chloroform was discovered in 1831, by "Soubeiran, Guthrie, and independently in 1832, by Liebig." Its true constitution was discovered by Dumas, in 1834. The most economical method of preparing chloroform is the distillation of alcohol with chloride of lime.

Chloroform may be contaminated with alcohol, ether, and empyreumatic oils. Pure chloroform sinks in a mixture of equal parts of oil of vitriol and water. According to "Kessler," chloroform containing alcohol diminishes in volume on the application of this test. The presence of alcohol causes opalescence when the chloroform is mixed with water, whereas, pure chloroform remains clear. Chloroform containing alcohol acquires a green color when mixed with chromic acid or with sulphuric acid and acid chromate of potassium. Pure chloroform produces no green color. Chloroform prepared from wood spirit is much less pure than that obtained from alcohol. The former is specifically lighter than the latter, has a repulsive empyreumatic odor, and produces unpleasant sensations when inhaled. According to Gregory, impure chloroform may be recognized by the disagreeable odor it leaves after evaporation on a cloth which has been moistened with it, and by the yellow or brown color which it imparts to pure oil of vitriol when agitated therewith.

Pure chloroform placed upon oil of vitriol produces a contact-surface convex downwards; impure chloroform gives a plane contact-surface. According to Roussin, the purity of chloroform may be tested by means of dinitrosulphide of iron, $Fe^6H^2S^5N^4O^2$ (a salt obtained by the action of ferric chloride or sulphate on a mixture of sulphide of ammonium and nitrite of potassium). Pure chloroform shaken up with this salt remains colorless; but if it contain alcohol, ether, or wood-spirit, it acquires a dark color. Pure chloroform is a transparent and colorless liquid, of specific gravity 1.491 at 17° C. It boils at 61° (Regnault). Its vapor density is 4.199 according to Dumas, 4.230 according to Regnault. Chloroform remains liquid and transparent at —16° C., and may be solidified by the cold produced by its own evaporation. It has a very pleasant penetrating odor, a sweet fiery taste. Chloroform preserves meat, 200 times its weight, from putrefaction.

Chloroform dissolves slightly in water, imparting its sweet taste to the liquid. It mixes in all proportions with alcohol.

Chloroform decomposes when exposed to air and light, with the formation of chlorine, hydrochloric acid, and other products, but when kept under water it remains unaltered.

This is the second agent of importance in use as an anæsthetic, and one of the most powerful and most agreeable of all the forms. It is also the most rapid in its action and less under our control than ether. It has been found by the recent investigations of Dr. Henry I.

Bowditch,* of Boston, that ether and "chloroform resemble each other in their effects on those nerve centres whose activity is connected with the conscious perception of pain. The latter, however, acts much more powerfully than the former upon those centres which regulate the arterial blood tension, and thus effects profoundly the condition of animal life. Ether and chloroform are both anæsthetics, but chloroform is something more." And what is this something more? Namely, great *prostration* without warning.

In England, it has been stated that the deaths from chloroform are at the rate of one a week during the year. It has been proposed in France to seek the aid of the legislature to put an end to its employment. In Scotland,† it is stated that it is not the chloroform which is to blame, but the mode of administration, and yet there is nothing new in their method, only great care, with all the materials at hand in case of fainting, asphyxia, sudden paralysis of the heart, and one carefully instructed person who takes the entire charge of this powerful anæsthetic.

Report of Twenty-one Cases Chloroform Administration.‡

	Min.	Sec.
Shortest time taken to place the patient under anæsthetic influence of chloroform,	2	30
Longest time,	14	30
Average,	6	24
" time under influence,	12	48
Smallest quantity used in any one case, 1 drachm,		
Largest " " " " 8 "		
Average " " " " 3 " 9 minims.		

Great Prostration in one Case after Administration.—The chloroform was administered by means of a handkerchief or towel folded in the form of a cone.

---

* The Influence of Anæsthetics on the Vaso-motor Centres, by Henry I. Bowditch and C. S. Minot. Boston, 1874.

† On the Administration of Chloroform, by George H. B. Macleod, M.D., Professor of Surgery, University of Glasgow.—*Brit. Med. Journal.*

‡ By Surgeon-Major J. H. Porter, Assistant Professor of Military Surgery, London, 1875; Netley Hospital; Erichsen's Surgery, p. 50, Phila. 1878.

Vomiting occurred in 2 cases after the administration of the drug; excitement occurred in 10 cases during or after administration.

The following is a description of a simple form of inhaler for the administration of chloroform, devised by Dr. Allis, of this city.* See Fig. 16.

" It consists merely of two tin cones soldered apex to apex, with a tube projecting from the upper or receiving cone into the lower. Around the base of the larger cone a piece of linen is tied. When the instrument is to be used, a towel is properly folded and pinned around the larger cone, presenting, when complete, a cone of sufficient size to cover neatly the mouth and nose.

" This cannot be called an inhaler with any more propriety than can a towel or a napkin; but, while it resembles the latter in principle, it has in practice very many and important advantages.

Fig. 16.

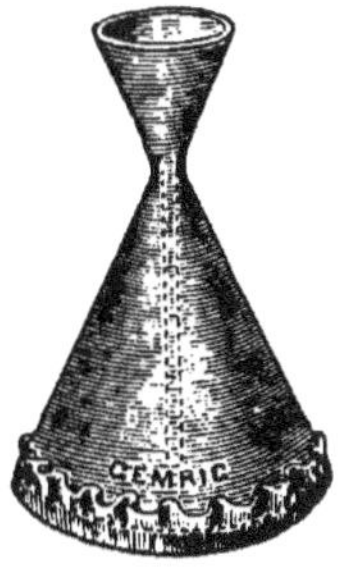

" 1. The chloroform falls through the tube upon a single layer of linen to both sides of which the air has ready access, and is accordingly instantly evaporated.

" 2. Every drop is conveyed to the patient.

" 3. A few drops at a time are all that are ever required, and all the patient can breathe with comfort.

" 4. The dropping may be more or less constant, as the instrument need not be removed from the face, and by means of a 'dropper' (see Fig. 7), the operator can gauge the amount to the necessities of the case.

" 5. The anæsthetic influence is gained gradually, imperceptibly, and rapidly, and with a minimum amount of chloroform. I seldom use more than a drachm and a half in adults.

" 6. As only a few drops need be added at a time, the danger must be far less than when an indefinite quantity is poured on from a bottle at once.

" 7. There is no exclusion of the air, but the air that

* Philadelphia Medical Times, Number 162.

is breathed is impregnated with a fresh supply of chloroform.

"8. The time consumed is usually from three to ten minutes.

"9 The influence once obtained may be easily maintained.

"We have used this repeatedly for nearly four years, and have found it all that we could desire.

"It is exceedingly convenient as a frame-work about which to pin the towel, and as a receiver of the chloroform, and so simple in construction that any tinsmith could make or repair it should it be broken.

"*As to its rendering the use of chloroform safe, I can only say that safety does not lie in an inhaler, but in him who uses it.*"*

"Chloroform is eight times more dangerous than ether. When to the deaths by chloroform we add those not infrequent chloroform accidents, where artificial respiration alone restored the patient, when life was hovering on extinction, and when the faintest attempt at respiration was so anxiously watched for, and heard with such intense relief (though such cases do not come under immediate publicity), it must indeed be admitted they would tend very much to intensify the distrust which is more or less acknowledged, and is the real impediment of this 'pain destroyer,' when we are about, by its means, to use the words of a modern surgical writer,† reducing the patient to a condition in 'which, to the uninitiated, he appears in articulo mortis,' and in 'which very little more would place the circumstances in a most critical relation.'"

Dr. M. Sims, of New York, considers that it is the safest plan to relinquish the use of chloroform altogether except in obstetrics. Yet, in this department, deaths have occurred from chloroform, one very recently. Prof. Depaul, of Paris, has stated that sudden deaths from the obstetric use of chloroform are not unknown to him.

We give the following case recently reported: "Death from chloroform at the Lyons Maternité."

"A young woman, twenty-five years of age, who had

---

* Prof. Morgan, of Dublin, op. cit.
† Prof. Miller, of Edinburgh (Surgery), p. 582.

already borne children, was admitted into the Maternité of the Charité, at 3 P.M. on March 23, 1876. The pains continued all night, and at about 7 A.M. of the 24th, the liquor amnii having been discharged, it was ascertained that there was a shoulder presentation.

"In order to effect version, chloroform was administered, under the sole direction of the sister intrusted with the service; neither the chef-de-service nor the interne on duty having been summoned to the case.

"As, after the operation was terminated, the patient did not revive, the interne was now called, but the patient died ten minutes after his arrival.

"The reporter justly observes that the death cannot be properly charged to chloroform without its being known what precautions were taken; but, he adds, that such a circumstance should so happen in the first maternité of Lyons is indeed as astounding as deplorable."— *Lyons Méd.*, April 9.

Employment of Anæsthetics in Labor.

M. Piachaud read a paper before the International Medical Congress of Geneva (*Gaz. Médicale*, October 20, 1877), in which he advanced the following conclusions, which are not generally approved of by the majority of gynæcologists, only a few holding to these views :—

1. The employment of anæsthetics is, as a general rule, advisable in natural labor.

2. The principal substances which have been used for this purpose up to the present time—chloroform, amylene, laudanum, morphia hypodermically, chloral by the mouth and by injection.

3. Of these, chloroform seems to be preferable.

4. It should be administered according to the method of Snow, that is, in small doses at the beginning of each pain, its administration being suspended during the intervals.

5. It should never be pushed to complete insensibility, but the patient should be held in a state of semi-anæsthesia, so as to produce a diminution of the suffering.

6. The general rule is never to administer chloroform except during the period of expulsion; but in certain

cases of nervousness and extreme agitation, it is advantageous not to wait for the complete dilatation of the os uteri.

7. Experience has shown that anæsthetics do not arrest the contractions of the uterus or abdominal muscles, but that they weaken the natural resistance of the perineal muscles.

8. The use of anæsthetics has no unpleasant effect on the mind of the mother or upon the child.

9. In lessening the suffering, anæsthetics render a great service to those women who dread the pain; they diminish the chances of the nervous crises which are caused during labor by the excess of suffering; they make the recovery more rapid.

10. They are especially useful to calm the great agitation and cerebral excitement, which labor often produces in every nervous woman.

11. Their employment is indicated in natural cases until the pains are suspended or retarded by the suffering caused by maladies occurring previous to or during labor, and in those cases where irregular and partial contractions occasion internal and sometimes continuous pain, without causing progress of the labor.

12. In a natural labor, chloroform should never be used without the consent of the woman and her family.

On the Necessity of Caution in the Employment of Chloroform during Labor.

Professor Lusk read a paper at the annual meeting of the American Gynæcological Society,* on the Necessity of Caution in the Employment of Chloroform during Labor. "He protested strongly against the popular idea that the administration of chloroform in obstetric practice was absolutely free from danger. In all cases in which a profound anæsthesia was produced by the administration of chloroform, the uterine action was weakened, and in some cases entirely suspended. It was extremely dangerous to continue the administration of

* Reported in Boston Medical and Surgical Journal, June 7th, 1877, p. 685.

the chloroform after the termination of the third stage, since in such cases there is great risk of a dangerous hemorrhage taking place. He believed that sudden death from the action of the chloroform, on the heart, was as liable to occur in obstetric practice as in cases of surgical operations."

Dr. Wilson, of Baltimore, dissented from the views of the writer as to the danger of using chloroform in obstetric cases.

Dr. Albert Smith, of Philadelphia, thought that chloroform was to be preferred to ether in those cases in which a rapid anæsthesia is to be desired.

In a recent case, which came under the writer's notice, where three pints of chloroform had been employed in a tedious labor, there was great retardation, and ultimately, when the forceps were applied, the infant was so narcotized from the effects of the chloroform that every means employed to restore it failed.*

A full account of Nelaton's Method of Resuscitation from Chloroform Narcosis.†

Dr. Charles James Campbell, the distinguished accoucheur of Paris, has recently written two papers on anæsthesia in obstetrics, in which he ably sustains the views long taught by Nélaton, that death from chloroform is due to syncope or cerebral anæmia. And amongst other strong arguments to prove his position, he gives a graphic description of a case of chloroform narcosis, which occurred in my practice in Paris, where M. Nélaton, by his method, unquestionably saved the life of the patient. She was young, beautiful, and accomplished, and belonged to one of the oldest and best families in France. Married at twenty, she gave birth

---

* In this case the baby's color, form, and features were most beautifully preserved by the chloroform for several days, without the use of ice, in hot weather.

† Read at the forty-second annual meeting of the British Medical Association, held in Norwich, August, 1874, by J. Marion Sims, M.D., Surgeon to the Woman's Hospital of the State of New York, etc.

to her first child a year afterwards. The head was enormous (hydrocephalic), impacted in the pelvis nearly twenty-four hours, and the delivery of a dead child was ultimately accomplished with instruments. Dr. Bouchacour, of Lyons, was called in consultation, and applied the forceps. In a week afterwards the urine began to dribble away, and in a fortnight an immense slough was thrown off. The case, surgically considered, was one of the most interesting I ever saw, and the operation was one of the most difficult I ever performed on any one in her station of life. The base of the bladder was destroyed, and the fundus fell through the fistulous opening; it was therefore inverted, and protruded between the labia majora as a herniary mass of the size of an apricot, its external covering being the internal or lining membrane of the bladder, which was of a deep vermilion-red color. The vaginal portion of the cervix uteri and the posterior cul-de-sac were destroyed; and by the reparative process the cervix and the posterior wall of the vagina were blended into one common cicatricial mass, which was firm, inelastic, and immovable. The case appeared desperate, and M. Nélaton had pronounced it incurable. A preparatory operation was necessary, viz., to open the cervix uteri, by dissecting it from the posterior wall of the vagina, and thus to reconstitute the canal of the vagina up to the canal of the cervix; and by a subsequent operation, to draw forward the flap thus formed, secure it to the neck of the bladder anteriorly, and thereby close the fistula. The first, or preparatory operation, was performed at the country house of the family, near Dijon, on November 3d, 1861, Dr. Dugast, of Dijon, assisting, and giving chloroform. The second, or operation for the radical cure, was performed on the 19th of the month, at St. Germain, about an hour's distance from Paris by rail. M. Nélaton, Dr. Campbell, Dr. Beylard, Dr. Johnston, and Mr., now Dr., Alan Herbert, were present. I seldom give an anæsthetic in private practice for operation on the walls of the vagina, as the pain is generally not sufficient to call for it. But in this case, as the slightest touch was unbearable, an anæsthetic was indispensable. Dr. Campbell was selected by the family, as well as by M. Nélaton and myself, to administer the chloroform, especially as he was in the daily habit of giving it in his large obstetrical practice, and we all had entire confidence in his caution, skill, and judgment. The patient was soon anæsthetized. The operation was begun at 10 A. M., and I thought it would require about an hour to finish it.

Many years ago I imbibed the convictions of my countrymen against chloroform in general surgery, and have always used ether in preference, never feeling the least dread of danger from it under any circumstances. It is otherwise with chloroform, and in this particular case I felt the greatest anxiety, frequently stopping during the operation to ask Dr. Campbell if all was going on well with the patient. At the end of forty minutes the sutures (twelve or thirteen) were all placed, and ready to be secured, and I was secretly congratulating myself that the operation would be finished in a few minutes more, when all at once I discovered an unusual bluish-livid appearance of the vagina, as if the blood were stagnant, and I called Dr. Johnston's attention to it. As this lividity seemed to increase, I felt rather uneasy about it, and I asked Dr. Campbell if all was right with the pulse. He replied, " All right, go on." Scarcely were these words uttered, when he suddenly cried out, " Stop! stop! No pulse, no breathing; " and, looking to M. Nélaton, he said, " Tête en bas, n'est-ce pas?" Nélaton replied, " Certainly; there is nothing else to do." Immediately the body was inverted, the head hanging down, while the heels were raised high in the air by Dr. Johnston, the legs resting one on each of his shoulders. Dr. Campbell supported the thorax. Mr. Herbert was sent to an adjoining room for a spoon, with the handle of which the jaws were held open; and I handed M. Nélaton a tenaculum, which he hooked into the tongue, and gave in charge to Mr. Herbert; while to Dr. Beylard was assigned the duty of making efforts at artificial respiration, by pressure alternately on the thorax and abdomen. M. Nélaton ordered and overlooked every movement, while I stood aloof and watched the proceedings with, of course, the most intense anxiety. They held the patient in this inverted position for a long time before there was any manifestation of returning life. Dr. Campbell, in his report, says it was fifteen minutes, and that it seemed an age. My notes of the case, written a few hours afterwards, make it twenty minutes. Be this as it may, the time was so long that I thought it useless to make any further efforts, and said, "Gentlemen, she is certainly dead, and you might as well let her alone." But the great and good Nélaton never lost hope, and by his quiet, cool, brave manner, he seemed to infuse his spirit into his aids. At last there was a feeble inspiration, and after a long time another, and by and by another; and then the breathing became pretty regular, and Dr. Campbell said, "The pulse returns, thank God! she will soon be all right again." Dr. Beylard, who always sees the cheerful side of everything in life, was disposed to laugh at the fear I manifested for the safety of our patient. I must confess that never before or since have I felt such a grave responsibility. When the pulse and respiration were well re-established, M. Nélaton ordered the patient to be laid on the table. This was done gently. But what was our horror, when, at the moment the body was placed horizontally, the pulse and breathing instantly ceased. Quick as thought the body was again inverted, the head downward and the feet over Dr. Johnston's shoulders, and the same manœuvres as before were put into execution. Dr. Campbell thinks it did not take such a long time to re-establish the action of the lungs and heart as in the first instance. It may have lacked a few seconds of the time, but it seemed to me to be quite as long, for the same tedious, painful, protracted, and anxious efforts were made as before, and she seemed, if possible, more dead than before; but, thanks to the brave men who had her in charge, feeble signs of returning life eventually made their appearance. Respiration was at first irregular, and at long intervals; soon it became more regular, and the pulse could then be counted, but it was very feeble, and would intermit. I began again to be hopeful, and even dared to think that at last there was an end of this dreadful suspense, when they laid her horizontally on the table again, saying, "She is all right this time." To witness two such painful scenes of danger to a young and valuable life, and to experience such agony of anxiety, produced a tension of heart, and mind, and soul that cannot be imagined. What, then, must have been our dismay, our feeling of despair, when, incredible as it may seem, the moment the body was laid in the horizontal position again, the respiration ceased a third time, the pulse was gone, and she looked the perfect picture of death? Then I gave up all for lost; for I thought that the blood was so poisoned, so charged with chloroform, that it was no longer able to sustain life. But Nélaton, and Campbell, and Johnston, and Beylard, and Herbert, by a consentaneous effort, quickly inverted the body a third time, thus throwing all the blood possible to the brain, and again they began their efforts at artificial respiration. It seemed to me that she would never breathe again; but at last there was a spasmodic gasp, and, after a long while, there was another effort at inspiration; and, after another long interval, there was a third; they were "far between;" then we watched, and waited, and wondered if there would be a fourth; at length it came, and more profoundly, and there was a long yawn, and the respiration became tolerably regular. Soon Dr. Beylard says, "I feel the pulse again, but it is very weak." Nélaton, after some moments, ejaculates, "The color of the tongue and lips is more natural." Campbell says, "The vomiting is favorable; see, she moves her hands; she is pushing against me." But I was by no means sure that these movements were not merely signs of the last death struggle; and so I expressed myself. Presently, Dr. Johnston said, "See here, doctor; see how she kicks; she is coming round again;" and very soon they all said, "She is safe at last." I replied, "For heaven's sake, keep her safe; I beg you not to put her on the table again until she is conscious." This was the first and only suggestion I made during all these anxious moments, and it was acted upon; for she was held in the vertical position till she, in a manner, recovered semi-consciousness, opened her eyes, looked wildly around, and asked what was the matter. She was then, and not till then, laid on the table, and all present felt quite as solemn and as thankful as I did; and we all in turn grasped Nélaton's hand, and thanked him for having saved the life of this lovely woman.

In a few minutes more the operation was finished, but, of course, without chloroform. The sutures were quickly assorted and separately twisted, and the patient put to bed; and on the eighth day thereafter I had the happiness to remove the sutures in the presence of M. Nélaton, and show him the success of the operation.

I have detailed the circumstances of this interesting case at great length, because I believe it goes as far to establish a principle of treatment as any one case ever did, or possibly can.

Nitrite of Amyl as an Antidote to Chloroform.

Within the last few years the nitrite of amyl has assumed considerable importance as a remedy in all spasmodic affections. The first notice of its effects was by Prof. Guthrie, who, while distilling nitrite of amyl from amylic alcohol, observed that the vapor, when inhaled, quickened his circulation, and made him feel as if he had been running. There was flushing of his face, rapid action of the heart, and difficult breathing. In 1861-2, Dr. B. W. Richardson, of London, made a careful and prolonged study of the action of this singular body, and discovered that it produced its effect by causing an extreme relaxation, first of the bloodvessels, and afterwards of the muscular fibres of the body. To such an extent did this agent relax that it would even overcome the tetanic spasm produced by strychnia, and relieve the most agonizing of known human maladies—*angina pectoris*. Even tetanus has been subdued by it in two instances. In asthma, my own experience coincides with that of others that it will, in certain spasmodic forms, instantly arrest the paroxysm. An exceedingly convenient mode of carrying the drug was by means of thin glass globules of nitrite of amyl, containing respectively ℳiiss and ℳv, suggested by Hubbell, of this city. When required, one of the bulbs is broken in a handkerchief or towel, and its contents immediately inhaled. I have employed this agent in spasmodic ear cough, also in tinnitus aurium, in which there is spasm of the muscles of the ear bones, in which case I directed the patient to carry a small glass-stoppered bottle, and to inhale five or six drops on a handkerchief, or even hold the nose for a second to the mouth of the bottle containing a small quantity.

At times I have been very much disappointed in the effects, and on examination of the drug, even obtained from a first-class store, it was found to be amylic ether, and not nitrite of amyl. Dr. Burrall, of New York, has recapitulated the experiments performed upon cats and dogs by others and himself, and set the amyl down as an agent which should always be in the armamentarium of the medical man who went prepared to meet any emergency that might arise while producing anæsthesia with chloroform.

Dr. W. L. Lane has repeated numerous experiments on animals with the nitrite of amyl, and states, " When inhaled in small quantities it produces recovery from chloroform insensibility (see experiments, *British Med. Journal*, Jan. 7, 1877) by dilating the arterioles of the brain, and thus removing the cerebral anæmia due to the chloroform. It also helps to produce recovery from the chloroform insensibility by raising the temperature, which is always lowered by chloroform, and by removing the paralysis of the heart due to chloroform; this action is well seen by the nitrite of amyl making the heart's beats fewer and sounds louder. This action of the nitrite of amyl in flushing of the face and eyes, causing increased heat, and making the heart beat slower, but with an irregular action, we have experienced in our own person in doses of two mimims and a half by inhalation."

Dr. Lane also states by way of caution, that, where the pure nitrite of amyl is inhaled in large quantities, instead of producing recovery from chloroformic insensibility, it not only retards it, but it may cause death by paralysis and over-distension of the heart and engorgement of the venous system. In large doses (inhaled), it produces a fall of temperature.

The Influence of Nitrite of Amyl in Counteracting the Depressing Effects of Ether and Chloroform during Anæsthesia.

Dr. Mundé (in *Am. Journal Medical Sciences*, Jan. 4, 1878) states: "The beneficial effects of nitrite of amyl in stimulating the heart, and thus permitting the continued administration of ether (in an operation for ovariotomy), were witnessed by all the physicians present, and are unquestionable. He also states that two cases of resuscitation from chloroform syncope by amyl-nitrite have been reported by Dr. Pilcher in his report on croup and diphtheria; and very recently* I find a case published in which the inhalation of the nitrite of amyl, which fortunately was at hand, according to the testimony of physicians present, revived the patient from sudden chloroform collapse, and saved her life."

Nitrite of Amyl in Threatened Death from Chloroform.

The Editor of the *British Medical Journal* says: We have received the following interesting report for publication from a physician:—

"On the 9th instant I was asked by a professional friend to administer chloroform to a patient of his, from whom he was about to remove a fatty tumor situated in the left lumbar region. The patient in question was about forty-nine years of age, married, the mother of several children; of thin, spare habit, but otherwise in good health. She was nervous, and apprehensive of the result, entreating me not to give her too much chloroform. Having previously examined the heart and found all sounds normal, I gave her about two teaspoonsful of brandy undiluted, and after waiting a few minutes, and placing her in a recumbent posture, I commenced the administration. The chloroform I used was Duncan & Flockhart's, upon the purity of which we can always depend. I poured a measured drachm upon a piece of lint enveloped in a

---

* British Med. Journal, August 18, 1877.

towel. I held it some little distance from her mouth and nose, and let her inhale slowly. My friend noted her pulse, whilst I carefully watched the respiration. The first dose did not produce any effect, and I then used another drachm, which soon caused a good deal of excitement, incoherent talking, and struggling, the patient striving several times to snatch the inhaler from my hand. This gradually subsided, and she appeared to be passing into the third stage of anæsthesia, when she made an abortive attempt to vomit, raised her head from the pillow, and, to my friend's great alarm, the pulse flickered and stopped altogether; she gave a gasp; foam gathered on her lips; her jaw became rigid, and to all appearance she was dead. I immediately withdrew the chloroform, my friend dashed some cold water in her face and pulled her tongue forward, whilst I commenced artificial respiration, after Marshall Hall's method, but without success. We then poured some nitrite of amyl on lint and held it to her nostrils. In such emergencies it is impossible to judge the flight of time correctly, but I should say in ten seconds there was a flushing of the face, the pulse was again felt, and, to our great joy, the all important function of respiration was again restored, the woman being rescued apparently from the very embrace of death."

J. T. Clover, Esq., in a note to the writer dated London, Dec. 20, 1875, in answer to a query in regard to chloroform and his "bag apparatus," writes, "I beg to say that my opinion of chloroform and of the bag apparatus for administering chloroform has not altered since the publication of the late Dr. Sansom's book."

In another published statement this same good authority writes:* "For giving chloroform, with or without ether, I use a modification of my bellows and bag apparatus. The favorable opinion as to the greater safety of ether, and the *increased alarm* as to chloroform, together with the improvements in the way of giving ether, have induced me within the last four or five years to give ether much oftener than chloroform."

* British Med. Journal.

Mixed Narcosis.—"During the past two or three weeks," says the *Lancet*, December 1, a "novel mode of producing anæsthesia, called mixed narcosis (*gemischte narkose*), has been employed by Thiersch, of Leipzig, whereby insensibility to pain may be procured without the total abolition of consciousness. The credit of the discovery is ascribed to Professor Nussbaum, of Munich. Although suitable for all kinds of operations, it is especially serviceable for operations about the mouth and jaws, in which blood is apt to flow into the trachea, or down the œsophagus into the stomach, and subsequently to cause vomiting. In some cases of removal of the upper jaw lately performed by Thiersch, the patient allowed the blood to accumulate for a while at the back of the pharynx, and then spat it completely out, when asked to do so; and we are informed that in one instance the patient watched, with evident interest, the motion of the saw that was dividing his upper jaw-bone.

"A subcutaneous injection of morphia, from a quarter to half a grain, is given as soon as the patient is placed upon the operating table, and immediately afterward the administration of chloroform is commenced. After inhalation for about five minutes the operation may usually be begun, but the chloroform must be renewed at intervals. The patients lose all sensibility to pain, but evidently retain a considerable degree of consciousness and control of voluntary movements. Within the last month mixed narcosis has been employed five times sucessfully, as far as the annihilation of pain is concerned, and without any bad effects."

The dose of morphia which is given in the communication in the *Lancet* is too large for safety, as there are many persons on whom even one-quarter of a grain of morphia hypodermically will act as a powerful poison, while half a grain even produces death. The injection of morphia should be small, say from one-eighth to one-quarter, and this should be given, according to Claude Bernard, from forty minutes to one hour before the chloroform is employed. The question should always be put to the patient, have you ever employed morphia? And, if so, what effect has it upon you? The great advantage claimed for this method is that the stage of excitement is rendered always *nil*, and less chloroform is needed to induce sleep than under ordinary circumstances. It must always be borne in mind that nausea and vomiting are not uncommon at the commencement if the morphia is quickly absorbed. This, with the vomiting which accompanies chloroform, will, we fear, be apt to complicate a delicate operation, and then you have the double risk of two such poisonous agents.

Deaths from Chloroform.

" The following account, with the *post-mortem*, is full and accurate.* On Friday, January 5, 1877, a death following the administration of chloroform occurred in the office of a dentist of Rahway, New Jersey. Walter E. Lewis, a lad, aged 14 years, shortly after taking a hearty supper, stopped, in company with a younger brother, at the office of a dentist in that place for the purpose of having a tooth extracted. He was accordingly seated in the operating chair, and the administration of the anæsthetic commenced without delay. An ordinary folded napkin was placed over his nose and mouth, and he instructed to take forced and deep inspirations. After several of these had been taken, and a slight struggling had been controlled, the tooth was extracted, immediately after which there was a *gasp for breath*, a *deep sigh*, and the head of the boy rolled to one side, and he was dead. The dentist, in alarm, left the boy in a sitting posture and ran for help. The nearest available help was Dr. Daly, but he being absent, Mr. Marsh, a student of his, answered the summons, and repaired to the place with a galvanic battery. It was not until his arrival, a period estimated at a quarter of an hour, that the deceased was placed in a recumbent posture upon the floor and any efforts made at resuscitation. Dr. Sclover arrived shortly afterwards, resorted at once to artificial respiration, applied the galvanic battery, and administered hypodermic injections of ammonia, but all to no purpose. At the time he saw the child the pulse had ceased to beat.

* Medical Record, January 7, 1877.

"An autopsy was held Jan. 8th, at the instance of the county physician, Dr. F. B. Gellette, of Plainfield, N. J., assisted by four physicians. The body was spare, but well nourished, cadaveric rigidity marked. On removing the coverings of the chest the muscles were found to be of a darker hue than normal. The pericardial sac contained a slight excess of straw-colored serum. The heart was normal in size, the right ventricle showing the usual amount of adipose tissue upon its surface. The vessels of the heart were ligatured previous to removal, and on being severed a quantity of dark blood escaped. The right ventricle was flaccid, and contained about half an ounce of the same character of blood noted above. The left ventricle was quite firmly contracted, and was entirely empty. No thrombi were found. All the valves of the heart were sufficient, and the muscular substance, on microscopical examination, was found to be free from fatty degeneration. The liver was of normal size, but congested throughout, and both lungs were in the same condition, slightly crepitant on pressure, and discharging from the cut surface of the smaller tubes a frothy mucus.

" The stomach was filled with a full and but partially digested meal, a portion of which found its way into the œsophagus by *post-mortem* gravitation. The mucous membrane of the organ was apparently healthy, and showed no evidence of *post-mortem* digestion. The larynx and trachea were entirely free, as was also the fauces, which fact destroyed the probability of choking during any possible effort at vomiting. Both passages were, however, markedly injected with venous blood; the same was the case with the small intestines and kidneys, which otherwise presented a healthy appearance. The bladder was half full of urine. The peritoneum, except a slight congestion, was also normal.

"The brain was carefully examined. Its substance appeared normal. Its surface shared in the general venous congestion to a slight extent. No abnormal amount of fluid was found in the ventricles."

" With the recent Rahway tragedy still fresh in our minds, we are called upon to record another victim to the administration of chloroform, whilst in a dentist's chair. In this instance the case was that of the wife of a prominent citizen of Rock Island, Iowa. As far as we can learn from the report furnished us, every precaution, save allowing the patient to sit in the chair, was taken to guard against the accident. The gentlemen who administered the anæsthetic was an experienced physician, and had performed a similar service to the patient before. Death appeared to be instantaneous from paralysis of the heart. If it were necessary to prove the dangerous character of chloroform as an anæsthetic in dentistry, we could hardly select a more direct case in point than the one under consideration. In the Rahway case the patient had a full stomach at the time of the accident, and there were other circumstances which more or less directly invited the issue; but in the Rock Island case there would seem to have been every chance for escape, except for the fact that the chloroform was given for tooth drawing, and the patient was at the time in the dentist's chair. In this connection we must refer to still another death from chloroform, occurring as an accompaniment of an equally trifling operation."

"We regret to have to record a death from chloroform, which occurred last week at University College Hospital, and, as has been frequently noticed in other instances, it occurred during only a trifling operation. We are indebted for the details to one of the house-physicians. The man was sent up to the ward from the out-patient room about four P. M., for the removal of a piece of carious bone from the stump of an arm. He was placed lying on a bed, with loosened dress, and as he felt pain very acutely, chloroform was ordered; it was not measured, but from one to two drachms were poured on lint, and afterwards the administration was continued *guttatim*. After a good deal of struggling he became suddenly under the influence, and the operation was commenced. He breathed equably for a few seconds, but when Mr. Heath grasped the bone, the breathing suddenly stopped. The pulse seems to have ceased about the same time. He is said to have been of rather dark complexion, and the administrator did not notice any marked change of color, though others thought it became bluish. Artificial respiration by Silvester's method was the principal remedy adopted, and energetically applied about half an hour, but to no purpose; brandy was not given. On the supposition that possibly some substance was fixed in the larynx, Mr. Heath performed laryngotomy as a last resource. At the *post-mortem* examination, the heart-substance was found in a state of marked fatty degeneration. We may say that the man's age was thirty-seven, and not twenty-eight, as stated in the newspaper reports. We have no clear history of his habits. He had taken ether safely at a previous operation. At the inquest, Dr. Crocker stated that the death occurred from misadventure, and the jury returned a verdict to that effect."*

If these and similar experiences serve as nothing more than new and forcible illustrations of old and acknowledged facts, a particular reference to them will not be in vain.

"Dr. Charles A. Jourdan, a dentist, was put under the influence of chloroform for the purpose of having the left eye extirpated, which had received an injury five months previously while he was living in Texas.

"The patient was placed on the operating table, and chloroform was administered in the usual way, which soon brought on that sleep that knew no wakening; the eye was speedily removed, when the pulse and breath simultaneously ceased, and all efforts to resuscitate were unavailing; he never breathed after the first alarming symptoms were noticed. He had a good constitution and no organic disease of any kind, which was proven by *post-mortem* examination."†

A death during the inhalation of chloroform, preparatory to undergoing an operation, has occurred in a village near Llanelly, South Wales. The patient, a collier, twenty-nine years of age, in fairly good health, suffered from fistula in ano, for which Messrs. Buckley and Thomas, surgeons, determined to operate. After inhaling the anæsthetic for a few minutes, the patient became suddenly blanched in the face, and breathed feebly, and in spite of the endeavors of the surgeons, who perse-

---

* British Medical Journal, January 20, 1877.
† American Journal of Dental Science, May, 1877.

vered for an hour in performing artificial respiration, died. The autopsy revealed a hypertrophied condition of the heart, and at the subsequent inquest the jury returned a verdict of "accidental death during the administration of chloroform."*

Dr. Taylor† states that "Fatal cases have been proportionally much more numerous from the use of chloroform vapor than from ether vapor. In one case, witnessed by a friend of Dr. Taylor's, the heart suddenly ceased to beat four minutes after the vapor had been withdrawn. The digital arteries, which had been divided in the surgical operation, ceased to beat. The man was dead. Two fatal cases are reported in the *Brit. Med. Journ.* for August, 1873, p. 230. In one, a man, in good general health, died suddenly after having inhaled one drachm of chloroform in vapor. Fatal syncope came on after the chloroform had been withdrawn. In the other case, a lady died at Brighton under the influence of chloroform, while having a tooth extracted. In this case, it is said, there was fatty degeneration of the heart. It is to this condition of a fatty or flabby heart that the fatal effects are usually ascribed. Assuming this to be to some extent the true cause of the fatality, it must be admitted that fatty and flabby hearts have become exceedingly common since the introduction of chloroform vapor for surgical and other purposes! But this theory is not necessary to explain the fatal results. They are simply cases of poisoning. In January, 1866, a healthy man died in three minutes from the effects of two drachms of chloroform given in vapor. This death occurred on the operating-table of a London hospital; the vapor having been administered by a gentleman who had given it previously to 300 or 400 patients. Death was sudden, and took place after some deep inspirations and expirations had been made. It was on this occasion candidly admitted that the body was quite healthy. I have been unable to procure any reliable information respecting the statistics of deaths from chloroform in

---

* London Lancet, Dec. 8, 1877.
† On Poisons, op. cit., p. 62.

surgical operations. Hospital authorities are unwilling to place their fatal cases before the public."

The *London Lancet* of February 10th, 1877, records the death, in the Peterborough Infirmary, of a man fifty-two years of age. The patient was placed under the influence of chloroform (two drachms in all being used) for the reduction of a strangulated inguinal hernia. It is the old story. The pulse and respiration suddenly ceased, and, although efforts at resuscitation were promptly employed, the man never rallied.

The last case was that of a woman for whom ligature of the carotid was to be performed for an aneurism of the aorta. The patient suddenly ceased to breathe, when laryngotomy was performed. The left innominate vein, as was afterwards discovered, being occluded, some veins crossing the larynx were much dilated. These were unavoidably wounded in the operation, a quantity of blood entered the air-passages, and, although it was promptly sucked out, the delay was fatal. The patient had taken but little chloroform when the obstruction to respiration occurred. In neither case is there any report of a post-mortem examination.

"A case of death whilst under the influence of chloroform recently took place at the Derby Infirmary. Deceased, who was fifty-six years of age, was about to undergo an operation for fistula and hæmorrhoids; but before he was ready for operation, the respiration suddenly became very irregular, he struggled violently, and the pulse, which had up to this time been good, ceased. In spite of all the means resorted to for a considerable time, he showed no signs of rallying from the first. The quantity of chloroform which had been poured into the lint-holder was in all about three drachms. The post-mortem examination did not reveal any organic disease."*

Another case, the patient being a boy, aged eight, is recorded in the same journal for November 11, 1876.

"Dr. Gustav Judell, privat-docent and chemical assistant in Professor Leube's clinic at Erlangen, was, on October 26th, found dead in his bed. He had been ac-

* Brit. Med. Journ., March 17, 1877.

customed to take chloroform at night as a remedy for sleeplessness, by which he was much troubled; and a bottle containing the anæsthetic was found near him. It appears that vomiting was excited by the chloroform, but that he was too deeply narcotized to eject the contents of the stomach, so that portions of the food remained in the œsophagus and caused death by suffocation."*

In the month of February, 1878, a Miss Wilson died in a dentist's chair in Brooklyn, after the extraction of ten teeth under the influence of two doses of chloroform. The coroner's jury, in summing up the evidence, gave as its opinion, that the hapless woman died from asphyxia, caused by the use of chloroform, and they condemned the use of anæsthetics in dental operations. We do not wonder that dentists who are not always familiar with the number of fatal cases of death from the inhalation of chloroform employ it, when they see it recommended by some of the most distinguished surgeons of the land, in the face of the almost constant deaths from its direct influence. These latter are the culpable ones, for they sin against the knowledge of its fatal character. If no other anæsthetic could be found there might be some reason for their wilful misrepresentations. Where ether and nitrous oxide can be had almost perfectly safe, why should such a dangerous agent be recommended?

The subjoined abstract of remarks by the editor of the *Brooklyn Eagle*, shows the popular impression in regard to the use of chloroform:—

"The obvious reason why, in the opinion of this jury, anæsthetics should not be administered ' in such operations,' can have no possible reference to the operations themselves. Tooth-pulling is an art of easy attainment by any human being of stout nerves and moderately powerful wrists, and in the simplicity of the operation lies its principal peril. Since any fool can extract teeth, a great many fools do, and the law requiring no special education of dentists in the study of physiology, the profession is overrun with quacks. Since the introduc-

* Med. Examiner, November 18, 1877.

tion of anæsthetics into dental operations, every quack finds himself called upon to administer the soothing drug to a patient, and, without any knowledge of the human frame, he does it—frequently with fatal effects. What does he know of the effects of anæsthetics? What theory can he possibly have of their action? What does he know of ganglia and their lesions, which render the administration of chloroform to some patients certain death from paralysis of the pneumogastric nerve? All he knows is that some dentists give their patients a drug which deprives them of consciousness, and therefore of pain. Chloroform is the best known of these drugs, and since no embargo is laid upon its miscellaneous sale, it is easily procurable. Like all articles of merchandise, it has its grades. Good, pure chloroform is at best a hazardous anæsthetic, which should be employed with the utmost caution, while the inferior quality may be regarded as usually fatal in effect. This opinion prevails among scientific men who have made a study of it. The dentist—a retired farmer, a discharged dry goods clerk, or a politician out of office—knows nothing of this, however, and goes on administering chloroform without hesitation. Ether, on the other hand, is a comparatively safe agent, and *competent dentists* prefer its use to that of chloroform. Of ether and nitrous oxide, and other mitigating drugs, the quack dentist is as ignorant as could be expected, and hence he cleaves to his fatal chloroform; comes before a coroner's jury every now and again, with blanched cheeks and a general air of perplexity, until habit accustoms him to the office of executing his fellow creatures without surprise or remorse.

"Since the operations of dentistry are extremely painful, it would appear that they offer to the beneficent discoveries of science in banishing pain a most fruitful field, but inasmuch as the avoidance of fatal consequences from the use of anæsthetics depends upon the knowledge of the practitioner, it would appear to be a matter of some importance that the *dentist should be a person of education* in at least this particular branch of physiology. He should, at all events, understand the conditions under which his practice may become dangerous to life or health, and to show that he does so understand, he should be called upon to exhibit a diploma. In other words, dentistry having advanced to a science, none but scientific practitioners should be allowed to perform its duties. It was all very well for the barber of a century ago to pull out the teeth of his patrons, or write their prescriptions, open their veins, and otherwise contribute to their general happiness and enjoyment of life, but we have left those days behind, and the good of the community demands that important trusts be confided only to those who are capable of discharging them."

Experimentation on Death from Chloroform.

The first series of experiments I remember to have made were commenced in the years 1850 and 1851, and had reference to the mode and cause of death under chloroform. At the time named chloroform had been in use a little over two years for preventing the pain of surgical operations, and already nineteen deaths in man had occurred from it.

These calamities had produced very painful and anxious feelings amongst medical men, and my researches had for their intention the elucidation of many points of practical importance. The mode of procedure was to narcotize the animals, with various degrees of rapidity, with varying percentages of chloroform vapor in the atmosphere, and during various atmospherical conditions; to note carefully the phenomena produced on the heart and on the respiration, and the duration of the four stages of narcotism. In some instances the animals—rabbits were usually subjected to experiment—were allowed to recover; in other instances the narcotism was continued to death. When the narcotism was made to be fatal the immediate cause of death was noted, and the body left until the rigidity of death could be recorded. Then all the organs were carefully inspected, in order to see what was the condition of the lungs, the heart, the brain, the spinal cord.

The results obtained by these inquiries were of direct practical value. By them I showed in various lectures and papers the following major facts:—

1. That the cause of the fatality from chloroform does not occur, as was at first supposed, from any particular mode of administration of the narcotic.

2. That chloroform will kill, in some instances, when the subject killed by it exhibits, previous to administration, no trace of disease or other sign by which the danger of death can be foretold.

3. That the condition of the air at the time of administration materially influences the action of the narcotic vapor. That the danger of administration is much less when the air is free of water vapor, and the temperature is above 60°, but below 70°, Fahr.

4. That there are four distinct modes of death from chloroform, and that when the phenomena of death from its application appear, they are infinitely more likely to pass into irrevocable death than from some other narcotics that may be used in lieu of chloroform.

5. That all the members of the group of narcotic vapors of the chlorine series, of which chloroform is the most prominent as a narcotic, are dangerous narcotics, and that chloroform ought to be replaced by some other agent equally practical in use and less fatal.

6. That so long as it continues to be used there will always be a certain distinct mortality arising from chloroform, and that no human skill in applying it can divest it of its dangers.

That knowledge of this kind respecting an agent which destroys one person out of every two thousand five hundred who inhale it was calculated to be useful, no reasonable mind, I think, can doubt. To me, who, many hundred times in my life, have had the solemn responsibility of administering chloroform to my fellow-men, it was of so much value that I should have felt it a crime if I had gone blindly on using so potent an instrument without obtaining such knowledge.—BENJAMIN W. RICHARDSON, in "*Nature.*"

Conclusions in Reference to the Use of Chloroform.

In what class of cases can chloroform be employed with safety? In my own experience, and after my experiments,

I would limit the use of this most potent of all the anæsthetics to very young children who are weak, strumous, or overgrown. To puerperal eclampsia, in very violent convulsions, in male adults, or in females during delivery, where rapidity of dilatation of the os uteri is absolutely necessary to save the mother's life.

In some rare cases of painful operation, where, after continued efforts, no complete insensibility can be produced by ether, I would feel justified in the use of a portion of chloroform on a clean sponge or inhaler. In a certain class of inebriates, no amount of ether will be of much use in reducing a severe dislocation at the hip or shoulder-joint. In those cases accustomed to the free use of stimulants, chloroform may always be resorted to, using all the usual precautions. By a reference to the recent cases of deaths from this agent, I am fully satisfied that no amount of care or precaution, or mode of administration, or amount inhaled, will prevent, in certain cases, the fatal result, and yet physicians and others will resort to the use of chloroform on account of its pleasant taste and odor, rapidity of action, cost, and comparative bulk. I have given its advocates every opportunity to state where, when, and how it can be given with safety, omitting nothing through prejudice or favor, having in my practice resorted to its use before being aware of the great risk incurred to every patient.

In a recent pamphlet,* by an *ophthalmic* surgeon, Dr. Chisholm, of Baltimore, he advocates the exclusive use of chloroform as the "Anæsthetic," and considers ether unsatisfactory, on account of the great distress occasioned by its forced inhalation in a concentrated form, its offensive odor, the large amount required, the excessive nausea induced, and the irritable cough often excited; and yet why will distinguished surgeons, like Drs. Jos. and Wm. H. Pancoast, Agnew, Ashhurst, Brinton, Morton, Allis, Levis, and others, give chloroform up on account of the greater safety to patients, and resort to the use of ether, some of them after years of its careful administration? At the Pennsylvania, Episcopal, University, Jefferson,

---

* What Anæsthetic shall we Use? By J. J. Chisholm, M.D. pp. 23. Baltimore, 1877.

with the exception of Prof. Gross, Presbyterian, St. Joseph's, St. Mary's, German, and Jewish Hospitals, of Philadelphia, chloroform is not used but in rare cases, ether almost exclusively.

The following are given by Dr. Chisholm as his proofs of the safety of chloroform: "At the Edinburgh Infirmary, during a period of twenty-eight years from the introduction into surgical practice to the present time, only two deaths have been attributed to chloroform, which, according to Ker, is one death in 86,500 administrations." Grant, in his admirable *Treatise on Surgery*, says: "I have seen chloroform given in some thousands of cases during upwards of twenty years, both in hospital and private practice, without a single death, or even an approach to a fatal termination." Elser, of Strasburg, had used chloroform 16,000 times, and had never seen a fatal case. Kidd, of London, had seen it administered upward of 10,000 times, and had seen no fatal case, either in his own practice or that of his friends. The French surgeons in the Crimea reported 30,000 cases of chloroform administered, and not one fatal issue. In the English army in the Crimea, chloroform was administered 12,000 times, with one single death reported as attributed to it. In the Confederate service, chloroform was exclusively used in a great many thousand operations without a death, as far as I am aware of, or have been able to ascertain after diligent inquiry among leading surgeons of the army. Surgeon McGuire, of Jackson's Corps, reported 18,000 administrations without one death. Richardson had seen it used in the London hospitals 15,000 times before he met with the first fatal case. Bilroth, of Vienna, had administered chloroform 2500 times before he met with his first accident. Clover has recorded 3000 administrations without a single death. Erichsen has only witnessed one single death under chloroform in twenty-five years, at University Hospital. No official statistics, that I am aware of, have been published of the use of chloroform in the Federal army, nor in the recent wars of the French, German, and Austrian empires.

Dr. J. Mason Warren, in 1867, published his *Surgical Observations*, with cases and operations, in which he mentions that in the Federal army chloroform was almost exclusively used in field operations. "The returns indicate that it was administered in no less than 80,000 cases. In 7 cases, fatal results had been ascribed with apparent fairness to its use, a proportion of 1 death in 11,428 administrations. Enough," he states, "has been already said, however, to prove that, under careful administration, deaths from chloroform must be among the rarest of accidents—so rare that it should not be seriously considered.

To the testimony above I will add my own individual experience. I have been practising surgery twenty-five years, and have used chloroform largely during that entire period, in private and hospital practice, in the army as well as in civil life, and have administered it to the extent of fully 6000 cases. Now let us sum up the evidence which I have collected, and here we find an array of *over* 250,000 *administrations of chloroform with* 12 *deaths;* even attributing them all to idiosyncrasy, which calls for a most unbounded charity, and we only have 1 death in 20,000 cases. Can any stronger proof," he observes, "of the excessive rarity of the fatal idiosyncrasy in chloroform be needed?"

Now, on the other hand, what do other reliable authorities state, without going into much detail? *There have been* 210 *deaths faithfully recorded and reported*, with the additional ones in this work, *from chloroform* (see *Medical News and Library*, Philadelphia, 1869), and these mostly occurred in the hands of the most experienced surgeons, and many of them in large hospitals where every appliance was to be had, and all the known means employed to prevent death. Where are the large numbers of deaths unreported which, like fatal operations in surgery, never see the light of day, and are therefore of no use to the seeker after truth?

In the recent admirable work on surgery by Erichsen,* he discussed the question, Do anæsthetics influence the rate of mortality after operation? and concludes by stating: "I am inclined to believe that the rate of

* The Science and Art of Surgery, p. 42. Philadelphia: H. C. Lea, 1878.

mortality has increased since the use of anæsthetics in operative surgery." Again, "I cannot but think that chloroform does exercise a noxious influence on the constitution, and does lessen the prospect of recovery in certain states of the system, more especially when the blood is in an unhealthy state." He states the most dangerous condition in which to administer chloroform is that in which, in consequence of renal disease, the blood is loaded with urea; in such cases epileptiform convulsions are readily induced.

In 1856, Mr. Erichsen,* in a letter to Dr. S. D. Townsend, of Boston, said, that "when a patient was fully under the influence of chloroform he was on the verge of death."

Prof. Frank H. Hamilton, of New York, says: "In nearly all my surgical operations I prefer ether to chloroform."

The following correspondence explains itself, and I regret reporting that this distinguished surgeon still gives his influence in favor of the most dangerous of anæsthetics.

1502 WALNUT ST., Jan. 28, 1878.

PROF. S. D. GROSS:

DEAR DOCTOR: Knowing from your works that you advocated and employed chloroform as an anæsthetic for many years, and having been informed you had for good and sufficient reasons given up its use, will you oblige me by giving me in a few words your reasons for so doing, and allow me to publish them in a little work I am about to have issued, and to which I have devoted considerable attention during the last two years?

Yours truly,
L. TURNBULL.

S. E. COR. 11TH AND WALNUT STS.,
January 29, 1878.

DEAR DOCTOR TURNBULL: There is not one word of truth in the report that has reached your ear to the effect that I have abandoned the use of chloroform; on the contrary, I employ it nearly, if not quite, as frequently as ever. It is only in operations upon the mouth, and in elderly, dilapidated subjects, that I prefer ether, and even in them it is questionable whether it possesses any de-

---

* Records of the Boston Society for Medical Improvement, vol. iii. p. 34.

cided advantage over chloroform. As a rule, ether is undoubtedly the safer anæsthetic; but, with proper care in its administration, harm will seldom, if ever, befall our patients iu the use of chloroform.

I am, dear Doctor, very truly, yours,
DR. LAURENCE TURNBULL.   S. D. GROSS.

Chloroform versus Ether.

Timothy Holmes, F.R.C.S., Surgeon to St. George's Hospital, London, author and lecturer, prefers chloroform to ether for the purpose of producing relaxation in the reduction of hernia and dislocations. It is more speedy and effectual in its action than ether, and he considers the dangers no greater. The Boston *Medical and Surgical Journal* prefixes the statement of Mr. Holmes's views with " Anno Domini 1877 !"

We are surprised at the use of chloroform by Mr. Holmes in hernia, as in the majority of cases the system of the patient is very much depressed, and requires the stimulation of ether as well as its relaxing effects. We do not object so much to the use of chloroform, as we have before stated, in the reduction of severe dislocations, especially in beer-drinking and intemperate cases; and Dr. Frank H. Hamilton, of New York, states that more complete muscular paralysis is more quickly and certainly attained by chloroform than by ether.

We cannot conclude this part of our subject in more emphatic language than by noting the following: Another case of death from chloroform is recorded in the *British Medical Journal* for Feb. 2, 1878.

Dr. Moses Gunn, the distinguished surgeon of Chicago, now uses ether exclusively, using his great influence in its favor.

CHAPTER V.

Original observations and experiments with hydrate of chloral. Liebreich on the impurities of chloral in cakes, test of purity, etc. Experiments of Dr. John A. Campbell at Garland Asylum, Carlisle. On chloral as an anæsthetic in children, by Dr. Bouchut, of Paris. M. Couty, of Paris, on death from chloral. Prof. Ore, of Bordeaux, venous injections of chloral. Dr. J. M. Fothergill, of London, on the great utility of strychnia in chloral poisoning. Case of death from the use of chloral, and post-mortem appearances. Drs. Taylor and Tuke's opinions upon the effects of the long-continued use of chloral. The use of chloral for a long period with no serious results.

Hydrate of Chloral.

THIS new and valuable sleep-promoter, which has been so *recently* introduced into practice, has already been employed in thousands of cases.

Chloral conforms to all the tests of Drs. Liebreich and Richardson, being solid, of a white color; taste pungent and disagreeable, like that of a stale melon and chlorine. It dissolves with some difficulty in cold water, more freely in hot water, but requiring equal parts, by weight, for a perfect solution; is unaffected by nitrate of silver, and is slightly clouded by a solution of permanganate of potash. Its physiological and therapeutical action has been tested upon man and frogs.*

According to Liebreich, *it is altogether impossible* to purify cake chloral. Chloral in dry, transparent crystals alone is reliable, not in needles but in rhomboidal plates.† Thus chloral hydrate which is not perfectly pure may sometimes be observed to become acid. This increase of acidity is not due to the decomposition of chloral hydrate itself, but to the decomposition of an accompanying impurity (chloro-carbonic acid), which sets

---

* Original Observations and Experiments with Hydrate of Chloral, by Laurence Turnbull, M.D. Medical and Surgical Reporter, Aug. 24, 1872, and Aug. 31, 1872.

† Prof. Maisch, of this city, says the shape of the crystals is no proof as a test of the purity of hydrate of chloral. Ib., March 9, 1878.

free hydrochloric acid. When this occurs in the stomach it gives rise to great irritation, and when it occurs in the blood it causes great constitutional excitement.

Owing to the excessive alkalinity of the blood in typhoid fever, ten grains of chloral hydrate will often suffice to produce hypnotic effects, while in the state of excitement of delirium tremens twenty to thirty grains are necessary; by hypodermic injection, fifteen grains.

Impure chloral hydrate is apt to produce nervous excitement; which state of excitation overcomes the hypnotic effects. Chloral hydrate poisons by paralyzing the heart, and its effects are observable in retardation of the pulse and respiration. Hence Dr. Liebreich has been led to urge the use of strychnine in combating these effects. The results of his experiments* have been confirmed by subsequent observers.

First Experiment.—To a large frog was administered hypodermically near the inner part of the thigh half a grain (gr. ss) of hydrate of chloral in twenty minims of distilled water (xx ℳ).

Nine minutes after, the frog was examined. The respiration was increased to twenty (20) a minute, but not the slightest narcotic result was perceived; skin cooler than natural. Waited thirty minutes, and again injected (gr. ss) one-half a grain. Soon after there was a drooping of the head, relaxation of the limbs, closing of eyelids (but no alteration of pupil), followed by profound stupor. In the course of ten minutes this animal became quite rigid, in fact, cataleptic; for, when the limb was stretched out, it retained that position. There was no tactile sensibility, not even when pricked or cut. When the web of the foot was placed under the microscope, two hours after the second injection, the blood, of a dark-red color, was found in active movement. This was witnessed by my son, Mr. (now Dr.) Charles S. Turnbull, and Mr. (now Dr.) G. B. Dixon. At this time the animal seemed almost dead, and no movements of respiration could be seen. The only motion was a feeble one of the heart, confirming Liebreich's views that

* Trans. Ac. Med., Berlin.

the heart is the last part that dies while under the influence of hydrate of chloral.

Experiment Second.—Another frog was treated in a similar manner, with one grain (gr. j) of hydrate of chloral in solution, but it passed rapidly into the death-like state. The heart's action was so feeble as not to be noticed.

Experiment Third.—A third frog was treated with three-quarters of a grain of hydrate of chloral, and was then carried to a meeting of the Philadelphia County Medical Society, where it was exhibited to the members present, in the apparently dead condition; and yet there was a movement of the circulation under the microscope. On removing the sternum, one hour after, the heart was found acting slowly, but soon stopped; and on stimulating it by friction the heart would again act, as in all cold-blooded animals.

It will be seen, by the above experiments, that there are three stages of the action of chloral on animals. First, soporific; second, sedative; third, relaxant.

Second, deep sleep, with diminished sensibility, and cataleptic state, with rigidity. The third state is a sleep so profound that it looks like death; and, unless altered, death supervenes.

Experiment Fourth, which demonstrates the fact that in small or moderate doses, from ℨss to ℨj, hydrate of chloral is not an anæsthetic, but is a hypnotic, or a producer of sleep. Lady, aged 45, suffering from gastric fever, with distressing nausea and vomiting, and diarrhœa, but unable to sleep for several nights, even under the influence of the camphorated and simple tincture of opium, also Dover's powder (pulv. ipec. et opii, U. S. P.), by enemata. Dissolved gr. xx of hydrate of chloral in a wineglassful of sweetened water, which was administered at 8 P. M. There was considerable heat of skin; pulse rapid and feeble. It was taken while in the recumbent position, and, her stomach being empty, no sickness or disagreeable results followed. In half an hour she was sound asleep.

At 12 P. M., pulse quiet and slow; breathing so gentle as not to be noticed; when, feeling uneasy on account of the very quiet sleep, she was simply touched on the hand; she at once awoke, inquiring "if we wanted to wake her?" She changed her position, and again went to sleep, and slept without interruption until 8 A. M. the following morning.

Experiment Fifth.—Lady, aged 34; has had a tumor removed from the uterus, and some months since she began to suffer the most distressing pain, with swelling in the region of the right ovary. All the domestic remedies, as mustard plasters, hot fomentations, with hops, etc., had been tried in vain, also the application of opium and chloroform, but without benefit, being unable to take either morphia, opium, or any of its preparations. She was directed gr. xx of the hydrate of chloral in water and syrup. This was taken in two doses, resulting neither in sleep nor relief of pain. She was then directed thirty grains (gr. xxx), after taking which she had three hours of sleep, and by repeating the half-drachm doses she was entirely relieved of the pain, and was able to sleep without being disturbed by noises or touch.

In this case the hydrate of chloral did not act as an anæsthetic until fifty grains (gr. l) had been administered.

Experiment Sixth.—Young married woman, aged 25, with typhoid fever; pregnant, and threatened with abortion at third month; pulse 100; temperature of skin 107°; dry, with petechial eruption on abdomen on fourteenth day; unable to sleep; had taken at various times Dover's powder, bromide of potassium, tincture of opium, morphia, etc., but with very unfavorable effects. Directed the hydrate of chloral in water and syrup of orange flowers. The first night she took twenty grains (gr. xx), but it was rejected by the stomach, still she slept for a short period; second night she had ten grains (gr. x), still rejected; third night, five grains (gr. v), and slept longer than any night since she has had the fever; less fever; heat of skin reduced to 96°, and pulse 90.

On the fourth night she aborted, and fœtus was discharged, softened; lost considerable blood; placenta retained. The os was plugged, and in the morning removed the plug; but the placenta did not all come away for several days; convalescent at the end of the sixth week. The hydrate of chloral was employed from the

10th of February until the 16th of March. There is no doubt that it hastened the recovery very materially, by reducing the temperature of the skin, allaying pain and nervous excitement, which kept up the fever. The point of importance that these cases teach is that small doses are to be employed with persons of feeble constitution, or where there has been loss of blood. It also proves that it reduces the temperature of the skin; this fact we have since proven in numerous cases.

Experiment Seventh.—A comparison between the effects of morphia and hydrate of chloral. Mrs. N., aged 34, has suffered with paroxysm of intense pain in the hypochondriac region, with obstruction of the bowels, followed by inflammation of a diphtheritic character, evidenced by cast being discharged. The only means of relief was by the use, hypodermically, of from half a grain (gr. $\frac{1}{2}$) to three-quarters of a grain (gr. $\frac{3}{4}$) of morphia, which, although it gave her almost instant relief, was invariably followed by much distress in her head, with nausea and vomiting. By the use of seventy grains of hydrate of chloral she was relieved of her pain, and slept; and the most agreeable feature about the effect was that she awoke from her slumbers without any of the unpleasant symptoms in the head and stomach.

Experiment Eighth.—Mrs. R. M., aged 30, suffering in like manner, was relieved by sixty grains (so that 60 to 70 grains of chloral were about equal to half a grain of sulphate of morphia).

Experiment Ninth.—Cases of gout and rheumatism are better treated by adding soda or potassa in conjunction with chloral, or the bromide of potassium. Samuel H., aged 54, was exposed to a sudden change of temperature of twenty degrees reduction, without being suitably clad, and was attacked with acute rheumatism of the limb and knee; he was directed an anodyne and a stimulating liniment with Dover's powder (pulv. ipec. et opii ℈j), gr. xx, but without relief. A mixture was then ordered him of aromatic water and syrup, of fifteen grains of potassæ bicarb., and thirty grains of hydrate of chloral; he took but five such doses, when he was free from nervous excitement and pain, and finally slept. By its occasional use he had no return of the disease.

Experiment Tenth.—John H. B., aged 45, while suffering with acute gout in his hands and hip, was ordered three ten-grain doses of chloral in water and syrup, but as it caused him so much excitement, the soda bicarb. was ordered with it to get rid of the soda salts in his joints. This had the desired effect, and by its use for ten nights all his acute symptoms disappeared; only a certain amount of stiffness remained.

Experiment Eleventh.—Men require, as a general rule, larger doses than women, and in brain difficulties bromide of sodium is an admirable addition.

John H. N., aged 56, suffering from amaurosis from atrophy of the optic nerve, was exposed, and contracted bronchitis, and the inflammation passed along the Eustachian tube to the middle ear, causing otitis media, followed by intense pain. He was ordered thirty grains of hydrate of chloral, without relief; a second dose of the same quantity, with a drachm of bromide of sodium; this relieved the pain, and gave him a quiet, good night, and he awoke, with a slight discharge from the ear, but free from pain.

Experiment Twelfth.—Its value in diseases in little children.—We have tested it in three typical cases during the heat of the summer of 1871, in little children suffering from restlessness and cholera infantum. In almost every instance the child was able to sleep without pain or disturbance of the brain, by the soothing hypnotic influence. The chloral was combined with an aromatic syrup; also chalk, and a small portion of port wine or syrup of brandy (made by burning the strong brandy with sugar). Our dose was, for a child of 12 months, one grain of hydrate of chloral, half grain of prepared chalk, and half grain of powdered gum arabic in each tablespoonful; also, some mint, aniseed, or cinnamon water, so as to disguise the disagreeable taste. The hydrate of chloral should be increased in the proportion of one grain for each year.

Experiment Thirteenth.—Frank N., aged 21 years, of strumous tubercular habit, laboring under an attack of congestion of the lungs, with the pleura involved, pain very intense, respiration hurried, temperature 104°; pulse 120; directed a blister and fifty grains (gr. l) of hydrate of chloral in two doses. His mother, in her desire to relieve him, gave it at one dose. The effect was good, and his sleep profound; skin so cool and clammy that she became alarmed and woke him suddenly; yet, when he was thus awakened, he was not confused, was able to answer all questions directed to him, and was entirely free from pain, with free expectoration, and breathing much relieved.

Experiment Fourteenth.—It is a most valuable agent in severe affections of the nervous system.

The mother of the above lad, aged 45, had a most severe shock to her nervous system, owing to the sudden and terrible loss of two of her boys, aged respectively 10 and 11 years, by drowning, which was followed, in her case, by nervous fever, with delirium and insomnia, and unwillingness to take a particle of food for twenty-four hours. By prescribing and administering equal parts of syrup of chloral and fluid extract of valerian (each ʒj), with beef essence as food, she finally obtained sleep and recovered her reason, and was ultimately restored to good health. This will partially account for the large dose she gave her son, having had such faith in it herself. But in all diseases of the heart and lungs great care must be employed to commence with small doses, or to combine the chloral with a small quantity of morphine or tincture of Indian hemp.

Experiment Fourteenth.—Miss J. W., aged 18, with panophthalmitis and destruction of the eye; pain and distress were relieved by three thirty-grain doses of hydrate of chloral, and was able to sleep.

J. W., aged 52, father of the above, had his right eye penetrated by a percussion cap July 4, 1871, and had been under the care of a homœopathic physician for treatment before coming to the hospital. He was pale, nervous, and in great agony, with entire loss of vision. The eye was removed, and thirty-grain doses of hydrate of chloral kept him free from pain. The only other means employed was the use of the ice-bag. It is very useful in some forms of eye diseases of a strumous or neuralgic character, associated with quiniæ sulphas, but not in other forms.

Experiment Fifteenth.—Heat toxæmia, thermic fever. —G. C., aged 22, male, a resident of Mexico, while on a visit to Darby, July 18, 1871, had to walk a mile and a half in the broiling sun; was overcome, and obliged to retire to the shade, and was unable to proceed. Since which time he has had constant pain in the head, with heat of skin and almost complete insomnia. Reasoning on the former experiments of the cooling influence of chloral, and its effects upon the nervous system, I ordered him ten-grain doses every three hours, in water, with ice to his head. After using it six hours he was able to sleep four hours; arose and took some nourishment; he was free from pain in his head, and his skin reduced to 90°. Took the chloral again at 11 P.M., and had a good, quiet sleep, until 7 A.M.

In some few instances the chloral will disturb and distress the stomach, say in about three per cent. of the cases; but if incorporated with a portion of mucilage, it is rapidly absorbed. If given by the rectum, at the rate of double the quantity required by the mouth, it will in some instances produce swelling of the eyelids, and even cause intoxication and dimness of vision.

In cases of chorea, epilepsy, and convulsions, arising from irritated nerves or reflex spinal irritation, it can be given with advantage alone, or in combination with the bromide of potassium or tincture of hyoscyamus. In acute mania, simple or puerperal, it is more valuable than Indian hemp, or bromide of potassium, or morphia, as numerous cases have demonstrated.

Experiment Sixteenth.—Case of acute mania treated by cold, sedatives, morphia, etc., without inducing sleep, accomplished by the use of hydrate of chloral. Mrs. Letitia B., aged 49. Sept. 13, 1871. Has been suffering with acute mania for ten days, without any known cause except distress in regard to her rent. When I visited her she was in bed, with a wild expression, pupils dilated; her hands were tied to prevent her from destroying everything she could get hold of; talk incoherent and rambling; refused all food, which had to be administered by force; had not slept, except a few hours, for ten days. After trying morphiæ sulphas hypodermically, to the extent of one grain, other agents having been employed previously to my seeing her, hydrate of chloral in ten-grain doses was administered every three hours. She slept the first night for three hours after using thirty grains. She continued its use on the 15th, 16th, 17th, 18th, and 19th, sleeping longer each night, and on the morning of the 20th, when she awoke, she was rational, able to eat some soup, and desired to see her little girl. She also spoke to her sister, who before she would not look at. In corroboration of the above, we cite the observations of Dr. A. Höller, Attending Physician of the Insane Retreat in Klosterneuburg, and Dr. Campbell. Dr. Höller remarks:—

1st Case. The hydrochloral, during a period of three and a half months, failed only twice to produce sleep; while, in forty-six days, the exhibition of morphine was followed nine times by a negative result.

2d Case. Catharine B., aged 47 years, suffered from religious melancholy; was greatly troubled night and day with *tinnitus aurium*, causing her to pass entire nights without sleep. The employment of scruple doses of hydrochloral produced several hours of uninterrupted sleep. In the course of time it became necessary to augment the dose to two scruples. Her pulse sank in the mean time to 66, and the quantity of urine (as had already been noticed in other cases) was increased. The disturbance of hearing diminished very decidedly.* Mr. Aldridge examined the eyes, with the ophthalmoscope, of patients under the influence of chloral hydrate, and the deductions, if any might fairly be drawn from such a small number of instances, would be that the chloral hydrate increases the calibre of the arteries, and consequently the vascularity of the retina, until such times as the patient falls asleep, and that the anæmic appearances seen at the latter period are those which are said to be characteristic of healthy sleep. This fact was first observed by Dr. Hammond, and published in the New York *Medical Journal*, February, 1870, p. 469.

* The Journal of Psychological Medicine, April, 1872, pp. 371, 372, and 404.

Dr. John A. Campbell* gives the following results of experiments at Garland Asylum, Carlisle:—
1. That both chloral and tincture of hyoscyamus are sure sedatives to maniacal excitement.
2. That of these two medicines, chloral is the most certain sleep-producer.
3. That chloral acts more quickly than tincture of hyoscyamus.
4. That though bromide of potassium, in gr. xc doses, is a sedative to maniacal excitement, and to a certain extent hypnotic, yet it is not a sufficiently powerful sedative to allay intense excitement, or an hypnotic to compel sleep where great insomnia exists.
5. That a two-drachm dose of tincture of hyoscyamus is not quite equivalent to thirty grains of chloral. Two and a half drachms would probably be as nearly an equivalent as could be given.

Experiment Seventeenth.—In two cases of delirium tremens, from excessive use of mixed drinks, and in one after a severe injury, both instances were relieved, the first by thirty grains of hydrate of chloral, and in the second seventy-five grains were ordered, which gave the patient a quiet night, with no delirium, and the cases ultimately did well.

A third case of the above disease was treated with equally good results, but its use had to be discontinued, owing to so copious a flow of tears obscuring the vision, etc.

Experiment Eighteenth.—Case of dysmenorrhœa, pain relieved by hydrate of chloral. Miss C. G., aged 31, stout, and of large frame, has suffered with most distressing and painful menstruation for some time; the pain so severe as almost to produce convulsions; menstrual fluid coming in a gush and then retained. Administered thirty grain doses every three hours, with the most happy results of relieving the spasm, increasing the flow of the fluid and urine, and great relief to the pain. The writer has also used it in inflammation of the ovaries with equally good results.

* Journal of Mental Science, January, 1872. The Practitioner, April, 1872, pp. 255-6.

Toxical effects on the human system: This drug has been employed in hundreds of thousands of cases by medical men without producing but very few deaths, yet in the hands of persons not in the profession several deaths have followed its indiscriminate use, or rather abuse. According to Dr. B. W. Richardson, the maximum dose is 90 grains, and with 140 the sleep would be dangerous. Yet deaths have been reported from 60 to 100, or even 45 grains; but, as stated before, not ordered by a medical man, except in one or two instances. In recent cases reported by Mr. B. Browning, recovery took place after the use of 100 grains, and as much as seven pounds has been used, in increasing doses, by one individual without any very injurious results. See also two cases of death reported in op. cit., vol. xxvii., August 17, p. 160, one after four days' use, and one after twelve days, quantity not stated.

Means to be employed in case of accidents in which a fatal dose of chloral has been administered: First, apply warmth, and furnish warm air. Second, sustain the body by an abundance of food, especially warm milk, with a little lime-water, and stimulants, say every two or three hours, one or two ounces of brandy or whiskey to half a pint. Third, keep up artificial respiration by a small double acting bellows or other means. It is useful to add to this, as in Mr. Browning's case, small doses of morphine by the hypodermic method.

Although it is a most useful agent in all convulsive diseases as a pain reliever, it will not always, nor could it, take the place of morphine. It has been found very valuable in causing sleep, and even curing cases of tetanus and trismus. There have been, up to June, 1871, thirty-six cases of tetanus treated by this agent and the galvanic current, in which there has been twenty-one recoveries and fifteen deaths. In one case the dose was 60 grains every half hour, and the patient took seven doses and recovered. It has been found useful in the paralysis of the insane, and yet in some instances it produces a partial paralysis of the organs of deglutition; also restlessness, and even coma.

It is antagonistic to the poisonous effects of calabar

bean and strychnia, and yet is given in combination with them.*

Dr. H. Griffin reports a successful case in 1872 by means of chloral, morphine, and galvanism. M. Garnier refers to several cases in which chloral was used in the treatment of tetanus occurring in very young persons; two cases were cured. The writer finds another case of death from chloral, reported by Dr. W. H. Lathrop, occurring in the practice of another physician, in which 100 grains were given; after the last dose of 20 grains the two physicians left the house, when they were called back to find the patient dead, who prior to their leaving, it is stated, complained of a slight paralysis in the right lower extremity, which no doubt extended to the heart. A post-mortem examination revealed nothing. This is like one or two fatal cases related by Dr. N. R. Smith, of Baltimore, in which, when given in large doses (60 gr.), and where the system may have become charged with it, it overwhelms the powers of life, as is the case in some instances by the hypodermic use of morphine, aconite, strychnia, etc. According to Dr. Richardson's observations, it should be given in repeated doses, at the rate of ten grains every two hours, or seven grains every hour; but the pulse, heart, and skin should be carefully watched. Dr. Nathan R. Smith describes its effects upon the fingers, attended by desquamation of the cuticle and superficial ulceration; but so far as our observation goes, and that of many physicians, no such results followed its use, and his cases are exceptions which it will be well to remember as results which may be encountered.

Hydrate of chloral has been found to act beneficially in a number of cases of puerperal convulsions; and Dr. Liebreich is disposed to explain this by accepting Frerich's theory, that the convulsive attacks are connected with the transformations of urea into urate of ammonia, and by supposing that besides the production of chloroform there is a formation of hydrochloric acid, which neutralizes the ammonia. Among other diseases in

* See table by Dr. Joseph R. Beck, p. 299, in the St. Louis *Medical and Surgical Journal*, June, 1872.

which there has been a general agreement of opinion as to the beneficial effects of hydrate of chloral, Dr. Liebreich mentions senile nervous asthma, not noticed before in this paper, dental convulsions in children, seasickness, etc. The following are our conclusions, as drawn from our experiments, observations, and the most recent literature upon this interesting subject:—

1. The action of chloral hydrate differs from that of chloroform.

2. That the action is the result of the conjoined use of chloroform and formic acids upon the blood.

3. A part of the chloroform formed by the action of the alkali of the blood is eliminated by the pulmonary mucous membrane; a part of the formic acid is eliminated by the urine as formiate of soda, as shown by experiments of "Byasson" (French Academy, June 12, 1871).

4. There are three degrees of the operation of chloral on animals and man, as shown by our own experiments.

The first degree is feebly soporific, and slightly nervous sedative action.

The second degree is an intense soporific action, with diminution of sensibility; at this period there is a deep sleep of variable duration, without apparent trouble of the principal functions of life.

The third degree, complete anæsthesia, with total loss of general sensibility and muscular power, cataleptic state. Death almost always follows this degree of action, as was seen in our experiments on animals.

5. Under the microscope the blood was seen moving, with some bright red, or dark red particles. According to "Ralph," starchy bodies are also met with in both urine and blood.

6. Death takes place last at the heart, which is kept in action long after all signs of death in the animal were present, as shown by removing the sternum, etc.

7. Sleep, with diminished heat of the surface one or two degrees below the natural standard.

8. Small doses do not produce anæsthetic results, these requiring from forty to fifty grains. In typhoid and typhus fevers one must commence and continue in small doses; five grains is the average quantity required.

9. It increases the flow of the menstrual fluid.

10. Seventy grains of the hydrate of chloral is equal to ½ grain of morphine employed hypodermically, and is not apt to cause so much disturbance of the stomach.

11. Gout and rheumatism must be treated with an excess of alkali, potassa, or soda, to obtain the best results from its use.

12. Males require a larger dose than females.

13. It is very valuable in diseases of little children, but care must be exercised to commence with small doses, gr. j for each month, and it should be mixed with nothing but water, as it is so apt to change and become worthless in contact with organic matter.

14. Hydrate of chloral will be found useful in phthisis, and even some forms of acute affections of the lungs, but not when the heart is involved.

15. It is a most valuable agent in nervous affections.

16. In affections of the eye it requires care to use it, as it is apt to cause swelling and redness and excessive flow of watery secretions, with obscuration of vision.

17. In sunstroke or heat toxæmia it is a most valuable aid to produce sleep in that restless state after reaction produced by frictions of ice and ice-water to the head and body.

18. In tetanus it has been found a most pleasant agent in arresting the fearful paroxysms and giving the patient rest, and assisting materially to the cure, causing a relaxation to the affected muscles, and by counteracting the effects of the spasm.

19. In cases of impending death the means are to support the system by heat, food, and artificial respiration, with stimulation and small doses of strychnia.

20. It has been found a most valuable agent in acute mania and in the paralysis of the insane, delirium tremens, dysmenorrhœa, and tinnitus aurium.

21. Comparatively, trials prove it more valuable in maniacal cases, in producing sleep, than tincture of hyoscyamus or bromide of potassium.

22. Chloral is very useful in the convulsions of children (when there is no severe affection of the bronchi, heart, or lungs), but care must be employed not to administer it if the infant or child is very anæmic or in an exhausted condition, as in the case of a wasting disease.

23. The necropsy in case of death from hydrate of chloral shows anæmia of the brain, acute œdema of the lungs, hyperæmia of the abdominal organs, and dark fluid blood in the vessels.

On Chloral as an Anæsthetic.

The London Medical Times and Gazette, Oct. 21, 1876, states that at the late Medical Congress at Brussels, Dr. Bouchut "observed that he took that opportunity of again directing attention to the fact that children can be placed in a state of absolute anæsthesia by means of chloral given by the mouth in doses of three or four grammes, and without producing pyrosis, gastritis, vomiting, or diarrhœa. It commences a quarter of an hour after the injection of the chloral, and is complete at the end of an hour. If, at this period, an abscess be opened, caustic applied, or a tooth extracted, the sleeping child may heave a sigh or move a limb, and again become immovable, waking up four hours afterwards quite unconscious of what has passed. This is a new proof of the difference which exists in the action of certain medicinal substances in adults and in children.

Mr. Couty, of Paris, finds that when animals are killed by chloroform, ether, or chloral, the muscles and motor nerves retain their irritability much longer than when death is produced by bleeding, compression of the heart, or asphyxia. This is especially marked in the case of chloral. We have repeated these experiments with *chloral* on frogs, and showed the results before the Philadelphia County Medical Society, and published the results in the *Phila. Med. and Surg. Reporter*. Mr. Couty considers the cause of this phenomenon to consist, not on any action of the anæsthetics on the spinal cord, but in a direct modification of the nerves and muscles by them through the blood, similar to that which occurs in poisoning by carbonic oxide.

Prof. Oré, of Bordeaux, has introduced the intravenous injection of choral as a means of producing general anæsthesia; he employs the following formula:—

℞.—Hydrate of chloral, 10 grammes.
Distilled water, 30 grammes.

A graduated hypodermic syringe is employed, gold trocar and canula. A band is placed on the arm above the point selected, and when the vein has become prominent it is pierced through the skin and 50 centigrammes are to be injected after removing the band. If anæsthesia is not produced, one gramme is added at a time until the patient complains of a strong inclination to sleep, when the canula is withdrawn. From six to ten grammes are stated to be required for an adult. The author adds this caution: It is an indispensable precaution to have an electrical or galvanic apparatus at hand, in order to arouse the patient from his insensibility by passing a current along the course of the pneumogastric nerve. Advantages: Absence of stage of excitement, and of nausea, and vomiting. Accurate graduations of dose, absolute characters of the anæsthesia, muscular relaxation and prolonged blunting of the patient's sensibility, which protects him from shock. Risks: Thrombosis and embolism, irregularity of the heart's action, presence of blood and albumen in the urine, and above all, risk of fatal syncope and death.

Chloral Poisoning.*

Dr. J. Milner Fothergill, of London, recommends (in *Medical Times*, Phila.) the great utility of strychnine as a true expectorant in bronchitis when the stage of free secretion is reached, and the air-tubes are full of mucus and the patient is in danger of choking. A combination of carbonate of ammonia, tincture of nux vomica, and tincture of squill, is a most excellent mixture for patients suffering from dyspnœa, and generally procures them "more breath," as they phrase it. One of the most important matters connected with such use of strychnine is its relation to sleep. In a case seen recently by him of complex lung and heart mischief, to which was added chloral poisoning, the good effects of strychnia were well marked. The patient was almost at once relieved from the attack of dyspnœa, in the middle of the night, to which he had long been subject. By

* The Council of the British Pharmaceutical Society passed a resolution that chloral hydrate and its preparations ought to be regarded as poisons within the meaning of the Pharmacy Act.

the use of strychnia during the day, a narcotic pill at bed-time is often deprived of its tendency to produce nocturnal dyspnœa. We might add that strychnia, in combination with ammonia and senega, might be found very useful in the after-treatment of congestion of the lungs, from the excessive use of sulphuric ether and alcohol; it is surely worthy of trial.

Hydrate of chloral, when given in large doses, sometimes causes dangerous symptoms, followed by sudden death. Several instances are recorded of medical men who have taken it incautiously and have died from its effects; two cases are reported in the *Med. Times and Gaz.*, 1871, vol. i. p. 367, and of late they have become numerous. The deaths have been sudden, and no remarkable symptoms have preceded dissolution, as observed by Dr. Taylor.* The person has passed at once from sleep into death. One case proved suddenly fatal by causing paralysis of the heart (*Lancet*, 1871, vol. i. p. 440). "In the fatal cases which have occurred, the principal *appearances* noted were congested state of the brain and its membranes." Drs. Taylor and Tuke have given it as their opinion, based upon *one* case, that the long-continued use of chloral might have produced a diseased condition of the brain, which, by the sudden withdrawal of the narcotic, might have rendered the party accused of murder (a man in a fit of passion, for some trivial cause, throws a petroleum lamp at his wife, which ignites her dress, and death is the result by burning). I have directed the employment of chloral hydrate in solution in medicinal doses for one year as a sedative and narcotic, and the only disagreeable result complained of by the patient was that it caused a hot feeling, with free perspiration, as if she was in a hot bath; it was withdrawn at the end of that time without producing the least disturbance of the brain, inflammation of the skin, or loss of memory or intelligence. We have had no fatal cases of this kind, therefore, I believe that other causes besides the hydrate of chloral may have produced some of the recorded results.

In the treatment of large doses of the hydrate of

---

* On Poisons, op. cit., p. 616.

chloral, the stomach pump should be used and the stomach well washed out with strong decoction of green tea, and the same treatment as from poisoning by opium.

CHAPTER VI.

Nitrous oxide gas as an anæsthetic. Practical observations and experiments of Dr. J. D. Thomas. The Thomas inhaler, description and mode of use. Mode of manufacturing nitrous oxide for inhalation. Impurities and mode of purification. Mode of administration Use of *prop* in extracting teeth, while under its influence. Risks, and treatment of accidents. Coxeter's form of cylinder for liquid nitrous oxide.

Nitrous Oxide Gas.

IN entering upon the subject of nitrous oxide it is not my purpose to go into its discovery, early history, etc., as a short statement is made in another part of this work, and numerous references are given for those that are interested. This anæsthetic can be employed in a few operations in surgery; these are, extraction and surgical operations on the teeth and gums. With it the ophthalmic surgeon can operate for ordinary strabismus, or removal of small tumors, or even the diseased eyeball. It is very valuable in examining the urethra for stricture, and even cutting of an impervious stricture has been performed with success. A recent luxation, or stiff joint, or the tenotomy of tendons for the relief of club foot, etc., have all been performed while under its influence. My chief object will be to treat of this anæsthetic in its practical relation in connection with dentistry.

Thomas's Inhaler.—The late Dr. Thomas had constructed a valuable inhaler, which he employed in his numerous operations, and his brother, Dr. J. D. Thomas, has continued to use it, with so much satisfaction that at my desire he has described it as follows (see Fig. 17), and

I have had a cut made, and approved by him. The inhaler is turned from a piece of vulcanized rubber, eight inches long by three inches square, leaving the mouth-piece one inch and a half across. The diameter of the opening is a little more than one-half an inch, with stopcock in the centre, in which is the inhaling valve, which is con-

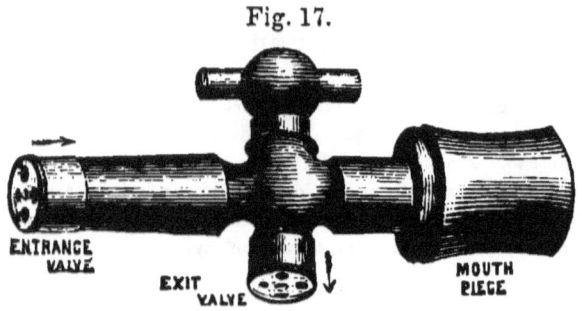

Fig. 17.

structed of a simple piece of rubber dam secured by a pin to a stopple, in which are three oblong apertures, as is the inhaling valve at the extremity of the inhaler. The aperture being of sufficient size, is made not to obstruct the free passage of the nitrous oxide gas, the valves are three-quarters of an inch in diameter, and the stopple is of vulcanized rubber. His method of using it will be described in his lecture.

Manufacture of Nitrous Oxide Gas.

Nitrous oxide gas ($NO-N_2O$) is prepared from nitrate of ammonia. This is a crystalline salt, but for convenience of introduction into the retort, should be in a granulated form, which can be obtained of the manufacturing chemist.

The second important matter is to be furnished with a convenient gasometer, an illustration of which is seen at Fig. 18, and these can be obtained from the various dental depots.* Having obtained one of these convenient gasometers, care is required in the selection of the bottles for

---

* Of Dr. S. S. White, in the chief cities of the United States.

MANUFACTURE OF NITROUS OXIDE GAS.

Fig. 18.

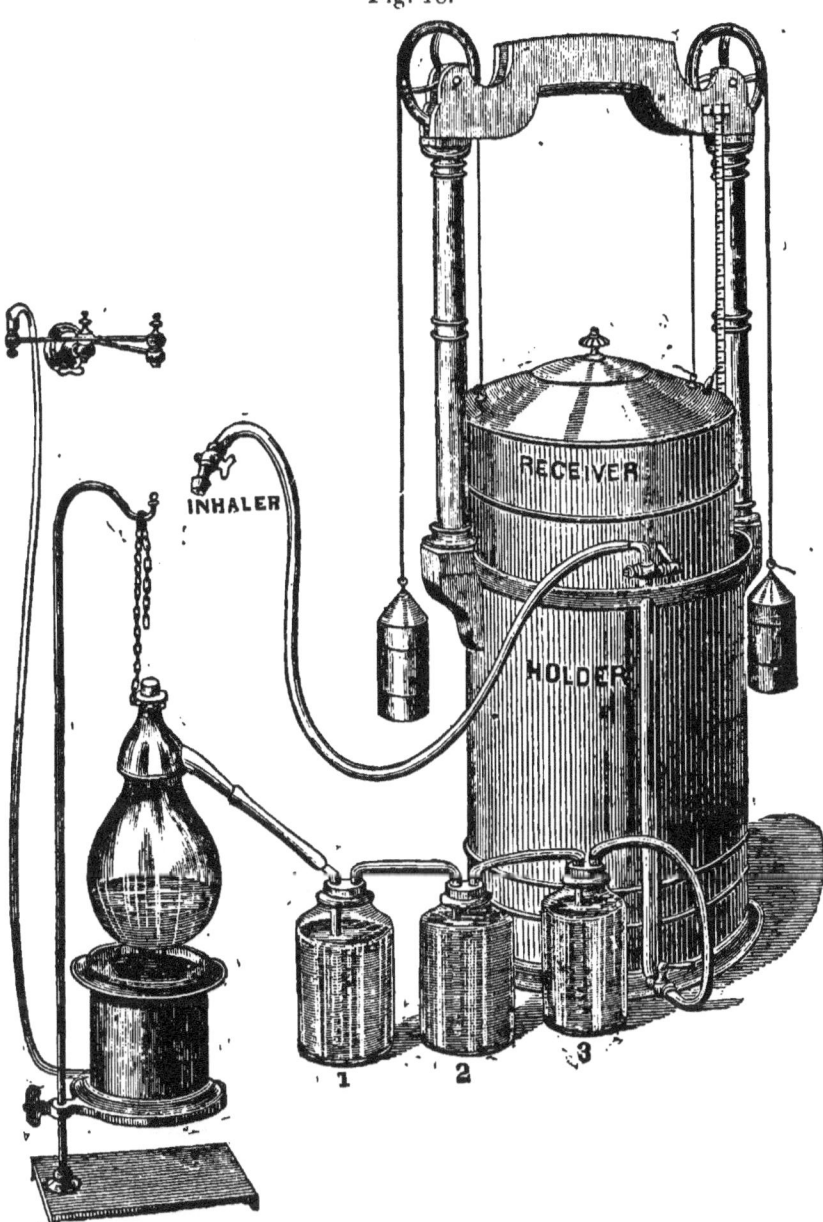

Fig. 19.

washing and purifying the gas. Fig. 19 represents a very good form, which is furnished with perforated rubber cork and glass tubes bent at right angles, the long tube is pierced with small holes at the bottom to compel the breaking up of gas, and so insure its more thorough washing. In purifying the gas some employ a solution of sulphate of iron in one bottle and pure water in the other two. To remove chlorine gas, which is sometimes present, and can be noticed by its green color and irritating vapor upon the respiration, a small stick of caustic potash is added to one of the bottles containing the water.

When no chemical agents are employed in the purification of the gas it should be well washed through fresh water, and allowed to stand for some few hours over the water in the gasometer, to remove any impurities that may have passed over.

Fig. 18 represents the gasometer in position. The holder is first filled with water to within one and a half or two inches of the top; while this is being done take off the weights and open all the spigots, to allow the air to pass out and the receiver to remain in position. When the holder is filled, close the spigot and arrange the weights; it is then ready to receive the gas. The wash-bottles are placed as represented in the cut, Nos. 1, 2, and 3, which are connected one with the other, and to the retort and gasometer, by means of rubber tubing. The first bottle, No. 1, is placed next to the retort, and is simply used to catch the drip resulting from condensed vapor.

The long pipe of bottle No. 1 must not dip under the water, for the tubing thereby becomes choked with dense vapor and the free passage of gas is interrupted.

Into wash-bottle No. 2 place about four ounces of sulphate of iron, and add sufficient water to cover the end of the dip-pipe, about one and a half to two inches.

Into wash-bottle No. 3, Fig. 19, it is unnecessary to

place anything but fresh water; yet some, fearing the chlorine, add a stick of caustic potash.

Sufficient water should be employed to cause the pipe which dips into the water to sink the same depth as it does in No. 2.

When the bottles are prepared, connect them by the piece of rubber tubing B, and to the spigot of the gasometer. If they are arranged properly, a current of air, blown into the tube intended to connect with the retort, will cause the water to bubble in the wash-bottles, Nos. 2 and 3, and if the spigot A is open, the receiver will commence to ascend.

Having the bottles in readiness and properly connected, place the quantity of nitrate of ammonia, which will be required, into the retort (one pound of the granulated salt will produce about thirty gallons of the gas). D is a stove-like arrangement heated by gas-burners, with a sand-bath for holding and heating the retort. Connect the retort with the long pipe of the first bottle by the rubber tubing, and then open the spigot of the gasometer.

The heat must be applied gradually, first to melt the ammonia, about 226° F., and then to cause it to boil; and give off gas at 460° F., and so regulate this heat as to keep it boiling at 460° F. to 480° F., until it is nearly all decomposed. When the gas has ceased to come over, take a cloth and disconnect the retort from the tubing and close the spigot of the gasometer.

The inhaling tube is attached to the spigot at the top of the holder.

There is a register which shows the number of gallons of the gas in the receiver.

The water and solutions contained in the wash-bottles should be changed after each operation, and the water in the holder once in a month. When nitrous oxide gas is thus obtained, it is colorless, almost inodorous, of a sweetish taste. The chemical decomposition is as follows: nitrate of ammonia resolves itself into nitrous oxide gas and water; thus, $NO_3NH_4 = OH + 2NO$. The heat necessary to cause active evolution of gas is stated to be 460° F., and this heat should be kept up, else a portion of the salt will sublime. The heat should never be allowed to rise above 482° F., as the nitric oxide is apt to be given off in the form of an orange-colored vapor. To determine the proper temperature a thermometer is prepared which can be passed into the cork and into the retort, so that no risk need be incurred by the introduction of poisonous materials into the gas.

By condensation nitrous oxide gas will become a liquid,* and as such is sold in Coxeter's form of cylinders, and is to be had of Mr. Samuel S. White, of this city.

Messrs. Coxeter's test of the purity of their nitrous oxide is the appearance of the gas, and its freedom from red fumes as it comes from the retort, and the smell.

"The complete apparatus consists of an iron cylinder containing at least 100 gallons (usually more) of nitrous oxide, liquefied, to which is attached by means of a nickel-plated union the necessary tubing, gas-bag, and inhaler; nickel-plated wrench and key; the whole inclosed in a stout morocco case.

"The inhaling tubing is made of the best material known for the purpose.

"The gas-bags hitherto sold have been a source of annoyance and complaint on account of their flimsy character and their liability to burst. Those now offered cannot fail to give satisfaction. They are made of stout muslin, thoroughly coated on both sides with pure 'steam vulcanized' para rubber.

"Their parts are all cemented together before putting them in the heater, insuring a strong vulcanized seam.

"The advantage of this method of construction is seen at once. If accidentally cut or burnt, or mutilated on the outer surface, they are still good and serviceable, as the inner coating remains intact, and will prevent all leaking."

"†After this brief description of the process of its manufacture, as it has been set forth, I would remark that some use the fused and others the granulated nitrate of ammonia. I consider the granulated preferable, only from the facility with which you can fill the retort. After the gas is made, it should stand over water from

---

* "Liquefied Nitrous Oxide," Dental Cosmos, vol. xx., No. 3.
† From Dr. J. D. Thomas.

seven to ten hours before using, but this will do little towards insuring absolute purity of the gas; neither will washing it through solutions of iron and potash purify it perfectly. Should there be chlorine present (which is the poisonous element) in the ammonia, I have found that no amount of washing through solutions will obliterate it. The ammonia should always be tested before using, which is done by dissolving about a teaspoonful in half a tumbler of distilled water, and applying a few crystals of the nitrate of silver. If the ammonia be pure, the solution will remain perfectly clear; but, should chlorine be present, it will show a clouded appearance, and the ammonia must be discarded altogether.

Next to pure gas, a perfect inhaler is the most essential object to the successful administration of nitrous oxide; it must be one with a tube large enough to admit the gas so freely that the most nervous as well as patients with weak lungs can inhale through it without exertion; and it must be perfectly air-tight. The majority of inhalers are so constructed that it is only with using great effort that patients can supply the lungs to their natural capacity, causing them to struggle for air, or go to sleep with such feelings of suffocation and depression that they will drift into dreams of the most frightful character, and become almost unmanageable in their excitement.

It is necessary that the valves should be perfectly air-tight, so as to administer the gas free from any atmospheric air, one breath of which is sufficient to dilute two or three of the gas, and should there be a continual supply through the valves, it will require three times the quantity of gas, and the anæsthesia so produced will be of such a nature as not to render the patient utterly oblivious to the effects of the operation.

Inhalers which cover the face or any part of it are objectionable. In cases of gentlemen with beard, it is impossible to give the gas without the admission of some air. In instances, such as harelip, or where, from swelling or other cause, the muscles of the jaws become so contracted as to render it impossible to pass the mouthpiece between the teeth, I would recommend Dr. Barker's rubber hood, which is soft and pliable, and answers admirably in such cases, though not desirable for universal use. The color of the blood, as shown through the mucous membrane of the lips, is one of the principal guides to the condition of the patient during the inhalation of the gas; and if they are covered from view by the hood or otherwise, we have lost *that* means of rendering success to the operation.

Unlike chloroform and ether, the muscles of the patient become rigidly contracted while under the influence of nitrous oxide in a large number of cases, which render the use of props indispensable. These are made of hard wood of various sizes, and have strings attached to assure the patient against the possibility of swallowing them, and are placed in the mouth on the side opposite from where the tooth is to be extracted. By their use one has a fair opportunity to perform the operation to his entire satisfaction; but without them there is danger of the patient bruising and possibly breaking the front teeth by biting so hard upon the mouthpiece, with the probability of recovering from the effects of the gas before the mouth can be gotten open sufficiently wide to admit of the extraction of a tooth. (Here a number of inhalers were exhibited, and their qualities explained. After which, the mode of administering was illustrated, together with position, the importance of an assistant, and the symptoms during the inhalation. In extracting, the kinds of forceps required, and how to use them, and the importance of having in the mind just what was to be done, so as to instantly commence the operation.)

Nitrous oxide must always be fresh to insure success, though some have recommended it after it has stood over water one or two weeks, and even a month, but it is impracticable.

Two years this fall my brother, who is now deceased, was attending medical lectures at the Jefferson College. Dr. Rand, the late Professor of Chemistry at that institution, advocated old gas; and, to practically demonstrate the difference, we allowed some gas to stand for two weeks, then invited him to test between that and the new. He invited his assistants, Drs. Green and Smith, and tested by inhaling with deep inspirations to the full capacity of the lungs, first of the new, then the old, and it required five times the quantity of the old to produce the effect with the new, which proved quite convincing. Besides requiring an excessive quantity, the anæsthesia produced by old gas is not so complete but what the patient will mostly receive some undefined impression of the operation, and they will often complain of giddiness and a fulness in the head, and feeling generally miserable for the balance of the day. With fresh gas, sickness will never occur, except with patients of very delicate organizations, who are easily disturbed by nervous excitement, and those who are affected by the sight of blood, or the contemplation of a wound of any kind.

In its pure state the gas may be given to almost any one, I believe, with impunity, if judiciously administered, for I have given it to a large number of patients afflicted with heart disease and consumption, also to cases subject to epileptic fits, St. Vitus' dance, persons of apoplectic tendency, and women advanced in pregnancy, and have never yet met with any but the most satisfactory results.

Among the difficulties you may meet having the appearance of danger in administering nitrous oxide, the most common will be the constriction of the glottis or swallowing the tongue. The use of the prop cannot be overestimated in such cases. The patient becomes very dark in the face; there is a violent exertion of the diaphragm, and presents every indication of approaching asphyxia, which, having the mouth well propped open, is very readily relieved by catching hold of the tongue with a dry napkin and pulling it out of the mouth, and at the same time raising the body forward; as soon as the patient has taken two or three inspirations the tension is relaxed, and he will recover in a minute's time. I recall to my mind a case of this sort in Exeter, England, where the patient died some time ago.*

The most formidable appearance of danger is when your patient is attacked with syncope while under the influence of the gas. You want first to be sure the air-

---

* Described in "The Dental Cosmos," May, 1873.

passages are open by getting the tongue forward. Then, the patient being in a sitting posture, bring the head and body forward with considerable violence, which will invariably prove sufficient. You may, however, meet cases which will require more effective remedies. The object is first to get the head on a level or below the heart, so the blood may flow freely to the brain, which is done by laying the patient on the floor, then throwing cold water by the tumblerful violently in the face. In my experience I have found the most effectual remedy is to place the finger far down the throat, which will produce involuntary retching, and is the most efficient action to bring about restoration, after which you treat the same as any ordinary case of fainting, giving a little brandy, and allowing him to lie on the lounge until he has become strong enough to walk in the fresh air, when he will soon recover completely."

In the hands of so skilful and careful an operator as Dr. Thomas, no great risk attends the employment of this anæsthetic; but those who are less skilful and are inexperienced should reject cases of great physical exhaustion, or patients with a feeble or fatty heart. The distension of the right cavities which accompanies the disappearance of the radial pulse, and the general lividity of the features, may be attended with some degree of risk, and the danger must be increased when, the muscles of the trunk and limbs being convulsed, the pressure of the contracting muscles upon the veins drives the blood forcibly towards the right cavities of the heart, and so adds to their distension.

CHAPTER VII.

Physiological action of nitrous oxide gas. Resemblance between the effects produced by nitrous oxide and asphyxia. Summary of the facts bearing on this subject. Not merely a passive agent. Dr. Evans' (of Paris) experiments with nitrous oxide and other gases, and his conclusions Dr. J. H. McQuillen's experiments in 1868, and his repeating them in conjunction with the writer. Personal experiments of Dr. Jeannel in 1869; he dwells upon the non-fatal character of nitrous oxide, and the rapidity with which its effects pass away. Also the corroborative experiments of M. Limouzin. Original experiments of `Dr. Robert Amory in 1870, with his conclusions, and opinions of Dr. Johnston. Mode of action of anæsthetics. Experiments of Professors Heinrich Ranke and D. C. Binz on morphia, chloral, ether, chloroform, amylene, bromoform, and bromohydrate. Physiological action of nitrous oxide gas, by the editor of "Binz's Therapeutics." List of authorities on the nature and action of chloroform, ether, and nitrous oxide. Deaths from the inhalation of nitrous oxide. Post-mortem changes, etc.

Physiological Action of Nitrous Oxide Gas.

THE marked resemblance between the effects produced by nitrous oxide and those resulting from asphyxia was observed by the earlier experimenters with ether; and a few eminent physiologists at once expressed this opinion; but at the present day it is not very generally entertained.*

The following is a summary of the various facts bearing on the subject, *i. e.*, in regard to the physiological action of nitrous oxide :—

" It would seem that this accumulated evidence is sufficient to show that the anæsthesia produced by the inhalation of nitrous oxide is *simply* asphyxia; yet it is

---

* A Treatise on Therapeutics and Toxicology, p. 241, 2d ed. Dental Cosmos, from Jan. 1869, to April, 1870; continued in five numbers. J. B. Lippincott, Phila.

stated that it produces in man, even when mixed with air, a feeling of exhilaration, which would indicate that it is not merely a passive agent." "Dr. Evans,* of Paris, states that he can call to mind no word in modern medical literature which is used with less definiteness of meaning, and which is more frequently misused, than this word asphyxia. Understanding, however, by the word asphyxia, the condition which arises from an insufficient oxygenation of the blood, or from the accumulation in the blood of carbonic acid, he is by no means inclined to regard such conditions as identical with that produced by the inhalation of nitrous oxide. If there is a close resemblance between these, he states, there are also marked differences.

Nitrogen, when inhaled, is supposed to act upon the animal economy solely by the exclusion of oxygen. Nitrogen, when taken into the lungs, gives rise to no feeling of exhilaration, but to malaise and a sense of impending suffocation, and only occasions symptoms of narcosis and insensibility after an interval of time considerably greater than that usually found necessary when nitrous oxide is used.

In animals, after death following the inhalation of nitrogen, Dr. Evans has generally found less venous congestion, particularly of the portal system, than is to be observed after death from nitrous oxide. The blood is also lighter in color, and the liver nearly normal in appearance.

There is, however, one condition strikingly similar to that observable after death from nitrous oxide, *i. e.*, the condition of the lungs. These organs are found neither voluminous nor collapsed, of a light pink or rose color, and generally with one or more small circular, well-defined ecchymotic spots, usually on their posterior surface. These spots, the *ecchymoses sous pleurales* of French writers, are considered by Briand and Chandé as peculiar to death by suffocation, and as distinguishing that kind of asphyxia from the asphyxia of drowning, hanging, and strangulation. The phenomena occasioned by the presence of carbonic acid were then

---

* Physiological Action of Nitrous Oxide Gas, by Thomas W. Evans, M.D., D.D.S., Paris, France.

carefully studied by experiments by Dr. Evans. This gas, when pure is irrespirable; the mixture which he employed was 30 per cent. of carbonic and 70 of common air. This mixture when inhaled produces the peculiar effects of carbonic acid, loss of power of motion, loss of conscious sensation, and finally, death. The insensibility is not preceded by a period of excitement, such as is witnessed during the inhalation of ether, and more especially of nitrous oxide. Again, the after-effects following a prolonged inhalation of carbonic acid are observed—the sense of weariness, headache, loss of appetite, nausea, etc.; none of these signs of nervous disturbance are commonly seen after inhalation of nitrous oxide. This is an important difference, not only practically, but physiologically.

After death from nitrogen or nitrous oxide, the lungs are moderately crepitant, and the blood which escapes from an incision is more or less full of gas bubbles. In case of death produced by nitrous oxide, the bubbles will be found in the bronchial ramifications mixed with mucus, and in one or two instances, Dr. Evans found the trachea filled with rusty, frothy fluid, so common after drowning as to have been referred to by Dr. Riedell as almost pathognomonic of that cause of death. The local effects of nitrous oxide were found to be less marked than those produced by carbonic acid. They both act upon the blood-corpuscles so as to darken them. The lividity upon the lips, and the darkening of the mucous surfaces seen every day in the operating room after administrations of nitrous oxide, are the result of this action. The inhalation of nitrous oxide is followed by an increased exhalation of carbonic acid; so is the inhalation of ether, chloroform, etc. Soon, however, according to M. Buisson, if the inhalation be continued, the exhalation of carbonic acid falls below the normal proportion to be found in expired air.

While it is perfectly evident that nitrous oxide has a strong affinity for the blood-corpuscles, it may usurp the place of oxygen in them, and prevent for a time that combination of oxygen with the hæmatin upon which the red color of the corpuscles is presumed to depend. Chemistry has not yet shown that it is decomposed in the blood, or exerts any of the chemical properties of oxygen on the constituent elements of the blood."

The conditions which obtain after the inhalation of nitrous oxide, ether, chloroform, and other anæsthetics, are, specific toxical properties, which first stimulate, then narcotize, then destroy nervous action: by (*a*) an interference more or less marked with the oxygenation of the blood, and the consequent imperfect accomplishment of certain chemico-vital processes; by (*b*) a retention in the blood of a portion of the usual pulmonary exhalations: the two latter and secondary conditions always finally co-operating with the specific action of the anæsthetic in the production of narcosis, the arrest of innervation, and in the suspension of every functional movement; in a word, in the death of the organism. Latterly it has been disproved both by experiment and observation, *i. e.*, the theory which for a time prevailed in the United States, "that nitrous oxide acts upon the blood as an oxygenating agent." No experimental proof has yet been furnished that nitrous oxide is decomposed in the blood, or forms chemical combinations with it. It enters into the blood as nitrous oxide, and as such is eliminated. It will naturally be inferred from this statement that the presence of nitrous oxide in the blood is not indicated by the appearance (except change of color), as before stated. This was very conclusively proven by Dr. J. H. McQuillen, Professor of Physiology in Philadelphia Dental College, which proofs are here given with the illustrations.

By the kindness of Dr. Thomas, of this city, of the Colton Dental Association, was placed his whole apparatus, with a large supply of recently made pure nitrous oxide gas, at the disposal of Dr. McQuillen and myself, and we repeated the experiments (see p. 148) in confirmation of the facts: that the gas had no positive poisonous qualities; second, that the blood-corpuscles were changed neither in form nor color under the microscope, and nitrous oxide is only known by the change of color, and even this varies much in individuals. A full report will be found at the end of his original communication.

Dr. McQuillen has placed this communication at my

disposal, with the cuts to illustrate it, and made such modifications of it as time and his mature judgment would seem to have dictated.

Action of Anæsthetics on the Blood-Corpuscles.*

In the October number of the *Dental Cosmos*, 1868, a report was presented of a series of experiments performed by me, on a number of animals, with the view of ascertaining whether the assertion made by Dr. B. Ward Richardson, that nitrous oxide, even under the most delicate manipulation, would prove destructive to life, could be possible. These experiments, which clearly demonstrated the assertion to be unfounded, were not performed in private, but in the presence of a number of gentlemen whose experience in the use of anæsthetics and whose scientific knowledge made them competent judges. First performed before the members of the Odontographic Society of Pennsylvania, they were repeated, after an interval of three weeks, on the same animals, in the presence of the members of the Biological and Microscopical Section of the Academy of Natural Sciences.

A month subsequent to the last-named occasion, one of *these animals*, a rabbit, in the presence of a number of gentlemen, was placed under the influence of nitrous oxide, and kept in a profound state of narcosis for *one hour and five minutes*, by alternating atmospheric air and nitrous oxide, removing the inhaler ever and anon for that purpose. Without question the animal could have been kept in the same condition double or treble the time without injury to it, for in a few minutes after removing the anæsthetic entirely, the animal was restored to consciousness, and leaped from the table to the floor, and for a number of weeks after this ran about my premises in a healthy and lively condition.

On examination no perceptible difference was observable in the blood-corpuscles under the microscope, even

---

* Republished in the Boston Medical and Surgical Journal; Monthly Microscopical Journal, London; Deutsche Klinick, Berlin; Dental Cosmos, March, 1869; Correspondenz Blatt für Zahnärzte; Giornale di Correspondenza dei Dentisti; Le Progrès Dentaire.

after this lengthened exposure to the anæsthetic, when compared with the blood of another rabbit, which was not under its influence. This result induced me to examine into the statements made by Dr. Sansom, relative to the action of anæsthetics on the blood-corpuscles, in his highly interesting and able work on chloroform.*

Prior to giving a description of my experiments in this direction, it may be proper to briefly refer to the prevalent theories on the physiological action of anæsthetics; also to the experiments performed and conclusions arrived at by Dr. Sansom. The view generally entertained is that first suggested by Flourens, that these agents act directly upon the nerve centres, producing regular and progressive modifications in the functions of the brain and spinal axis, first affecting the cerebral hemisphere, then the power of co-ordination in the cerebellum, then the conduction of sensation and motion in the spinal cord, and lastly, if the agent is pushed so far as to decidedly impress the medulla oblongata, suspension of respiration and circulation.

Dr. John Snow, regarding this theory as erroneous, and recognizing ether, chloroform, and other anæsthetics as non-supporters of combustion, advanced the theory that these agents, interfering with the introduction of oxygen into the system, induced their effect by the suspension of oxygenation; he therefore asserted that "narcotism is suspended oxygenation." This view is embraced and strongly advocated by Dr. B. W. Richardson, and in England apparently is being very generally adopted by writers on this subject; Dr. Kidd is, however, a prominent exception.

Dr. Sansom, accepting this theory, and knowing that nitrous oxide is not only an anæsthetic but a supporter of combustion, recognized the necessity of presenting something more conclusive in the support of the view than had heretofore been offered. He therefore, in a paper read before the Royal Medical and Chirurgical Society, in 1861, as the result of certain experiments performed on the blood-corpuscles of man and animals

---

* Chloroform, its Actions and Administrations. By Arthur Ernest Sansom, M.B., London: Lindsay & Blakiston, Philada.

out of the body, attributed the influence exerted by anæsthetics on the nervous system to their acting directly upon the blood-corpuscles, by modifying their form and integrity, and indirectly upon the nervous system through this altered condition of the blood, by interfering with its oxygenation. In this work he describes a series of six experiments; placing on glass slides, under a quarter-inch object-glass, human and frog's blood, and subjecting them to the *direct contact* of alcohol, ether, and chloroform, which resulted quickly in the disintegration of the blood-corpuscles, leaving nothing but their nuclei and débris of the walls of the corpuscles. From these experiments on blood *out of the body*, he states in the work referred to : "The effect, therefore, of these agents upon the blood is solution—destruction. At first there is a change induced in the cell itself and upon the nucleus (in the case of frog's blood). The globuline of the blood is acted upon as it were by a caustic. Finally the blood-corpuscle is destroyed and the coloring matter set free." . . . From the foregoing facts and other considerations, the author considers that certain conclusions in regard to the action of anæsthetics are warrantable. Anæsthetics are agents which, when absorbed into the circulation, exert an influence upon the blood. They are shown to have the power of altering its *physical character* and *physical properties.* By an action upon its constituent (proteinous) elements, they tend to alter and by a profounder action to destroy its organic molecules. Its physical perfection being interfered with, its function is held in abeyance ; the changes which contribute to constitute perfect life are retarded. Narcosis ensues ; and is due, not to the influence of a circulating poison, but to the influence of an altered blood. Further on he adds : "Narcotism (or to speak more particularly, chloroform narcotism) is due not to a special poison that 'mounts up to the brain,' but to an altered blood. Then 'narcotism is a suspended oxygenation.' Whatever produces, to a certain extent, insufficient aeration of the blood, produces narcosis; and whatever produces narcosis, produces, by some means or other, imperfect aeration of the blood."

In drawing these conclusions, of an altered condition of the blood, from appearances presented by the blood *out of the body*, Dr. Sansom evidently leaves it to be inferred that somewhat if not exactly analogous results are produced on the corpuscles *in the body*, when human beings or animals are under the influence of anæsthetics by inhalation. After a patient, oft-repeated series of experiments performed by me during the past three months, not only on blood out of the body, but also in cases in which human beings and animals have been placed under the influence of ether, chloroform, and nitrous oxide, and the blood drawn from them *prior* to and *after* the administration of these agents has been carefully *examined* and *compared*, the results obtained compel me to take very decided exceptions to such conclusions being justifiable in the premises.

First Series.—The experiments were as follows: In my examinations of the blood of man and animals, when ether and chloroform were brought in direct contact with it out of the body, under a fifth objective, the discharge of the nuclei and the disintegration of the corpuscles have invariably occurred, and in the frog leaving a result similar to that which is presented in the accompanying drawing (Fig. 20) from one of my specimens, wherein it will be observed that the field is occupied by the nuclei, débris of disintegrated globuline and corpuscles, in which the change of form, size, and other characteristics are most striking.

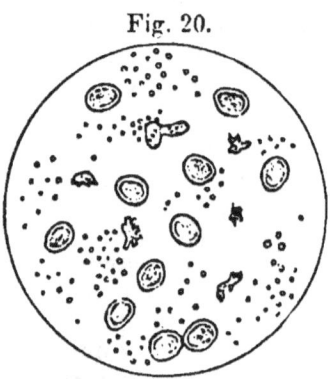

Fig. 20.

Frog's blood placed upon the slide, and chloroform brought in direct contact with it.

Second Series.—On placing, however, two glass slides containing frog's blood over watch-crystals, one holding chloroform and the other ether, and covering them with glass finger-bowls for half an hour, thus exposing one to an atmosphere of ether, and the other of chloroform, I found, on removing the bowls, and permitting the bloody sides of the slides to remain downward, until all the ether and chloroform had evaporated, that no disintegration or marked change in the form of the corpuscles was observable under the microscope, on comparing them with the blood of a frog unaffected by an anæsthetic. This forcibly demonstrates the difference between exposure to *direct contact* and the *vapor* of chloroform or ether, even out of the body.

Third Series.—Over and again in the presence of a number of gentlemen, I have placed frogs under the influence of ether, chloroform, and nitrous oxide, and examined their blood-corpuscles immediately after without finding any disintegration or change in the form of the corpuscle. In one instance, a frog was so completely narcotized by chloroform that it died; the thorax of the animal was opened, the lungs cut out, and the blood obtained directly from that organ, and even here, where, if the inference of an altered blood was correct, there should have been discharge of nuclei, disintegration, or *marked* change in the form of the corpuscle, nothing of the kind was evident, as will be seen by the accompanying illustration, drawn from the slide on which the blood was placed. (Fig. 21.) As already intimated, the experiments in this direction have been prosecuted on every available occasion within the past few months; and I have not confined myself to frogs, but, in the course of vivisections on a large number of animals (rabbits, dogs, cats, and pigeons), to illustrate my course of lectures on physiology this winter, when these animals have been placed under the influence of ether or chloroform, their blood has been examined and no change in the form of the corpuscle has been evident.

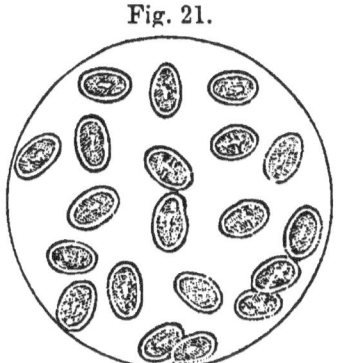

Fig. 21.

Corpuscles from the lungs of a frog which died under the influence of chloroform.

Fourth Series.—The examination of the blood of a number of human beings, drawn prior to and after having been under the influence of ether, chloroform, or nitrous

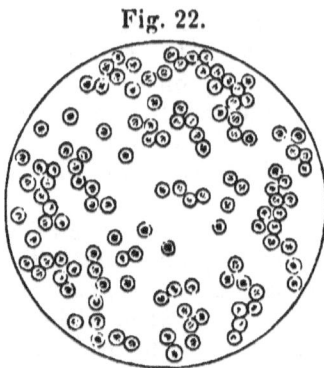

Fig. 22.

Corpuscles of a patient under the influence of chloroform.

oxide, has yielded similar results, as will be evident from the accompanying illustration of the blood, obtained from a patient (Fig. 22) while under the influence of chloroform. Any one accustomed to microscopical examinations will recognize the normal characters of the corpuscles, so far as it is possible to present them in a woodcut.

In conclusion, although it is not my intention in this communication to engage in an extended inquiry relative to how anæsthetics produce their effects, it seems to me that the above experiments demonstrate that we are not warranted in denying that these agents act directly upon the nerve centres. All the phenomena, indeed, attendant upon their administration, the gradual exaltation of the cerebral functions followed by the progressive impairment and temporary suspension of the special senses, the loss of co-ordination on the part of the cerebellum, and when the agent is pushed too far, the arrest of respiration and circulation through the decided impression made upon the medulla oblongata, seem to favor this hypothesis, in contradistinction to the theory that anæsthesia is due to suspension of oxygenation.

Experiments with Nitrous Oxide by Drs. McQuillen, Thomas, and Turnbull, December, 1877.—A large-sized frog was placed under a glass jar holding five quarts of nitrous oxide, and kept there sixteen minutes. With the exception of some change in the color of the skin, there was no apparent impression made the first five minutes, as he jumped about when the jar was moved in the pneumatic trough. After that he assumed the position of a frog sitting on a log, and maintained it until removed from the jar, when he was found in a semi-torpid state with the eyes wide open. On touching the eyes gently, the lids closed, and then opened immediately; the leg was retracted on pricking it with a pin. Two minutes after removal from the jar, he moved slowly about the floor, and ten minutes later hopped from a table on to the floor. After remaining out for thirty-five minutes, he was again placed under the jar, in a fresh supply of gas, and kept there for thirty minutes; on being removed he presented the same semi-torpid condition, and recovered from it in two minutes. In twenty minutes he was a third time placed in fresh nitrous oxide, and remained there fifteen minutes, with the same results as the previous trials; the confinement for one hour, in all, to the influence of nitrous oxide not having made any marked impression on him. Examined under $\frac{1}{5}$ objective and B. eye-piece, the blood-corpuscle presented no disintegrative discharge of nuclei, or change of form.

A small-sized rabbit was kept under nitrous oxide for two minutes, and in one minute after was completely restored to consciousness. He was then kept under the gas for five minutes consecutively, and recovered in $1\frac{1}{2}$ minutes. After this, for twenty minutes off and on, the animal was under the influence of the gas. In three minutes after removal from it he was running around the room as though nothing had occurred. The blood examined under the microscope gave no evidence of disintegration of the blood-corpuscles.

To test the quality of the gas used, Drs. Turnbull, Thomas, and McQuillen inhaled it, and each one was sensibly affected by their inspirations of it.

If we assume that the influence of anæsthetics is dependent not upon a direct action on the nerve centres, but upon an altered condition of the blood and the suspension of oxygenation, we must apply the same principle to all diffusible stimulants.

It will be noticed that it was in 1868 Dr. McQuillen published his experiments upon nitrous oxide. On the 7th of December, 1869, Dr. Jeannel read a paper[*] before the French Academy of Medicine on the protoxide of nitrogen or nitrous oxide as an anæsthetic agent. He states that there is no record of a fatal case from the use of the drug, notwithstanding its frequent application. He reported a number of careful personal experi-

[*] Gaz. Hebdomadaire, 1869, p. 786.

ments. He dwells at some length upon the rapidity with which the effects of this drug pass away, followed by the proper exercise of the natural functions, and concludes that his own and M. Limouzin's experiments authorize the presumption that this gas is an anæsthetic much less dangerous than ether or chloroform.

In August, 1870, Dr. Robert Amory published a number of experiments on man and animals* to show the physiological action of nitrous oxide. He commences his experiments with this proposition:—

"I have not, as yet, been able to find how the peculiar effects of this so-called anæsthetic agent are explained; nor has any one *directly* stated that the action may be explained by an accumulation of carbonic acid in the blood. A direct proof of this supposition it would be a difficult matter to give. An approximate idea I have attempted to show by a few experiments."

After making his experiments, which he gives in a table at page 13 (see pamphlet), he observes: "Now if we examine this table carefully, we should merely compare the figures in the last column with each other, as also the effects produced by this agent upon the same animal. If we do so, we shall find that the gas diminishes the amount of carbonic acid exhaled by almost one-half. This, then, would lead us to suppose that the effects produced by inhaling this gas may be due to the accumulation of carbonic acid in the blood; but a plausible explanation is that the oxygenation of the blood is prevented, and carbonic acid, the result of combustion, is withheld; the effects are by no means so rapid as when this agent is inhaled. Again, I do not quite accept a theory which supposes that an accumulation of carbonic acid in the blood will cause asphyxia and death in twenty minutes." At page 18 there is a paragraph which strongly corroborates Dr. McQuillen's experiments. "Two or three times it has happened to me, when I had thought an animal dead from asphyxia, after the inhalation of this gas, to be surprised by voluntary

---

* New York Med. Journal, August, 1870. Republished by James Campbell, Boston, 1870.

respiration recurring after I had removed the muzzle. In fact, I have now two dogs alive who have not respired for *one whole minute* several times when undergoing an experiment. Never has an animal died *unexpectedly*, and it was always very difficult for me to cause *asphyxia*, if the smallest modicum of air passed into the lungs."

At page 29 the author finally states: "Having proceeded thus far in my writing, I came across, accidentally, a lecture of Professor George Johnson, in the number of the *Medical Times and Gazette* for April 3, 1869. I was exceedingly surprised to see a confirmation of his theory in regard to the anæsthetic action of nitrous oxide. What he had arrived at by careful reasoning, I have been able to obtain by actual experiment. For example, he says:—

'Nitrous oxide is a rapidly-acting anæsthetic, causing complete unconsciousness in less than a minute. At a high temperature it is an oxidizing agent, but at the temperature of the body it gives up no oxygen, but is exhaled again unchanged. When inhaled in place of atmospheric air, it rapidly replaces the oxygen of the blood, and, this being done, the functions of the brain are completely suspended, and there is a state of profound coma, which quickly passes off when air is again allowed to enter the lungs. . . There is no reason* to conclude that the inhalation of either nitrous oxide or nitrogen causes an accumulation of carbonic acid in the blood.' Before this, he says: ' To produce oxidation of the brain, there must be (1) a free current of blood through the capillaries of the brain; (2) the blood must be duly aërated or oxygenized; (3) the blood must be unmixed with any material which prevents or impedes the giving up of oxygen from the blood to the tissues.'"

Then our author and experimenter says:—

"If we accept these three rules for the preservation of the nerve functions, of course, if one be wanting, the nerve functions are suspended. Now the experiments XIV, XV, and XVI, taken in connection with the accompanying sphygmographic traces (which are given), show an increase of capillary tension, with, as we should sup-

* Vide Experiments Nos. I, IV, etc.

pose, increased arterial pulsations; but finally, *arrest* of capillary pulsation in the brain. At this stage anæsthesia occurs. When the pulsation recommences and the tension falls, consciousness sets in. This effect, then, is a violation of Rule 1. Again, the blood having no oxygen to give up in the capillary system, there is a violation of Rule 3."

We do not think either Dr. Johnson or Dr. Amory has proven his propositions by facts; the one resorts to theory *alone;* and the other to supposition after experiments, by supposing an increased number of arterial pulsations, which is not proven, as the pulse before inhalation, is increased in frequency by the nervous excitement, and always decreases when the patient has begun to inhale the nitrous oxide. This fact has been recently proven by a large number of experiments.

We are fully convinced by experiments on animals and man that when death occurs, it is the result of syncope, caused by a capillary stasis of the blood, and the true anæsthetic action was discovered by Flourens, that nitrous oxide acts directly upon the nerve centres, producing regular and progressive modifications in the functions of the brain and spinal axis, first affecting the cerebral hemisphere, then the cerebellum, and lastly, the medulla oblongata, with suspension of respiration and circulation.

Mode of Action of Anæsthetics.

We have already given our own results and those of others as to how anæsthetics act under the several agents, viz.: chloral, ether, chloroform, and nitrous oxide. Their true action is still a subject of dispute, and I avail myself of the recent investigations of Dr. C. Binz, of Bonn,* and of Heinrich Ranke to further illustrate this complex subject. Binz concludes an article on the officinal sleep-producing substances in the *Archiv für Experimentale*

* Elements of Therapeutics. A Clinical Guide to the Action of Medicine. By Dr C. Binz. Prof. of Pharmacology of the University of Bonn. Translated from the Fifth German Edition. Wm. Wood & Co., New York, 1878.

Path. u. Pharm., by saying that these agents possess the power of producing a kind of coagulation of the substance of the cerebral cortex, whilst other agents, though nearly allied to the former in chemical composition, do not possess this power. Morphia, chloral, ether, and chloroform possess, these latter maintain, a strong affinity for the substance of the cortex of the brain in man, and when they are introduced into the blood they enter into combination with the cerebral substance, opposing or impeding the disintegration of the living substance, and thus rendering it unfit to discharge the functions required of it in the living state. In a paper on the subject in the *Centralblatt*, Aug. 25, 1877, Heinrich Ranke* observes that protracted study of the effects of anæsthetics has led him to very similar conclusions in 1867. He has found that the action of chloroform, ether, and amylene on frogs first produces a condition in which, just as in poisoning by curare, no contraction can be induced in muscle by any kind of irritation applied to the motor nerves, though the muscular tissue itself reacts to direct stimulation, and the current in the nerve remains constant both in force and direction. In a later stage of the anæsthesia the muscular tissue itself ceases to respond to the most powerful induction currents, though its proper electro-motor force remains unweakened; and lastly, at a still more advanced stage, the whole muscular tissue of the body passes into a condition of rigor. He has further found that a solution either of albumen from the brain or of myosin from muscle in very weak salt and water is precipitated by the vapor of the three above-named anæsthetics, and that their power of producing muscle rigor in the case of muscle depends on the coagulation of the myosin.

Additional experiments have lately been instituted by Ranke, which demonstrated that not only chloroform and chloral hydrate, when injected into the arteries, caused rapid stiffening of the muscles, but that the same influence was exerted by *ether, amylene, bromoform, and bromohydrate,* whilst, when tannin, cupric sulphate, mercury chloride, ferric sulphate, or spirits of wine were in-

* Translated in the London Lancet, Nov. 24, 1877.

jected, though strong fibrillar contractions occurred, and coagulation of the blood, followed by death, in no instance was rigor produced. Iodoform, indeed, appears to form an exception to the conclusion that the rigor-producing action of the anæsthetics is something peculiar to them, for it is not known to possess anæsthetic properties. If injected in solution in ether, rigor is immediately produced, but ether has itself a stiffening action on muscle. Nevertheless, Ranke thinks he can distinguish between the action of the iodoform, which is immediate and tense, and that of the ether, which comes on later and is less powerful; and he attributes the failure of iodoform to act as an anæsthetic to its insolubility merely, which, as it were, masks its proper action. Ranke was unable to find that solutions of morphia were able to exert any coagulating influence on muscle, either within or without the vessels. It may be asked what relation does the action of these agents on muscle bear to the process of anæsthesia, and in reply Ranke observes that anæsthetization obviously cannot depend on such a complete coagulation as admits of no further change, since the effects produced by anæsthetic agents are but transitory. But it is very conceivable that an action which in its final stages leads to coagulation of albumen may, in its earlier stages, render, to a certain extent, fixed and immovable the albuminous molecules in the ganglion-cells of the brain, and afterwards in nerve and muscle, the effect passing off with the removal of the cause.

This same hypothesis was maintained by the late Claude Bernard on similar grounds, several years prior to the publication of even that of H. Ranke. The editor of the *Lancet* adds: "It would have been exceedingly interesting if the view of 'Binz' to the effect that morphia acts also as a coagulating agent upon the ganglion cells could be corroborated, since, if such were the case, it wound tend to show that the various kinds of anæsthetics act essentially in the same manner."

The physiological action of nitrous oxide, as given in Binz's work by the editor, is as follows: "When inhaled pure it appears to produce anæsthesia by taking the place of the normal respiratory oxygen, and so preventing the proper oxidation of the nervous centres; for though it contains more oxygen than atmospheric air, this oxygen is perfectly inert, and remains throughout in chemical combination with its nitrogen. The gas is taken up by the blood and circulates with it, but though, as proven by the spectroscope, it enters into combination with hæmoglobin, it does not part with any of its oxygen to the tissues, being expired as such unaltered. It does not, however, prevent the escape of carbonic acid from the blood, for if the expired gas be passed into lime-water, a precipitate of carbonate of lime is thrown down." The editor gives no authorities for his conclusions, so they will have to be received with caution.

We would refer those interested to the following authorities, in part kindly furnished by Dr. Isaac Ott, of Easton, Penn., and from his recent work.*

CHLOROFORM. — Kussmal, Virchow's Archiv, xiii. p. 289; Böttcher, Virchow's Archiv, xxxii. p. 126; Hermann, Pflüger's Archiv, 1866, p. 27; Bernstein, Schmidt's Jahrbüch, bd. cxlii. p. 227; Bucheim u. Eisenmenger, Eckhard's Beiträge, v. 73; Dumeril et Demarquay, Archives Générales, 1848; Whestphal, Virchow's Archiv, xxvii. 409; Snow, on Anæsthetics; Husemann, Schmidt's Jahrbüch, bd. cli. p. 84; Hering u. Kratschmer, Berichte der Wiener Akademie, lxii. bd. ii.; Knoll, Sitzb. der Kaiserlich Akademie der Wissen., 1873; Vierordt, Archiv f. Physiolog. Heilkunde, 1856, 269; Gosselin, Archives Générales, 1848; Schienesson, Archiv d. Heilkunde, x. 37, 172, 225; Anstie, Stimulants and Narcotics; Bernard, Leçons sur les Anæsthetiques, et sur l'Asphyxie; Nothnagel, Handbuch der Arzneimittellehre, 1874; H. Köhler, Handbuch d. Physiolog. Therapeutik, 1876; Dogiel, Reichert's Archiv, 1866. Several references will be found in the body of this work.

ETHER. — Bernard, Substances Toxiques, 413; Wettich, Schmidt's Jahrbüch, bd. cxii. p. 212; Hermann, Archiv f. Anat. u. Physiologie, 1866, 27.

NITROUS OXIDE.—Jolyet et Blanche, Archives de Physiologie, July, 1873; Thompson, Phila. Medical Times, Nov. 1873; Hermann, Lehrbuch der Experimentellen Toxicologie, 1874.

---

* The Action of Medicines, by Isaac Ott, A.M., M.D., formerly Demonstrator of Experimental Physiology in the University of Pennsylvania: Philadelphia, 1878, pp. 143-4.

Deaths from the Inhalation of Nitrous Oxide.

We know only of one instance in this city of supposed death from this anæsthetic agent, and in this case it was subsequently discovered that one of the cork props, which had no securing-string attached, was found at the *post-mortem* examination in the larynx of the patient.

Second case. In June, 1872, in the *Dental Cosmos*, was an editorial by James W. White, M.D., on a death alleged to have resulted from the inhalation of nitrous oxide gas administered by Dr. Newbrough, of New York, at whose office the death occurred, and by whom the following (summary) of evidence was made before the coroner's jury. The patient, a middle-aged lady, desired the extraction of seven or eight front teeth, which were *loose*. Dr. N. advised that their removal would be so easy that an anæsthetic would be unnecessary; but the patient insisted that she could not submit to the operation without it. Dr. N. then procured a six-gallon bag of nitrous oxide gas; but the patient seemed equally fearful of anæsthesia as well as pain, and as soon as she had made the inhalation, rejected the bag and declared her willingness to have the operation performed without it. At sight of the forceps her courage again failed her, and she decided once more to try the gas. She took one inhalation, and again rejected it. By this time so much of the gas had escaped from the bag that the doctor replenished it. Of this she took two inhalations, and peremptorily refused to have anything more to do with it, declaring her determination to submit to the operation. The teeth were then extracted. "Immediately," says the doctor, "she fainted; her head dropping over sideways." The face rapidly became livid, and finally purple; respiration falling to about fifteen per minute. In about *thirteen* minutes, notwithstanding the prompt application of the galvanic battery and efforts to assist respiration, death ensued.

Dr. Otis, summoned by Dr. N., arriving in about ten minutes after the fainting, testified that he continued the usual restorative treatment for *forty-five* minutes, when death ensued. At *post-mortem*, found no disease of the heart; brain perfectly exsanguined in every part; no fluid in any of the ventricles; one lung was more engorged than the other, but healthy. As the testimony was very discordant in several particulars, we shall give only the conclusions of Dr. W., who carefully sifted the whole testimony:—

"In view of these discordant theories, it may seem presumptuous to express an opinion; but the conviction of the writer, based on personal experience, repeated hundreds of times, as well as on observation and reflection, is that nitrous oxide, when inhaled, acts primarily by a specific stimulant effect on the centres of innervation (over-stimulation, and consequent depression, if continued), and secondarily by *preventing* the oxygenation of the blood.

The various opinions held by different observers doubtless owe much of their diversity to the considerations of the phenomena presenting at different stages of the toxical influence of the agent.

That the inhalation of nitrous oxide continued, produces by some method of action, no matter what its primary effect, progressive depression of vital functions, which tends to death, and in which the anæsthesia, or temporary unconsciousness sought, is a more or less clearly-defined step in the downward path, there is no doubt.

Without discussing the processes of its manufacture, or the means by which its purity may be determined, or the best methods for its administration, suffice it to say, that immunity from danger can at the best be assured only by an intelligent and watchful guard, that its exhibition be suspended while yet the centres governing respiration and circulation are not too profoundly impressed.

Of the case under discussion, the inference seems entirely justified, that death was not caused by nitrous oxide gas, for the simple reason (if the evidence can be relied upon) that not enough was inhaled to produce such a result on any theory of its action. Nor was there any fact established by the *post-mortem* to justify such a conclusion; while the testimony renders it entirely probable that the cause of death was nervous shock, from dread of pain, and apprehension of fatal effects from the inhalation of an anæsthetic agent.

It may be remarked, however, that an examination by the coroner as to the possible lodgment of an extracted tooth in the air-passages would have eliminated that from the list of uncertainties.

Death from Nitrous Oxide.—The following case is reported in the *Medical Times and Gazette* of April 7th. As it is of considerable importance, on account of the extended use of the anæsthetic, we quote it in full:—

"An inquest was held last week, at Manchester, on the body of Mr. George Morley Harrison, aged fifty-three, a surgeon in good practice, and formerly lecturer on Medical Jurisprudence at the Manchester Royal School of Medicine, who died whilst under the influence of nitrous oxide gas, administered at his own request previous to having a tooth extracted by a neighboring dentist. Mr. Harrison, it appears, being unnerved and excited, partly from the suffering he had undergone, and partly owing to the want of proper food, which the condition of his mouth had prevented him from taking, insisted on the inhalation being pushed until he should snore, and—for, at any rate, part of the time—held the mouth-piece in his own hand, and inspired very vigorously. The first attempt at extraction was made before he was fully insensible, and was abandoned until more of the gas had been given. Eventually, however, two teeth were removed. The patient did not appear to be coming round properly after the operation, and the dentist, taking alarm, sent for medical assistance. On the arrival of a surgeon, Mr. Harrison was pronounced to be quite dead. At the *post-mortem* examination there was found some fat about the heart; the cavities on the right side were distended with blood, while those on the left side were empty. The lungs on both sides were gorged with dark blood. All the other organs were healthy.

The jury came to the conclusion that the deceased 'died from syncope, during the administration of nitrous oxide gas for the extraction of teeth, whilst laboring under fatty degeneration of the heart.'"

Post-mortem in the above case of Death from Nitrous Oxide.*—" The examination of the body took place seventeen hours after death. Rigor mortis was well marked, and there was considerable *post-mortem* lividity. There was a good deal of fat beneath the skin, in the omentum, upon the external surface of the heart, and in the usual localities. The heart and pulmonary artery were opened *in situ*. The right side of the heart was distended with fluid blood; the left side was empty. There were two or three slight patches of atheroma in the aorta, and upon one of the aortic valves. There was some little evidence of fatty changes in the slightly altered color and consistence of the walls of the heart. The coronary arteries were examined and found free from disease. The mucous membrane lining the trachea and bronchi was congested. Some mucus was found in these tubes, but no blood or other foreign body. There was distinct thickening of the aryteno-epiglottidean folds and of the vocal cords. The lungs on both sides were gorged with dark fluid blood; at the left apex there was an old fibrous cicatrix. The liver was enlarged, its tissue was very friable, and of a dirty yellowish-white color. The kidneys were full of blood; otherwise perfectly healthy. The bones of the skull were of unusual thickness. The visceral arachnoid was thickened and opaque. On removing the brain a large quantity of cerebro-spinal fluid made its escape, and the cornua of the ventricles were found dilated. The brain-substance was healthy, and its vessels full of blood."

In this sad case a most valuable life was sacrificed almost at the patient's own request. No man has any right to do as a patient desires, or allow him to be the judge of the quantity of an anæsthetic he should inhale, as a patient under such circumstances is not a competent judge.

The following are some observations of that veteran chloroformist, Mr. J. F. Clover, on this interesting case, addressed to the editor of the *British Med. Journal:*—

"SIR: In the *Times* of Good Friday last, there appeared a notice taken from the *Manchester Examiner*,

---

* Medical Times and Gazette, April 28, 1877.

of a death under nitrous oxide gas. The following was the verdict of the coroner's jury : ' Died from syncope, during the administration of nitrous oxide gas for the extraction of teeth, while laboring under fatty degeneration of the heart.'

The details of so unusual an event would be highly interesting to the medical profession, to enable them to judge of the safety or danger of the anæsthetic used. To form a correct opinion, we should at least know how long the inhaler was applied, the order and manner in which the movements of the heart and respiration became affected, and what had been swallowed previously.

The verdict was probably inaccurate in stating that the syncope occurred *during the administration* of the gas, as no symptoms of danger were noticed until after the extraction of the second tooth.

The most probable explanation of this sad case is that the extractions were difficult, and that the patient, on recovering from the effect of the gas, was susceptible to the shock of a severe operation ; and that this shock, and not the gas, was the cause of the syncope, which structural disease of the heart rendered fatal. Unfortunately, it appears that no third person was present, and we cannot expect the necessary evidence from the operator, whose attention was otherwise directed.

Those whose opinions of the effects of nitrous oxide are formed by inferences from Reid's *Experiments on Asphyxia*, and some cases of cardiac distress, first complained of after inhaling gas, will blame the latter. Those who daily witness the continuance of the circulation, in spite of the blood being black from the gas, and the speedy and cheerful recovery from it, will conclude that so unusual a result must have depended upon the peculiarity of the patient, whose heart was found in a state sufficiently diseased to account for sudden death."

As this work was passing through the press, my attention was called to the fatal results following the inhalation of nitrous oxide in the case of Mr. Samuel P. Sears, the operator being Mr. José R. Brunet, D.D.S.[1]

---

[1] Dental Times, vol. i. page 157, New York, 1864. See also Instructions in Nitrous Oxide, by Geo. T. Barker, D.D.S. Philadelphia, 1870, p. 56.

CHAPTER VIII.

J. F. Clover's improved apparatus for the combined use of nitrous oxide gas and ether. On the prevention of accidents from their use, and how to treat them successfully. Dr. F. N. Otis, of New York; his apparatus, and his opinions. Death under the administration of nitrous oxide and ether. Sir Henry Thompson, of London; successful use of these agents combined. Inhaler of Codman and Shurtleff, of Boston, for the use of nitrous oxide or ether combined or for each. Dr. J. D. Thomas's experiments with this inhaler. Letter of defence of Codman and Shurtleff. Bonwill's method of anæsthesia produced by rapid breathing of atmospheric air.

The Administration of Nitrous Oxide Gas and Ether.

WITH the addition of sulphuric ether to nitrous oxide gas, operations of any duration can now be performed. The writer has received from Mr. J. F. Clover, F.R.C.S., the following interesting account of his improved apparatus for administering nitrous oxide gas alone or combined with ether. This apparatus was on exhibition at our Centennial Exposition, being deposited and made by Mayer and Meltzer, of London, and was employed but badly managed in the Clinic of the University of Pennsylvania in a surgical operation:—

"The apparatus consists of a thin bag, oval in shape, and fifteen inches long; at one end connected with the ether vessel, at the other with the face-piece. Inside the bag there is a flexible tube also connected with the face-piece and ether vessel.

By turning the regulator (Re) the patient is made to breathe ether directly into the bag, or indirectly through the tube or ether vessel.

When the letter G is visible, the way to the gas bag is open; when the letter E is visible, the only way to the bag is through the tube and ether vessel; so that the more the regulator is turned toward E, the more ether is given, and *vice versâ*.

The other vessel contains a reservoir of water to prevent the temperature of the ether becoming too low; this is to be kept full.

The ether vessel is to be rather more than half filled, the precise point being marked against the glass gauge. A thermometer inside this gauge tells the temperature of the ether. Before using it, the vessel should be dipped into a basin of warm water, and rotated until the thermometer stands at about 68°.

If the room be cold, and if the patient have thin cheeks and large whiskers, the temperature may be 73°.

It is important that the face-piece should fit closely against the face. Those made by Mayer, of solid leather framework supporting a collar of inflated India-rubber, are the best, but sometimes they require to be warmed before using. For giving nitrous oxide only, the regulator is turned to G. The stopcock of the ether vessel is closed.

This vessel is hooked upon the strap round the neck. The strap is adjusted so that the ether vessel stands at a higher level than the face-piece.

The gas being turned on by rotating the foot-key with the foot, the gas bag is kept filled as fast as it is emptied by the patient. When the latter breathes out, the supply of the gas is stopped; and after the bag is fully distended, the escape-valve opens, and allows the expired gas to escape.

If the shape of the patient's face prevent the face-piece from fitting closely, the escape-valve should be closed by pressing it with the finger. Enough gas will escape beneath the face-piece during the expiration; but the bag, being slightly distended, will yield the gas so abundantly that no air will be drawn in at the same place during the inspiration.

If ether is to be used without gas, the gas-tube should be taken off the ether vessel; the regulator should be turned to G, and the face-piece should be first applied to the face during an expiration, and be held rather closer during expiration than during inspiration.

It is important not to oblige the patient to inhale after

the bag is empty, because the barometric pressure of air on the ether being diminished, the vapor would increase in strength, and make the patient cough, or perhaps vomit.

The regulator is gradually turned towards E, and thus the way is opened to the inner tube. The air breathed through it carries vapor from the vessel into the distal end of the bag.

As soon as one-half of the air passes through the ether vessel, the vapor becomes strong enough to cause insensibility in about two minutes, usually without any coughing. As the movement of swallowing is excited by a too strong, although less pungent, atmosphere than is generally needed to excite coughing, it should be watched for, and the regulator slightly turned back if it occur.

By far the easiest and least unpleasant way of getting a patient ready for a surgical operation is to use gas and ether combined, the gas being given pure during four or five respirations, and the ether gradually added as above described.

The supply of gas should cease when the ether is turned on; but if during the operation we have admitted so much fresh air that the patient seems conscious of the taste of ether, we may, instead of increasing the ether, give a liberal supply of gas until the patient is tranquil.

I find less sickness and less complaint of the taste of ether afterwards than when ether is used alone.

In operations on the eye, the muscular twitching and panting character of the breathing during the first few minutes of insensibility are objectionable; but if the operation be not commenced for five minutes, and the ether given as strong as it can be taken without exciting a cough, the patient begins to breathe stertorously, and now the face-piece may be removed every third or fourth inspiration, and as the stertor goes off, the eye will become quite steady.

I am, however, so well satisfied with a modification of my chloroform apparatus, by which I can give as much of ether or chloroform as I like, that when I have a choice, I prefer using these for cataract operations, and for the ligature of deep-seated arteries, etc.

With respect to vomiting, I think it most important that the patient should have an empty stomach, and prefer that neither food nor drink of any kind should be taken for from four to six hours beforehand.

There is less sickness after operations if done before breakfast.

In using this apparatus, as in using others, the breathing and the pulse should be kept under observation.

Whenever we see a patient swallow, it is probable he is taking the vapor stronger than is necessary, and the regulator should be turned back slightly.

If the patient cough violently, remove the face piece, and be sure that the apparatus has not been overheated, or filled with ether above the proper level.

As soon as any muscular twitchings, like those of paralysis agitans, are seen, give about a fourth of an inspiration of fresh air, and do not keep the face-piece quite close to the face till the twitchings have nearly ceased.

I have never seen any harm result from the condition which causes these movements. If air were not given, they would increase, and then stop; the respiration would become intermittent, and, some time after this, the heart would cease to beat.

The fact that death may be produced if signs of danger are disregarded, applies to all anæsthetics.

Whenever the breathing becomes jerking, sobbing, or intermittent, the face-piece should be removed, but applied directly the breathing loses that character, unless the pulse is much depressed.

It is much less important to watch the pulse whilst giving gas and ether than in giving chloroform; but it is desirable, for when it decidedly loses power, we may safely admit a little fresh air, and thus anticipate the need of removing the face-piece to a greater extent on account of muscular twitching or stertor.

If the finger be taken from the pulse to do something else, I would give a little air, unless the patient had only just begun to inhale, or was evidently but slightly under the anæsthetic.

Practical suggestions :—

As the apparatus would be injured by an excited patient taking hold of it, it is as well to have an assistant near in case of need.

It is a good plan to replace a handkerchief over a patient's eyes, and keep it there until he is asleep, and apply it again when he is about to awake.

In operations on the rectum, it is desirable that the bandage required for keeping him on his side should be applied before giving the gas.

Sudden distension and bursting of the gas-bag or gas-tube can scarcely happen when the gas-rarefier is used ; but if this be not used, or if the gas-bottle have become frozen, it is desirable to warm the bottle, and in doing so, the top end should be more warmed than the other.

Whenever there is much difficulty in getting the face-piece adjusted, it may be necessary to arrange a handkerchief or towel so that the air drawn in under the face-piece may be nearly the same as that which was breathed out.

In conclusion, the advantages of the apparatus are these :—

1. It lessens the waste of ether, and consequently the odor of ether about the house.

2. The patient usually goes to sleep without any struggling, and is ready to be operated on in from one to two minutes.

3. The percentage of ether need not be so high as to produce coughing or swallowing, and it can be made stronger or weaker, as we wish, by merely turning a regulator.

Lastly, patients recover rapidly, with less delirious excitement, and less sickness, than if ether be given in the usual way."

In April, 1877, Dr. F. N. Otis, of New York, exhibited Clover's apparatus for administering ether and nitrous oxide, and remarked that it had given him the best satisfaction of any apparatus he had ever employed, for anæsthesia was readily produced without a struggle upon the part of the patient. It could be used for the administration of laughing-gas without producing any of that dreadfully suffocative appearance so commonly attending its use by the methods usually employed. He thought well of prefacing the ether by the use of a moderate amount of nitrous oxide.

Death under the Administration of Nitrous Oxide and Ether.—" A death has recently taken place in London at University College Hospital during anæsthesia from nitrous oxide gas and ether, being, we believe, the first fatal case which has occurred in this country that can be attributed to this combination of anæsthetics. The patient was a woman fifty-five years of age, who was admitted to the hospital in consequence of strangulated femoral hernia. When admitted she was in a very weak and exhausted condition from constant vomiting, the hernia having been strangulated for over forty-eight hours. She was taken into the operating-theatre, and gas and ether administered by means of Clover's apparatus. In about four minutes she was well under the influence of the anæsthetic, without having exhibited any previous excitement. Taxis was then applied, when almost immediately the patient became pale and recommenced vomiting stercoraceous matter. At the same time the respirations became weak, and the pulse at the wrist imperceptible. The doors and windows of the theatre were at once thrown open, and artificial respiration was carried on for a few minutes. As no obvious benefit resulted, an enema, containing three ounces of brandy, was administered. Fumes of strong ammonia were applied to the nostrils, and ammonia injected into the right median basilic vein, but all without any good result, and the patient died within about ten minutes from the onset of the alarming symptoms. At the autopsy, stercoraceous matter was found in the trachea and right bronchus. The right side of the heart and the large veins were full of dark fluid blood. The ventricular walls were thin and flabby, and the cavities slightly dilated. The left ventricle was empty. The arch of the aorta presented numerous patches of atheroma."[*]

Sir Henry Thompson recommends Mr. Clover's plan of administering nitrous oxide gas for thirty seconds and then ether.[†] This is nothing but an attempt not to

---

[*] Med. Times and Gaz., March 17, 1877.
[†] London Lancet, Jan. 8, 1876.

give to ether all the credit of being a perfect anæsthetic when employed for long and painful operations like lithotripsy.

Inhaler for Nitrous Oxide Gas or Ether of Codman & Shurtleff, of Boston.

I have received a beautiful inhaler from the above firm, through the politeness of S. S. White & Co., of Philadelphia.

The points for which they claim superiority are:—

" 1st. Durability; being made of metal, they are not liable to be easily broken, as so frequently happens to the hard-rubber inhalers, and, as they are nickel-plated, they retain their brilliant polish without change.

2d. For convenience both to the patient and operator. With one hand the latter can apply the inhaler, and open or close the two-way stopcock, leaving the other hand at liberty to control the patient, or for such exigencies as may occur. As the elastic hood covers both nose and mouth, the patient is saved the necessity of having the nostrils closed either by clamps or the fingers; a part of the operation always very disagreeable, and, to very sensitive patients, positively frightful, as it produces a feeling of suffocation.

3d. Cleanliness. The rubber hood, which alone comes in contact with the face, is easily removed and replaced, and, as all the other parts are either metal or hard rubber, the whole instrument can be kept perfectly pure by washing, which is a point of great importance to the comfort of the patient.

4th. Durability and accurate working of the valves."

Upon this, perhaps, more than anything else, depends the successful administration of anæsthetics. If the exhaling valve does not quickly and perfectly close while the gas is being inhaled, air is taken with it, and the gas is so much diluted that it very much delays or wholly prevents the desired effect.

If, on the other hand, the inhaling valve does not work properly, the patient breathes back into the reservoir a mixture of nitrous oxide and air.

Fig. 23 is the inhaler with a hard rubber mouth-piece, A. The metal hood, B, is used for nitrous oxide gas.

Fig. 23.

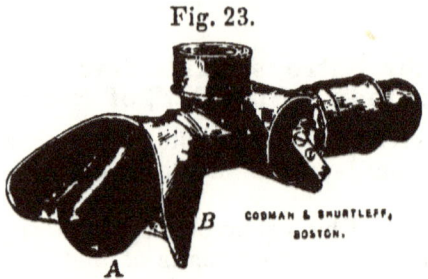

Fig. 24 is the inhaler for nitrous oxide gas: A, metallic hood, containing, B, flexible rubber hood, covering both

Fig. 24.

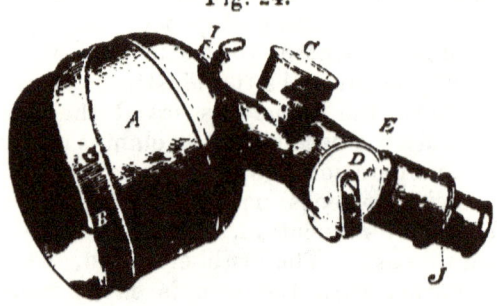

nose and mouth; c, exhaling valve; D, two-way stopcock; I, packing, through which a silk cord passes; E, sliding joint, where J is detached to connect the ether reservoir; J contains the inhaling valve.

Fig. 25. The inhaler arranged for using ether. This differs from Fig. 24 only in the addition of the hollow sphere, F, which contains a coarse sponge, on which the ether is poured through the opening, G; H, cover, closing the reservoir when not in use. This part is attached at the sliding joint, E, and will fit most inhalers made by Codman & Shurtleff during the last three years. By this arrangement waste of ether, by evaporating, is prevented, and it is stated that less than half the quantity is required to produce or keep up anæsthesia.

The operator also escapes breathing so much of the ether as he is compelled to do when using it from a sponge or napkin.

Fig. 25.

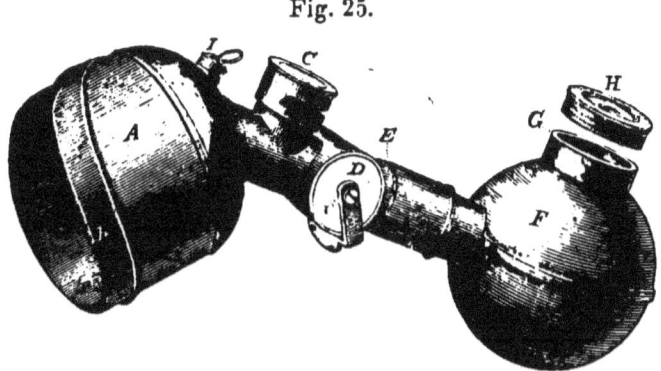

Experiments made with the Inhaler of Codman & Shurtleff, Boston.

First experiment with new inhaler, November 1st, 1876, with three patients, two males and one female.

In each was tested the ether attachment: two were unable to make the valve act quickly; in the third the operation of inhalation was a success, the exhaling valve acting with each respiration by a click.

Nov. 2d. Second experiment, two females and one male. With the females the soft rubber covering for the mouth, nose, and face fitted admirably; with the male the rubber cover could not be made to fit air-tight, owing to his having a beard, but it worked more satisfactorily. If the distance from the ether supply and the mouth-piece is shortened, the ether passes much more rapidly in the case of a patient who is feeble.

The exhaling valve should be screwed tightly, else it is apt in handling to become loose and will drop out.

Third experiment. Dr. Thomas has demonstrated that the gag was not suitable, for it should not project out of the mouth to prevent its perfect closure. Second, it did not fit into the teeth as that of his brother's form (a plug of wood or cork with two concave surfaces and a string attached in the centre).

I have received the following reply from the makers to a report of my experiments.

"Sir: We have received yours of the 3d. In regard to the fit of the rubber to the patient's face, we have had no complaints, except where the beard in male patients has prevented close contact, and in cases of children where the face is too small to fit the rubber. In the former class of cases the beard may be wet with water, or that failing, the mouth-piece used instead of the flexible face-hood, which is the plan to be pursued with children.

We have adopted this style of face-hood in preference to the English pattern, that having an air-tube attached to the metal hood, as being as well or better adapted to a great number of faces and not liable to get out of order, as that is almost sure to do after but few months' use, and as being removable for cleansing or removal without any expense or delay.

The Centennial Judges, who took ample opportunity to examine this inhaler, refer to it in the report accompanying the award to us of the highest prize, in the following terms, viz.: 'The novelty of design of the inhaler, perfection of its execution, and general suitability to the rapid and safe administration of anæsthetics.'"

Dr. J. D. Thomas, who has had extended experience from 75,000 cases, and who with a few exceptions extracts most of the teeth required by the other dentists of this city, has favored me with the following observations on the use of the inhaler of Messrs. Codman and Shurtleff, which I loaned him not only to lecture upon before the Philadelphia Dental College Class, but to experiment with upon four patients.

"The inhaler possesses qualities which I have seen in no others for sale. It is convenient, and being nickel-plated does not corrode.

The stop-cock is so constructed that a patient may breathe, and have the gas turned on to him unawares.

The small size of the mouth-piece is an objection (but one that can easily be remedied when ordering the instrument), as patients in most cases exhibit a strong desire to pull the lips away and get a little atmospheric air, in the hope to resist and delay the effects of the gas as long as possible. The covering to the lips is an objection, but this is removable at the pleasure of the operator. The aperture between the inhaling valve is too small to admit of a full free passage of the gas where the patient possesses large capacity. The opening of the tube is of good size, but the valve should be smaller. (This last objection I have no doubt will be obviated by the makers.)"

Bonwill's Method of Anæsthesia.

This little work would not be considered complete without some brief reference be made to the method for diminishing sensibility by rapid respiration proposed by W. G. A. Bonwill, D. D. S., of Philadelphia. It is described by Dr. A. Hewson in the Philadelphia *Med. Times*, March 4, 1876.

"You have, all of you, I have no doubt, experienced the effects of rapid and deep respirations, after violent running, or blowing hard to ignite a fire, especially the confusion of sight and bewilderment of mind. These Dr. Bonwill recognized many years ago, associated with numbness of sensient nerves, as dependent on the rapidity of the respirations. Pursuing the subject he has brought it to practical use in his profession—that of dentistry—in which he uses it constantly to diminish the sensitiveness of dentine, and even to produce such insensibility as to allow of the extraction of a molar tooth without pain. Of the latter I have had a demonstration in my own family, which has led me to the study of the subject myself, and with the most gratifying results. I have used it in stitching wounds, in handling over-sensitive parts, and in probings and the like." He then relates the case of a medical gentleman who tried the experiment with success who had no recollection afterwards of a " pin sticking him, much less of its having been firmly imbedded in his flesh, as he found it when he had ceased the rapid respirations, and the anæsthetic effect had passed off."

His second trial was upon a boy in the receiving ward of the Pennsylvania Hospital. The boy had fallen upon the ice an hour previously, and had sustained a severe injury of his left wrist. The doctor directed him at once to try the rapid respirations. This, in two minutes and a half by the watch, caused some dizziness in the boy's head, when the doctor picked up the limb and moved it about with the utmost freedom, diagnosing a bad sprain of the wrist, and the absence of fracture. When the boy was recovering he took to crying, on account, he said, of the dizziness and confusion he had experienced. Nothing, remarked the doctor, could have been more satisfactory than this case in its results.

Analgesic Effects of Rapid Breathing.

Dr. Addinell Hewson, of this city, communicates an interesting paper on the History of Nitrous Oxide Gas as an Anæsthetic, and on the Analgesic Effects of Rapid Breathing (Transactions of International Medical Congress, 1876). Our own experiments were negative, and in conversation with several of the most intelligent dentists and physicians of this city, they all pronounced that their experiments of rapid breathing produced a certain amount of anæsthesia, but thought most of the results obtained by the distinguished surgeon were owing to the impression that relief of pain was to be obtained by this certain method.

CHAPTER IX.

Ether, its local application in the form of spray. Rhigolene. Dr. Latamendi's new method of utilizing the anæsthetic effects of ether spray. Anæsthetic mixture of ether and camphor. Excision of cancer of the breast by scissor-cutting under ether spray. Extract of eucalyptus as a local anæsthesia in dental operations. Snow, ice, and salt. Carbolic acid. Sulphate of morphia applied to sound skin also when the epidermis has been removed.

Local Anæsthesia and Anæsthetics.

The method of local anæsthesia proposed by Dr. Benjamin W. Richardson is the one most generally adopted.

The process consists in directing ether on a given surface of the body, the strongest, freed from alcohol and water, in minute division or spray, mixed more or less with atmospheric air. This is accomplished by means of a hand-spray, an article which has become very popular in diffusing the various perfumed waters in a room. The apparatus consists of a bottle to contain the ether; through a perforated cork a double tube is passed, one extremity of the inner part of which goes to the bottom of the bottle; above the cork a tube connected with the bellows (a rubber bag) pierces the outer part of the double tube, and communicates by a small aperture at the inner end of the cork with the interior of the bottle. The inner tube for delivering the ether runs upwards to the extremity of the outer tube.

When the two rubber bags or bellows are compressed by the hand, a double current of air is produced; one current descending and pressing upon the ether, forcing it along the inner tube, and the other ascending through the outer tube and playing upon the column of ether as it passes from the inner tube. Rhigolene, a product obtained by the distillation of petroleum, is also for local anæsthesia. It is the lightest of all known liquids, its specific gravity being 0.625; it boils at 70°. This local anæsthesia, which is produced by the evaporation of these volatile liquids, which produce intense cold, can be used with advantage in minor surgery. It should never, by these agents, affect a large surface. Nor should it be long applied, else it will freeze and destroy the tissue, so that the death of the part may take place.

Dr. Letamendi[*] has discovered a new mode of utilizing the anæsthetic effects of ether spray. After applying Richardson's spray-producer for about two minutes, in which he employs perfectly neutral sulphuric ether, the skin has by this time become red, and is the seat of a disagreeable sensation of cold, but no sensation of burning in the part. If at this moment an incision, eight to ten millimetres long, is made with a convex bistoury in the centre of the reddened part, not being carried deeper than the papillary layer of the cutis, immediately the

---

[*] Archives de Physiologie, November, 1875.

incision is made there is suddenly produced an anæmic zone, which enlarges outwards from the point incised.

If the spray is again directed for a few seconds on the part which has thus become anæmic, the region becomes perfectly bloodless and completely anæsthetic. The tissues, when cut, are like frozen fat, and have lost their elasticity. Around the white circle there is a zone, in which the anæmia is not absolute. The spray directed on this zone speedily makes the anæmia and consequent anæsthesia complete. The anæsthesia can thus be carried around or along a limb.

The theory brought forward by Dr. Letamendi to account for the effect of the slight incision is, that the cold produced by the ether causes relaxation, and consequently dilatation of the vessels. The incision produces a sudden reaction, which converts the extreme dilatation into extreme contraction. The practical advantage is, that anæsthesia is obtained without a prolonged application of the ether spray.

Anæsthetic Mixture.
℞. Sulphuric ether, f℥j.
   Pulv. camphoræ, ʒiv.—M.
   Dissolve.

On applying the mixture for a minute or two to the part where a superficial operation is to be practised, local anæsthesia is temporarily produced.

Excision of Cancer of the Breast by Scissor-cutting under Ether Spray.

Dr. Benjamin W. Richardson writes on the subject in *The Lancet* as follows:—

"At this moment, when the dangers of general anæsthesia are so anxiously felt by the profession, the following clinical facts may prove of value. A lady, fifty years of age, consulted me in April last respecting a tumor in the left breast. The tumor had been present, and had at times been painful for a considerable period, but, as it remained of small size, she did not consider it of importance until this year, when it began steadily to increase in size. The nature of the tumor was sufficiently clear. It was a hard scirrhus, of the size of a small hen's egg, loosely held in the gland, with no adhesions to the muscular structure beneath. The family history of the patient confirmed the diagnosis; her mother had suffered from scirrhus of the breast. The diagnosis left no doubt respecting the proper mode of treatment. There could be no hesitation in advising that the abnormal growth, while it was yet easily movable and removable, should be excised, and to this advice the patient gave a willing assent. But now the question of the administration of an anæsthetic came under consideration. The action of the heart of this lady was so intermittent and irregular, and the power of her heart was so reduced, that the slightest external impression influenced it in its motion. She belonged, in a word, to that population which is prone to die suddenly from chloroform and the other narcotic vapors. Under these circumstances I proposed to the patient that the tumor should be excised under local anæsthesia; and, that the failure of the process, if failure should follow the recommendation, might fall upon me entirely, I performed the operation myself.

I operated on the 8th of May last, in the following manner. The patient having been placed in a semi-recumbent position on a narrow couch, I directed Mr. W. Perkins, who very efficiently conducted the local anæsthesia, to direct gently over the tumor a large spray of common ether, so as to chill thoroughly, but not to freeze the skin. I let him maintain this for a period of five minutes. Then I handed to him another tube and bottle for spraying over the already chilled part the light fluid called anæsthetic ether, a compound of ether of sp. gr. .720 with hydride of amyl. A few moments' application of this lighter ether was sufficient to render the whole of the breast frozen like a hard snowball. For a minute longer, that the deeper structures might become equally chilled, the spray was continued. When the structures were thus prepared, instead of using a scalpel for cutting, as in the ordinary way, I made the required incisions through the skin with a pair of small, strong, sharp, slightly-curved scissors. Commencing the incision by an angular cut at the outer margin of the part to be excised, I carried the lower blade of the scissors deeply into the breast, with the edge of the blade everted. In this way I cut the lower flap; then, commencing at the same angle, I cut in the same manner the upper flap. The rapidity and ease with which these incisions through the hardened tissues were made struck me most favorably. The incisions were deep enough to enable me to grasp the tumor firmly with the left hand. I now laid down the ordinary sharp-cutting scissors, and with a pair of strong, slightly curved, tooth-edged scissors, I proceeded to cut on each side of the tumor until I could fairly lift it up; then, by a few strokes made with the same scissors underneath, I cleared it completely away. The operation lasted precisely three minutes, and was unattended, during the whole time, by the escape of blood. The diseased mass removed, I had the ether spray withdrawn, in order to see if any vessels would bleed during reaction from the freezing. There was a little oozing of blood, which quickly subsided, and one artery was tied, both ends of the ligature being cut off close to the vessel. The wound, carefully cleaned with a soft, damp sponge, was closed; the edges of it were secured with five sutures; a pledget of cotton-wool, charged with styptic colloid, was placed over the wound; and a lint-pad and firm bandage completed the dressing. The patient passed a good night after the operation. She was allowed to rise and go into the drawing-room on the following day; and as she exhibited no rise of temperature beyond 99° Fahr., and that only for a few hours, and suffered from not one untoward symptom, the dressing was left untouched until the 13th of May, when, on removing it, the wound was found healed throughout its entire extent. The sutures were removed a few days later, when the line of incision was found fairly closed, without a particle of discharge or interruption of healing at any point.

During the whole of the operation the patient did not utter a single expression of pain, and I may here add her description of what she felt of the operation. The description was taken down by Dr. Platt, who rendered me his most able assistance, from the patient, immediately after the operation, and it is repeated in her own words: 'During the application of the ether spray the local feeling was that of gradually becoming cold, as in frosty weather, just as when the hands go numbed, but there was no actual pain. Felt pressure when the scissors went into the tumor, and experienced a kind of jar, but did not feel anything like an incision, and, in fact, was not aware when the incisions were made. Felt nothing of the next part of the operation, but when the tumor was held up and divided by three long cuts, experienced a feeling, not of pain, but as if the parts were put on the stretch or dragged; did not feel the tying of the ligature, but when some small substance (a bit of loose fatty tissue) was cut off, felt again as if the parts were being stretched. When the sutures were introduced, felt the pressure whilst the flaps were being held together, but was unconscious of the prick of the needle.'

In all respects this operation was, as an operation, completely successful, and one other success followed it I did not expect. As the recovery from the excision progressed, the irregular action of the heart became less marked, and ultimately disappeared altogether. In the month of July this lady called upon me, and was found to be restored to perfect health.

Soon after the recovery of the patient named above, another lady came under my care, who was suffering from a scirrhous tumor, situated a little above the right breast, towards the axilla. This tumor, as a small mass about the size of a hazel-nut, had been present for several years without undergoing change; but recently, upon the occurrence of a slight blow from a fall, it had commenced to rapidly increase in size. It was now a firm and well-defined scirrhus, of the size of a pullet's egg; it moved with moderate freedom beneath the skin, but not without conveying a suspicion, which afterwards proved to be correct, that it was attached to the pectoral muscle. Over the centre of the tumor there was retraction of the skin, and the nipple was slightly retracted towards it. The glands in the axilla were free.

The diagnosis in this instance was sufficiently clear, and the practice of immediate removal of the tumor seemed to me positive. But again the question of the administration of chloroform or of some other anæsthetic vapor pressed for careful consideration. The patient had been declared by one of her medical friends to be suffering from disease of the heart, and had been urged by him in the most forcible terms not to subject herself to general anæsthesia. Another medical friend, in less determinate but still serious expression of opinion, gave her similar advice. She herself had read of the danger she heard described, and her anxious dread alone was all but sufficient to preclude the administration of any narcotic vapor. On examination of the heart, I found an exceeding feebleness of action, an irregular and often intermittent beat, and at the apex a soft systolic murmur. I suggested, under these circumstances, the removal of the scirrhous tumor under ether spray, and on June 23, again very ably assisted by Dr. Platt, I performed the operation. The steps of the operation were much the same as those described in the previous history. For a few minutes an ether of a specific gravity of 1035 was sprayed over the breast, then the light anæsthetic ether was used until all the part was completely solidified. This condition attained, I made the incisions with sharp-cutting scissors, separated the tumor by a few lateral divisions with the same scissors, and then raising it, cut it out from its deep connections by means of the curved tooth-edged cutting scissors. The growth in this instance was firmly attached to the pectoral muscle over a space the size of a florin, but I found no greater difficulty than a little delay in separating it, together with a layer of connective tissue, from its attachment.

So far the operation was actually bloodless. I waited a brief period before closing the wound for perfect reaction to occur, and for observing if there were any hemorrhage. With the reaction one small artery yielded blood, but the bleeding was instantly and effectually stopped by torsion. The edges of the wound were brought together with five silk sutures, and the styptic colloid dressing, with cotton-wool, a soft pad and bandage, was applied.

This patient, like the last, bore the operation perfectly. She felt no pain from the incisions, and although the deep dissection which was required to remove the tumor from its attachment was felt as a severe drag or pull, it gave rise to no evidence of acute pain. The act of sponging the wound, and the insertion of one of the sutures, caused momentary expression of pain, but, on the whole, she was throughout brave, perfectly collected, and as quiet as if she had been asleep. This patient, like the previous one, progressed so favorably that she was allowed to get up every day. On the fourth day after the operation, as she complained of the pressure of the pad, I removed the dressing, and found the wound freshly healed throughout its entire length, without a trace of suppuration. In this act, however, a little misfortune occurred. A portion of the cotton-wool adhered firmly, through the styptic colloid, to a loose end of the upper suture, and, while I was extricating the wool, an accidental movement of the patient caused the ligature to tear out of the upper lip of the newly-joined skin. From this slight point there flowed as much as a drachm and a half to two drachms of bright, red, very thin blood. I stopped this bleeding, not very readily, by firm pressure with styptic wool; but a little further bleeding took place during the day, beneath the compress, and into the subcutaneous tissue, and gave rise to a superficial sore about the size of a sixpence. On the eighth day after the operation the patient was able to go out of doors, and, but for the slow healing of the small sore whence the hemorrhage proceeded at the first dressing of the wound, recovery rapidly succeeded.

One other fact closely connecting this with the preceding case is worthy of particular notice. As this second patient began to rally from the operation, the distressing cardiac symptoms entirely passed away, the stroke of the heart improved in tone, the irritability ceased, and the faint murmur became imperceptible.

The facts recorded call for one or two brief comments.

The effect of the local anæsthesia.—It is certain that in both these cases the local method afforded everything that could be desired in the way of anæsthesia. It saved all acute pain; it saved the patient the dread of death during the insensibility from a general anæsthetic, and it enabled me to proceed in our task without a thought as to the immediate safety of the patient. I may say more for it still. It warranted me in recommending the operation. I should certainly not have advised any friend of mine, whose heart was in the same condition of irritability and irregular nervous supply, to inhale an anæsthetic vapor, to the fatal effects of which such conditions of the circulation are so favorable. Applying then this same rule to a patient who in putting his life into my hands makes his life for the time mine, I should consider it actually wrong to recommend a risk I would not myself accept. But, taking advantage of the local method, I had no occasion to suggest a danger of any kind, while I secured my patients the benefits of anæsthesia. I saved them the dread of death from the effects of a general anæsthetic; I saved them possibly the symptoms of after-vomiting and faintness; and I saved myself and my colleagues during the operation the anxiety that ever attends the administration of a general anæsthetic to persons in whom disease of the heart is foreknown.

The method of cutting with scissors.—Local anæsthesia has many disadvantages. It is more troublesome than general anæsthesia as a detail of practice, and, as it leaves the consciousness alive, it fails at times in preventing the fears of the patient. But hitherto the greatest difficulty in operating under it has been the obstacle of cutting through the hard, frozen, insensible part. The resistance to incision by the best cutting knife, and especially to dissection by the knife, is such that I have seen the most skilful surgeons troubled by it; and I have never been able to complain of the objection that has been made to the method on this ground. The difficulty is now overcome by the process of scissor-cutting which I have here introduced. The advantage of the scissors over the scalpel will be at once proved by any one who will take a thick, firm structure, the cover of a book, for example, and try to cut through it. With the best of scalpels he will be troubled; but with scissor blades he will cut with the utmost facility, if the blades be well set. So, in cutting through the frozen animal tissue, the parts can be divided as rapidly as may be wished with the scissor blades, with perfect accuracy of incision, and as deeply as may be desired. The cutting is also made without any downward pressure, by which pain of pressure is saved. Also in deep dissection, the tissues, frozen as they are exposed, can be divided more easily than by the knife; for the harder they are solidified, the easier they are divided by the scissor blades. In a word, I believe that every cutting operation, in which local anæsthesia is practicable, may be performed neatly and effectively by scissor-cutting, and that a much larger number of operations may now be painlessly carried out under the local method.

Some little attention requires to be paid to the instruments used. The scissors for superficial or skin cutting should be exquisitely sharp, neat, and strong; and I prefer them slightly curved. For deep cutting, where there are many bloodvessels, the tooth-edged cutters are valuable. These pierce, crush, and divide at the same time, and they save blood. For other purposes, as for division of a sinus, some modifications are required, and Messrs. Krohne and Sesemann are now making for me a case of instruments for the special purpose of operation in the method under consideration.

Effect of the operation, on the heart, in the cases related.—No fact is more instructive in the history of the patients recorded in this paper, than the beneficial effect produced on the functions of the heart by the operation. In both instances the cardiac irregularity and irritability were purely due to irregular nervous supply, to nervous irritation and consequent muscular exhaustion. The irritation might have been in part due to the mental anxiety which naturally accompanies the disease, or it might have been due to the irritation of the tumor, and have been reflex in character. Whichever view be correct, the result of the operation was curative, and, as the cases are typical of a class of phenomena of disease, the lesson they teach is extended far beyond them as individual illustrations. They show that so soon as the heart obtains rest from the persistent nervous thrill that invades it, its muscular tone returns, and its irregular motion and excitability cease. Thus by operating early for the removal of cancer, the surgeon acts as physician also, and prolongs the general life by removing the local disease. I am convinced I have seen patients suffering from cancer, die from the mental and local irritation of the disease long before any development of the malady has advanced to kill by destruction of the part or organ involved. I infer, therefore, that if, without any danger to life from general anæsthesia, we can remove external malignant growths painlessly and promptly, so soon indeed as they are detected, we shall bring art, effectively, to the defeat even of cancer."

Extract of Eucalyptus.

This agent is recommended as a local anæsthetic in dental operations and toothache. Apply one drop on cotton to the sensitive dentine just before excavating for filling.*

Local Anæsthetics—Ice and Common Salt.

Snow or pounded ice makes a most valuable local anæsthetic, and by employing it in an elastic bag, like that of Chapman, it will be found of great utility in all superficial incisions. If the snow or pounded ice is mixed with common salt in alternate layers, and placed in a gauze bag, a more profound impression may, in from fifteen to twenty minutes, be produced, and the tissues can be completely frozen if permitted to remain for one hour, and even a deep-seated tumor can be removed without any pain from the knife. It is well to examine the operation of the mixture, as the parts may become frost-bitten.

Alcohol.

In the use of snow or ice there is more or less pain in the part until it is frozen. By substituting cold alcohol the parts can be immersed in it for a long time, so as to deprive them of ordinary sensibility, and, although the faintest touch can be perceived, cutting or pricking them can be well borne.

* Boston Med. and Surg. Journal.

Carbolic Acid.

Carbolic acid if applied to the skin at first is painful, but after a time that passes away, and leaves the surface in such a state that even the white-hot iron can be applied with impunity.

In some instances, I have simply painted the parts with a strong solution, or, when I desired to make one long incision, a line was drawn with a brush, charged with the liquefied crystals of the acid.

Morphia.

When sulphate of morphia is applied to the skin, even in the solution, or three or four grains to the drachm, it has but little result in relieving pain; but if the cuticle is removed, it then may be dusted over the surface with much better effect.

Prof. König says that he has combined the hypodermic administration of morphia with chloroform in a large number of cases with favorable results. It is seldom necessary to give more than from one-sixth to one-third of a grain.

If a solution of sulphate of morphia, one grain to the drachm of water, be made, and one-fourth injected by a hypodermic syringe, under a part to be operated upon, it will produce local anæsthesia.

CHAPTER X.

An abstract of the employment of chloroform and ether, alone and in combination. Chloral hydras. Butylchloral in practical medicine.

Chloroform.

WHEN a four per cent. solution of chloroform in atmospheric air is administered by inhalation to a human subject, the first effect observed is acceleration of the heart's action, accompanied by contraction of the arterioles; the primary influence of chloroform being that of a diffusible stimulant upon the nervous centres. In the later stages of its operation, when the vapor accumulates in the blood, entering the circulation more rapidly than it can be eliminated by the kidneys, the lungs, and the skin, a decided narcotic effect is produced, the frequency of the respiratory act is reduced, the pulse loses in force and becomes feeble, signs of deficient aëration of the blood appear in the livid color of the face and cyanotic lips, and finally the subject is rendered completely comatose, unconscious of surrounding objects, and is entirely insensible to pain. This state of narcosis or anæsthesia is attributed to two causes acting concurrently; first, a specific action exerted by chloroform upon the brain and medulla, and the origin of the pneumogastric nerves in the floor of the fourth ventricle, rather than by a direct influence upon the red blood-corpuscle, causing its contraction and interfering with its function as an oxygen-carrier to the tissues. As a consequence of this we may have death from respiratory paralysis, or, secondly, we may have the function of respiration so impaired as to lead to an undue accumulation of carbonic acid and marked diminution of oxygen in the blood; and this same result may be brought about by its second action preventing the normal absorption of oxygen by the red blood-corpuscles. A French physiologist, P. Bert, having declared that, when the amount of oxygen in the blood decreases to the amount of two or three per cent., narcosis is produced, it is seen that a plausible explanation of the anæsthetic effect is given; but there are reasons for believing that, in addition to this indirect action, chloroform has some specific, soporific effect upon the nervous system, which is peculiar to itself, in this respect resembling opium and the other narcotics. Experiment, moreover, has shown that its administration produces anemia of the brain, differing in this respect from ether, where no such effect takes place.

In chloroform-anæsthesia we notice a paralysis to a greater or less degree (1) of the sensory nerves; (2) of motor nerves; (3) of the function of organic life.

Chloroform is classed as a catalytic by J. G. Westmoreland,* and he recommends it in albuminuria from the fact that chloroform forms a gelatinous combination with albumen.

---

* Acology and Therapeutics, p. 177.

External Use of Chloroform in Substance or Vapor.—Chloroform is used in medicine both for its stimulant and narcotic properties, to increase force, subdue spasm, and relieve suffering. Given in large doses it abolishes pain and contraction, paralyzes muscle and nerve, profoundly depresses force, and leads to death. The largest amount of chloroform inhaled by one person was $112\frac{1}{2}$ drachms in one day; another took one pound in five days. According to "Stillé's" Therapeutics (vol. ii. p. 194), recovery has occurred after the swallowing of two ounces of chloroform.

After the continuance of the habit of chloroform-taking, the following symptoms generally appear, in the following order: (1) sleeplessness of a most distressing character, and only to be overcome by abstinence from chloroform; (2) deafness; (3) apathy and disinclination to society and to conversation; (4) tremulousness of the hands.

Experience shows that frequent chloroform inhalation is like "dram-drinking." Its effects are similar to those of alcoholism, and it will produce symptoms resembling mania-â-potu. In the report of the committee of the Med. and Chir. Society,* it is stated that a man who had been accustomed to the use of enormous doses of chloroform to relieve asthma, frequently inhaling forty drachms a day, was reported to have had this appearance "on admission to the hospital; he seemed in a constant *state of dulness,* or like a person *intoxicated.*"

Chloroform, by its wonderful power over pain and muscular spasm, has been employed by Dr. Gobrecht and others in cases of poisoning by strychnia, with decided success. Even should, as was proved by the late Dr. Anstie and others, it have no antidotal action, it is of great service in relieving the fearful suffering, reducing the pulse to its natural standard, and causing respiration to become more easy. Another important matter is that under chloroform- or ether-anæsthesia, the tetanic convulsions from the strychnia are so controlled that nutritive enemata may be administered and retained.

Chloroform is valuable in the treatment of acute ma-

* London.

nia, chorea, and convulsions, especially in children, also in puerperal convulsions; it has proved to be an efficient remedy in our hands in procuring sleep. In cases of delirium tremens, in the reduction of hernia, and the diagnosis of abdominal tumors, chloroform will be found most valuable.

The late Dr. Snow relates an interesting case of a scientific man who became insane and refused to take food. It was found that if chloroform were given and food offered, during the waking stage, the patient would take it. Chloroform was, therefore, administered before every meal for a long period It has also been employed in the delirium of fever in cases where the patient has been worn out, in spasmodic diseases of the air passages, spasm of the glottis, laryngeal cough, spasmodic croup, and whooping-cough, when in very dilute vapor.

Dr. Sansom has found great value from the use of chloroform in several cases of phthisis. The same authority states that in some cases of chronic bronchitis, in acute bronchitis, and in pneumonia, when danger may occur from stasis of blood in the lungs themselves, it is not advisable to employ chloroform by inhalation. In paroxysmal and violent cough, combined with morphia, glycerine, and water, it is often very beneficial; and in the early part of the treatment of asthma, thirty to fifty drops inhaled from a handkerchief relieve the spasm, induce narcosis, and prevent the paroxysms.

Dr. Hyde Salter, the great authority in the treatment of spasmodic asthma, says, "The inhalation of chloroform is, beyond doubt, one of the most powerful methods of treatment of the asthmatic paroxysm that we possess." Properly diluted, the vapor is not pungent, and instead of increasing any tendency to spasm, at once relaxes it. Dr. Salter has never seen any bad effects from chloroform administered in the height of a paroxysm of asthma, and persons sound asleep may be chloroformed without their being awakened. Anæsthesia cannot, however, be produced in any one partially awake, or even lightly sleeping, without their knowledge.

One of the secondary effects of the prolonged use of chloroform in asthma is an increase of the asthmatic tendency. The use of chloroform must no more be allowed to become a habit than the use of opium. We have repeated this experiment in seven cases of asthma, and, although we felt some apprehension, still no disagreeable symptoms presented themselves, and the patient was relieved of the attack, but it returned, and, fearing its injurious influence, we substituted hydrate of chloral during the paroxysms, especially when unable to sleep. Patients vary in the benefit which they derive from chloroform. In some, small quantities not only relieve the urgent distress, but also prevent its recurrence. The congestive chills of the South, or the cold stage of intermittent fever, may be shortened, so as to gain time for the introduction of quinine into the system, by the inhalation of chloroform. Dose, 20 drops, sprinkled on a fine net, permeable to the air, and repeated several times until the effect required is produced.

In epilepsy, the inhalation of chloroform has been found valuable, especially in the treatment of injuries and fractures, the result of epileptic attacks. It will also be found useful internally in the same disease, in combination with the bromides of potassium, sodium, calcium, and iron, with or without strychnia.

The following are a few of the preparations of chloroform:—

1. Tinctura chloroformi comp., B. P. (chloroform, rectified spirits, comp. tinct. of cardamon; 1 in 10). Dose, ♏xx-lx; for internal use, to relieve pain and spasm.

2. Linimentum chloroformi (chloroform ℥ij, camphor liniment ℥ij, olive oil ℥iv).

3. Mistura chloroformi (chloroform ℥ss, camphor pulv. gr. ix, yolk of one egg, water ℥vi). Add chloroform and camphor, rubbing them up well, then add the egg by degrees to form a nice mixture. Dose, a tablespoonful every hour.

In neuralgia, a few inspirations of chloroform vapor from a towel or handkerchief (sometimes enveloped in a cone of paper, flannel, or metal, for convenience of administration and to regulate evaporation) will often relieve the severe pain, almost magically. If the suffering be not of a serious character, and the affection be moderate in its extent, the relief may be permanent. If the stimulant effect should be desired over a larger portion of the body, the following liniment can be employed with advantage:—

℞. Chloroformi, f ℥jss.
Pulveris camphoræ, ℨj.
Spiritus terebinthinæ, f ℨss.
Olei lavandulæ, ♏ xx.
Olei olivæ, f ℨij.—M.

The camphor to be broken in small pieces and dissolved in the chloroform and turpentine; the olive oil should then be warmed and added gradually. Ointment for topical use in neuralgia: in the proportion of from 5 to 15 of chloroform to 30 parts lard; or by means of a speculum, the vapor of chloroform may also be carried into the vagina or rectum, remaining for ten minutes. Or we may use a mixture of equal parts of the chloroform liniment, of the Pharmacopœia, and the officinal camphorated soap liniment, for the same purpose.

Powerful agents act on the skin more effectually when dissolved in chloroform, as they promote the cutaneous absorption, and the addition of an equal quantity of alcohol hastens the process, so that when we desire to limit the anodyne effect to a small spot, we may apply a solution of camphor in chloroform, of equal parts by weight, or as a still more powerful sedative—

℞. Morphiæ sulphatis, gr. viij.
Atropiæ sulphatis, gr. iv.
Alcoholis,
Chloroformi, āā ℨij.—M.
S. To be applied with a camel's hair brush.

These two agents might be added for facial and dental neuralgia: Ext. gelseminum* fl., gtt. iij every three or four hours; croton chloral hydrate in pills, 3 grs. every three or four hours.

This prescription, in facial or sub occipital neuralgia, should not be spread over a large surface at one time, as both the atropia and the morphia are more readily absorbed after this solution in chloroform. Strychnia, aconitia, or quinia may also be combined with chloroform in a similar manner. A very good plan is to

---

* The effects of this remedy should be carefully watched.

cover a cup with linen and drop a portion of the chloroform or the mixture on its surface, and hold it in contact with the painful part for a few seconds, which will often produce a good result in pleurodynia or neuralgia of the chest wall. In more severe, general neuralgia, I have on several occasions been obliged to keep the patient gently under the influence of chloroform for a considerable time until the person obtains sleep, or the pain has been entirely relieved. If the neuralgia, in the form of hemicrania or sciatica, should be of malarial origin, we may resort at first to the following mixture:—

℞. Veratriæ, gr. v.
Morphiæ sulphatis, gr. iij.
Linimenti chloroformi, f ℥ij.—M.
Fiat lotio.

The part to be rubbed with this lotion during the paroxysm of pain, while two-grain pills of quinia sulphas are given every hour until its physiological effects are produced. Cinchonidia may be substituted in three-grain doses if the patient cannot take the quinia.

This same treatment, in conjunction with quinine, will often relieve sciatica. In acute earache or toothache, two or three drops on a small piece of cotton-wool introduced into the ear or tooth will occasionally cause complete relief; if too large a quantity is used, it will cause redness, smarting, and even blister. Equal parts of chloroform and opium or creasote are also useful in toothache. When mixed with an equal quantity of camphor, it forms one of the most valuable agents to relieve the local pain of sprains, etc. In cancer, where the skin is broken, leaving a foul and irritable sore, the surface may be deodorized and the pain temporarily relieved by the use of the hand-spray playing the vapor on the raw surface. The pain of other forms of cancer, such as of the os uteri, rectum, and mammary gland, may be also relieved by application of the same agent. In the photophobia of scrofulous ophthalmia, a few drops of chloroform held in the palm of the hand, close to the irritable eye, will cause the child to bear the light with less pain. In the itching of the ear, nose, and rectum, in which we have urticaria, lichen, or prurigo, the annoyance may be allayed by the use of an ointment composed of half a drachm of chloroform to an ounce of lard (it must be kept in a ground-stoppered bottle).

Pruritus Vulvæ.—In this most persistent, troublesome, and annoying disease, we have found chloroform useful in combination with carbolic acid and soap liniment, as follows:—

   R. Acidi carbolici,   gtt. xii–xxiv.
    Chloroformi,   f ʒij.
    Ol. olivæ,
    Linimenti saponis, āā f ℥ij.—M.

Apply with a soft sponge to the affected parts.

Internal Use of Chloroform.

Chloroform has been found extremely valuable in all cases of *colic*, and will often assuage even pain of *colica pictonum;* this is due to its local anodyne and stimulant carminative action. In flatulent distension of the stomach equal parts of chloroform and camphor will be found beneficial. In diarrhœa, after the removal of the irritating agent, equal parts of chloroform and alcohol with a portion of the tincture of opium and capsicum may be administered with great benefit. In insomnia, where pain prevents the patient from sleeping, the following mixture will often prove useful:—

   R. Morphiæ muriatis,   gr. iss.
    Alcoholis
    Chloroformi,   āā f ℥ss.
    Tr. cardamomi compos. f ℥jss.—M.

A dessertspoonful at bedtime to be taken in milk.

In nervous headache the accompanying prescription will often produce a happy effect:—

   R. Acidi nitro-muriatici diluti, f ʒij.
    Strychniæ,   gr. ¼–½.
    Alcoholis,
    Chloroformi,   āā f ʒiij.
    Tinct. zingiberis,   f ʒiij.
    Aquæ,   q. s. ad f ℥iii.—M.

A teaspoonful in water three times daily.

In combination with quinia, chloroform may be given where there is marked tendency to frequent chills. The following formula would be very appropriate for such malarial manifestations in a child, say four years of age:—

℞. Quinæ sulph.   gr. xxiv.
Mist. acaciæ,   f ℨij.
Chloroformi,   ♏xx.
Syr. Tolu,   ℨiv.
Aquæ cinnamomi,   q. s. ad f ℨiij.

ʒj s. t. d. for a child four years of age.—DA COSTA.

In certain forms of chorea and epilepsy the combination of bromide of potassium and chloroform will be found valuable as follows:—

℞. Potassii bromidi,   gr. x.
Tinct. conii,   ♏xxx.
Chloroformi,   ♏xx.
Tinct. valerianæ ammoniatis,   ♏x.
Aquæ camphoræ,   f ℨj.

For one dose ter die for an adult.

In some cases advantage is obtained by adding strychnia to this mixture in the dose of $\frac{1}{30}$ to $\frac{1}{10}$, omitting the conium and the valerian.

Ether.

This is a colorless volatile liquid; as it is also very inflammable, it must be kept carefully from the approach of fire or a light. It sinks in water, and is best administered mixed with spermaceti and sugar, or in mucilage of gum arabic. Its taste is hot, pungent, and irritating; and when placed in the mouth, ears, nose, or rectum, pain is produced. It dissolves in alcohol, whisky, or brandy; and when required as a powerful stimulant, as in fainting, exhaustion, or collapse, this is an excellent method for administering it. In using it for some time it is best given enclosed in capsules.

Gout.—In sudden attacks of gout in the stomach or intestines a useful mixture is the following:—

℞. Spiritus vini gallaci,
Æther.   āā f ℨj.—M.

Dose, one teaspoonful in sugar and ice-water, repeated until relief is afforded.

This same preparation will be found valuable in spasm of the stomach, or intestines, or heart. Ether has been proved useful in tape-worm, alone or combined with the oleo-resin of the male fern. The patient must live upon milk and a little bread for one day, and the following morning, fasting, take the full dose:—

   ℞. Oleo resinæ felicis, ʒss.
   Æther.   f ʒj.
   Mucilag. acaciæ, ad f ℥ss.—M

This is to be repeated in three hours. In the evening food can be taken, to be followed with a full dose of castor oil with twenty drops of spirits of turpentine. Some French authorities prefer to give f ℥iss of ether alone, administered at once, and followed in two hours by the purgative.

Ether is also one of our most potent remedies in hysteria, especially when associated with valerian, assafœtida, musk, or camphor. In the first with the fluid extracts, as follows:—

   ℞. Æther.
    Valerian. ex. fluid. āā f ʒj.—M.

Sig. A teaspoonful every hour.

In the second it is mixed with the tinctures as follows:—

   ℞. Æther.
    Tinct. assafœtidæ, āā ʒj.
    Mucilag. acaciæ, ʒj.—M.

Sig A teaspoonful every hour until relieved.

With musk:—

   ℞. Moschus,   Эij.
   Æther.
   Mucilag. acaciæ, āā f ʒj.—M.

Sig. A teaspoonful every hour.

With camphor ether is not only useful in hysteria, but all forms of "nervousness," in dysmenorrhœa, diarrhœa, cholera, abnormal sexual excitement, epilepsy, hysterical, puerperal, and strychnic convulsions. Camphor with ether is best administered as follows:—

   ℞. Vitelli ovi, ℥ij.
   Pulv. camphoræ, ʒij.
   Æther.   ℥ij.—M.

Add the ether to the camphor, and then the emulsion. Administer in tablespoonful doses every two hours.

According to Zuelzer, ether can be used as a stimulant in small doses by hypodermic injections. He states that the symptoms of collapse are relieved by it, and abscesses are rare; the quantity recommended is one cubic centimetre, or about sixteen minims.

Asthma.—Inhalation of ether is very valuable to obtain relief in spasmodic asthma, and obtain sleep for the patient. It can be employed alone or associated with tinctura digitalis or conium. The ordinary dose of the ether is from ten to forty minims, and the tincture of digitalis from ten to thirty minims.

The Ether Spray in Post-partum Hemorrhage.—Mr. W. Handsel Griffiths, of Dublin, reports in the *Practitioner* the use of the ether-spray in two cases of post-partum hemorrhage, in which the usual means of arresting the flow had been resorted to without effect. He directed the spray over the abdominal walls, along the spine, and over the genitals. In both cases the uterus contracted immediately, and hemorrhage ceased.

Coryza and Obstinate Hoarseness.—Drs. Chapman and Physick recommended the vapor of equal parts of Hoffman's anodyne or compound spirits of sulphuric ether with equal parts of laudanum in cases of recent catarrh, in coryza, and obstinate hoarseness, by inhalation.*

Chorea.—A jet or hand spray of sulphuric ether, free from alcohol, applied to the spine will relieve the most violent spasmodic or convulsive attack of chorea, with the subsequent use of Fowler's solution, five to ten drops three times a day in water, and occasional application of the galvanic current to the spine.

Nervous Aphonia, or Temporary Loss of Voice.—The vapor of ether has been highly recommended as a most valuable remedy in hysterical or nervous loss of voice. It has been the means of discovering malingerers, who were supposed or stated to be deaf and dumb,† and who, as soon as they came under its anæsthetic influence, were able both to hear and speak.

* I have also employed ¼ gr. of sulphate of morphia in the place of the laudanum, making a more elegant preparation, and with good success.

† See Turnbull's Manual of Diseases of the Ear, pp. 312–315. Phila., J. B. Lippincott & Co.

Diphtheritic Angina, or Pseudo-Membranous Croup.—Cases of diphtheritic angina have been treated with success by inhalations of ether and steam.

Whooping-Cough.—Ether alone by inhalation is extremely useful in the relief of whooping-cough; and a combination of ether sixty parts, chloroform thirty parts, and turpentine one part, has been found a most successful remedy, by confining the patient to his room, and making him, at every access of coughing, place before his mouth a small piece of cloth, folded several times, and wet with a teaspoonful of the mixture.* This remedy I have used with most gratifying results, at the same time employing, between the paroxysms, extract belladonna and quinine sulph. externally, with the inhalation of diluted carbolic acid in the patient's room.

Chloral Hydras ($C_2Cl_3O_2H+HO$).

I have, under Chloral Hydrate, given my views, experiments, etc.; still there are one or two matters which I think it will be well to state here. This agent has been found useful in all general convulsions and spasmodic diseases, which depend on direct disturbance of the central nervous system, but is contra-indicated in hysterical convulsions, owing, as stated by "Binz,"† to the initial excitement which is so often present. It is best to avoid it also, or give it with great caution, in ulcerations of the *primæ viæ*, in gouty states, in typhoid fever (see our experiments), and in disturbances of the circulation. (Liebreich.) Chloral hydrate should be given with great caution to patients with cardiac disease. (Rosenstein.)

Binz states the maximum of a single dose should be one drachm; but it is safer to begin with ten grains, and repeated, which, under special circumstances, may be followed by 10 or 12 grains every hour. It is best given in an aqueous solution with gum and sugar; the ordinary syrup of chloral contains 10 grains to each drachm, the dose of which is ℨss–ℨij.

* American Practitioner, July, 1875.
† The Elements of Therapeutics, Translation, by Edward I. Sparks (1878), pp. 34-35. W. Wood & Co., New York.

Dr. Bigelow, of Boston, reports in the *Practitioner* a case of tatanus, caused by a rusty nail, which was relieved by the introduction of a drachm of chloral into the wound, by a hypodermic syringe.

Butylchloral ($C_4H_5Ch_3O$), until quite recently, has been erroneously termed crotonchloral ($C_4H_3Ch_3O$). (Binz.) This is a new narcotic. The method of preparing it is to act upon aldehyde with chlorine. It forms foliacious crystals, which are volatile when heated, and have a burning taste. It is soluble with difficulty in cold water, more readily in warm, and dissolves quite readily in alcohol. It ought not to contain any chlorine which can be precipitated by nitrate of silver. Its first effect is to produce *anæsthesia of the head*, the rest of the body retaining its sensibility. This stage is followed by loss of function in the spinal cord, as evidenced by the general cessation of reflex irritability. The respiration and pulse remain unaffected. Still larger doses paralyze the *medulla oblongata*. Butylchloral, therefore, possesses the property of deeply narcotizing the brain without materially affecting the functions of the rest of the organism. It is given in doses of three grains, repeated until fifteen grains have been taken. It is given in the form of pills, or else dissolved in syrup and water or glycerine.

CHAPTER XI.

Medico-legal relations of anæsthetics. Case in Philadelphia of a surgeon dentist. The important question whether chloroform can be administered for improper purposes. Cases in France, England, and the United States. Dr. N. L. Folsom, R. M. Denig. Ether as a poison. Experiments of A. Martin Ewald, Hitzig, C. Bernard and Binz. *Chloroform ; its action as a poison*, with the treatment. Ether intoxication.

THE responsibility attending the use of anæsthetics is of great importance to medical men, as frequently their personal and professional reputation is at stake; it is therefore always better in the administration of an anæsthetic to a female to have some reliable person present. This is especially necessary when ether or chloroform is employed.

During the early period of my medical career, soon after graduating, I had in my Quiz class a young ambitious dental surgeon, one of the most gentle and amiable of men, who was desirous of obtaining the medical degree, which he ultimately attained. Soon after this the man was married, and settled in this city, and acquired a large business. At that time it was common for the dentist to administer the anæsthetics in their office in the extracting of teeth, etc. He had a young female patient to whom he administered chloroform alone, and who afterwards stated that he had taken improper liberties with her person during this state. This case caused great excitement in our city, and the public sympathy was with the young female, and a suit was instituted in which damages were claimed. The case was argued by distinguished lawyers on both sides, and voluminous testimony taken. The judge charged the jury, and the sentence was ten years' imprisonment. Subsequently the sentiment of the community changed, and it believed that it was all the result of her vivid imagination, and that she was laboring under a delusion. The majority of physicians and dentists signed a petition, and the sentence was remitted, but his professional prospects were ruined.

It is stated by Taylor,* "That the vapors of ether and chloroform have been criminally used in attempt at rape. In a case which occurred in France, a dentist was convicted of this crime upon a woman to whom he had administered the vapor of ether." Now this may be just such a case as the one in our own city. Ether, from its disagreeable taste and irritating vapor, would be much more difficult to administer forcibly and against the will of a patient. The numerous stories of anæsthesia by simply placing a few drops on a handkerchief under the patient's nose or mouth, are in the majority of cases perfectly absurd, as the shortest time required to bring a patient fully under the influence of either of

---

* Taylor's Medical Jurisprudence, Eng. ed., London, 1865, p. 1006.

these drugs, even when forcibly held in contact, is from two to ten minutes, and if subsequent rough handling takes place the patient is at once roused up to make resistance by struggling. We were once called to a woman who had been in the habit of employing chloroform by inhalation from a small bottle, to cause sleep; she accidentally when in a drowsy state let the open bottle drop on the pillow, and its contents saturated the covering, and she with her face in it; but instead of making her sleep soundly, it produced most distressing nausea, and the family were awakened by her efforts at vomiting, and so her life was saved, she not being able to arouse sufficiently to get rid of the offending matter, and which would have lodged in her trachea, or the contents of the stomach might have been brought into the bronchial tubes by a deep inspiration, and thus have caused suffocation.

The former case in Philadelphia settled the important point in the minds of medical men of this city that this incomplete unconsciousness does not coexist with complete motor and sensory anæsthesia, and therefore anæsthetics are employed without any fear in all important operations. These observations are in part corroborated by two learned authors in a recent and most admirable work* on medical jurisprudence, in which they state:—

"A question of some importance to the medical jurist naturally occurs here, namely, '*Whether chloroform can be administered for improper purposes?*' We know, however, that comparatively, the insensibility from chloroform (and more slowly from ether) vapor is only slowly induced. It would be difficult, therefore, to administer chloroform forcibly and against the will, while, of course, the stories of immediate anæsthesia produced by it are but idle fables. Still, it might be administered to persons asleep without much difficulty (*Lancet*, Oct. 5, 1872, p. 514, and Oct. 12, 1872, p. 549), and this seems the only possible condition under which it could be con-

---

* Forensic Medicine and Toxicology. By W. Bathhurst Wood, M.D., F.R.C.P., and Charles Maymott Tidy, M.B., F.C.S. Lindsay & Blakiston, 1877, p. 457.

veniently used for improper purposes, unless considerable force was employed to prevent the person struggling, which under ordinary circumstances would be an almost insurmountable difficulty to its use."

The following case (reported in the *Philada. Medical Times*, December 22, 1877), which quite lately occurred in England, more completely confirms our own observations and experiments on this important subject:—

"A case of the utmost importance to the whole profession, not in Great Britain only, but everywhere, was tried before Mr. Justice Hawkins, at the assizes at Northampton, on the 9th of November. It was a charge against a surgeon's assistant of criminal assault,—of rape upon a patient when under the influence of chloroform. If there is a dastardly crime, it is to take advantage of a woman's helpless unconsciousness to violate her person. And so the magistrate thought, who sent the accused to jail on the 14th of September, declining to hear anything in his favor, and resolutely refusing to accept bail. The charge was that a married woman named Child went to the surgery of her family medical attendant to have her teeth operated upon. She had been there a day or two before, but the attempt to put her under chloroform then failed. A second attempt was rather more successful. She evidently had some peculiarities or idiosyncrasies in relation to chloroform, for he gave it for an hour and yet she was never sufficiently under its influence to admit of the operation being performed. She was accompanied by a friend,—a Miss Fellows. At the end of the hour Miss Fellows went out of the room and saw Mr. Child. In a quarter of an hour Miss Fellows returned. The prosecutor maintained that on Miss Fellows's return she was quite conscious, but unable to speak. Finding it impossible to perform the operation, the accused accompanied the prosecutrix and her friend home. So far Mrs. Child had been unable to speak, but shortly after the accused left the house she complained to her husband that he had taken advantage of the absence of Miss Fellows to assault her criminally. Next day, when the accused called, he was told about what she had said, and he replied that she was laboring under a delusion. Under cross-examination Mrs. Child said that she told the accused that if he would admit the offence and quit the town (Birmingham) she would forgive him. This the accused declined to do, denying that he had committed any offence. He was then given in custody. The prosecutrix stated that the offence was perpetrated immediately after Miss Fellows left the room; that the prisoner went upon his knees and then assaulted her. Miss Fellows stated that on her return she found Mrs. Child in precisely the same position in the chair which she occupied when she went out of the room. Such were the facts of the case. It was quite clear that there had been either an assault committed, or that the woman was under the influence of a very pronounced delusion. The whole of the accused's conduct was in favor of the latter hypothesis. But in such a matter, where no third person was present, the statement of one of the two parties concerned must be taken. When a woman whose character was apparently without blemish (for in cross-examination no attempt was made to call her reputation in question) makes a definite charge against a man of assaulting her under circumstances which permitted of such an assault, the law could only send the case to a jury. In the mean time the unfortunate surgeon's assistant was sent to prison.

When the case came to be tried, a large number of medical men of repute came forward voluntarily to aid the accused's defence, and did this quite gratuitously. The chief witness for the defence was Dr. B. W. Richardson, F.R.S., whose celebrity is world-wide. As is well known, Dr. Richardson has studied anæsthetics very carefully and for many years. He stated that there were four stages or degrees in which chloroform operated. The first stage was that in which consciousness was not lost; there was resistance and a desire for air. In the second, consciousness is lost, but the operation is impossible, the patient screaming, often without provocation. The third stage is that of complete unconsciousness, and where all rigidity is lost. This is the stage which permits of operation. In his opinion the patient was in the second stage; the third never having been reached. He stated that in his own experience he had known persons in this second stage to have delusions as to what had taken place during that time. He related a number of cases, and stated that the fact of such delusions being induced by chloroform was one of the earliest objections raised to its adoption. He related one case where the patient, a female, was being operated upon by a dentist, and alleged that the dentist criminally assaulted her. And this she persisted in, though her father, her mother, Dr. Richardson, and the dentist's assistant were all present throughout the whole time. She persisted in her conviction long after the effects of the chloroform had passed away; and Dr. Richardson said she was probably of that belief still. This evidence of Dr. Richardson's was corroborated by the experience of Dr. Hawksby, of London, and by Dr. Saundby and Mr. J. F. West, of Birmingham. The judge asked the jury if it was necessary to sum up, and they replied it was unnecessary,—they were already agreed upon a verdict of acquittal. Mr. Justice Hawkins pointed out that such a verdict would not be the slightest imputation upon the absolute sincerity of the prosecutrix, who no doubt firmly believed every word of what she had said. He then congratulated the accused upon having had an opportunity of fully vindicating himself from the charge preferred, and said that the verdict of acquittal did not mean that there was insufficient evidence, but that the accused was entirely cleared of any imputation in respect to the charge preferred against him. There could be no doubt the prosecutrix labored under a delusion. The accused was then discharged from custody, having been in prison two months for no offence. It is not merely that this unfortunate man was imprisoned for two months for an imaginary offence, but that any man who is present when a woman is being put under chloroform is liable to have the same charge brought against him, that gives this case its gravity and importance.

Such being the case, it becomes necessary that a little more should be known amidst the profession, as well as the laity, as to the occurrence of erotic sensations in woman. The subject is not a very pleasant one, but that is no reason why it should not be investigated. If it is a fact, and there is no doubt about this, that women when being put under chloroform are liable to those erotic sensations which they experience from sexual intercourse, the sooner the fact is generally known the better. It is just the mystery which surrounds such facts that permits such a monstrous hardship as that mentioned above to be a possibility at all. Of course it is obvious enough to any one that it is a delicate matter to inquire into the subjective sensations of women. But if these subjective sensations take the practical form of a charge of rape, two months in jail, and a trial by jury, they pass from the domain of sentiment and enter that of stern reality. Few, comparatively few, of the profession seem to be aware that women are subject to conditions and sensations identical with those associated with the sexual act, which arise quite subjectively and without any extrinsic stimulus. The delusion of St. Catharine that the devil visited her every night and enjoyed her person when she was asleep and could offer no resistance, is no unique experience, but one common enough to woman. Every one familiar with asylum work knows that a certain percentage of women patients have the delusion, among others, that the medical superintendent comes nightly to their bed and violates their person during sleep. Of course there is no foundation of any kind for such a delusion, except the subjective sensations of the woman herself. How strongly such a delusion, however, may be fixed in a woman's mind is evidenced by the case related by Dr. Richardson, where the woman persisted in her belief though her own father and mother as well as others were present, and where such assault was physically impossible. Such being the case, it behooves every man who is to be present with a woman when she is to be placed under chloroform to see that there is at least one other person present, and that, too, the whole time, without intermission, during which the woman is under the influence of chloroform, and that such other precautions be taken as will preclude the possibility of such a charge being raised. That Mrs. Child charged this unlucky man in good faith need not be questioned for a moment. She was far from being hostile to him, for she offered if he would avow his guilt and leave the town she would forgive him. The charge was not pressed from any rancorous spite; that is abundantly clear. But it is equally clear that something had occurred to that woman which she interpreted into the sexual act, and that this was so firmly fixed in her consciousness that it could not be dislodged. It becomes necessary then that the subjective sensations of woman should be investigated and made the subject of scientific observations, and seeing that they exist they must have a scientific value; and that no prudishness should prevent attempts being made to ascertain what the actual facts are, and what is their interpretation."

The following is the experience of Dr. N. L. Folsom, of Portsmouth, New Hampshire, in the same line:—

"In 1854, a clergyman's sister came to my office for the purpose of taking ether and having a tooth extracted, and brought her brother's wife with her. I began to administer the ether to the patient, and whilst renewing it she got away from me, and seemed alarmed and offended. I did not attempt to compel her to breathe any more ether, but urged her to take it, and so also did her brother's wife, but she would take no more. She had the impression, so her brother told me, that I attempted to violate her, and that his wife assisted me. It was a long time afterward before she would fully give up that she was mistaken in the matter."*

We are almost certain after a number of careful experiments that chloroform and ether can be administered in sleep, so as to produce the first stage of anæsthesia, and can be carried to full completion or total unconsciousness. Still this is rare without disturbing the patient's stomach, causing nausea, or irritation of the lungs, with risk of sudden death, by its dense vapor, and thus rousing him or her to consciousness, or a condition in which the patient can resist its influence, if the party is willing to make the effort. Another important point is that loud talking or handling, even in some cases the slightest touch or pain in any way, will cause the patient to start, and rouse him to resist. In the case of ether the patient can almost always see indistinctly, and in some instances is able to talk during the anæsthetic state.

Dr. R. M. Denig,† of Columbus, Ohio, in an article on

---

* Med. Surg. Reporter, January 12, 1877.
† Ohio Medical Recorder, January, 1877.

the Medico-legal Relations of Chloroform, propounds the following queries:—

"1. Can they be administered successfully to persons during natural sleep without awakening them?

2. Can they be forcibly administered for criminal purposes in opposition to the will of the person to whom they are given?

3. Can a person give competent testimony as to what occurred during the anæsthetic state?"

His general conclusions are, that it cannot be used successfully for felonious purposes, and that a person in the anæsthetic state is not a competent witness. He gives the following example:—

"Most of you are cognizant of a transaction which took place in our city a few years since, and which for a time produced the wildest consternation. Two employés in the service of an express company were said to have been chloroformed during sleep, the keys to the safe abstracted from their pockets, and the safes robbed of their valuable contents. A sponge, which bore the decaying fumes of chloroform, was found near the head of one of the messengers, etc. The whole thing was well gotten up, and was calculated to deceive even the most incredulous, and excite a sympathy in behalf of persons who had not only been robbed but nearly strangled. In less than a week, however, the possession of large sums of money led to the arrest of the supposed chloroformed individuals, and to their incarceration in the Ohio State prison."

Chloroform; its Action as a Poison.

Chloroform is not a very *active poison*. In a case quoted by Taylor,* an individual swallowed four ounces. He was able to walk a considerable distance after taking this large dose, but subsequently fell into a state of coma; the pupils were dilated, the breathing was stertorous, the skin cold, pulse imperceptible, and there were general convulsions. He recovered in five days. (*Med. Gaz.*, vol. 47, p. 675.) A second case reported swallowed

* On Poisons, Philadelphia, 1875, p. 618.

nearly two ounces, and recovered ; and a third swallowed two ounces, but he died in six hours afterwards. In this case the pupils were fully dilated, the breathing was stertorous, and the skin covered with a cold perspiration. On inspection, the lungs were found much engorged with blood, and there were some apoplectic effusions in these organs. The stomach was slightly inflamed in patches, and the mucous membrane was softened. (*Am. Journ. Med. Sci.*, October, 1866, p. 571.) A physician, æt. 57, swallowed three ounces of chloroform. He immediately began to stagger, as if intoxicated. He vomited, and sunk into a deep stupor, and was in a state of complete anæsthesia. His skin was pale and tolerably warm ; the muscles were relaxed, the breathing short, and the action of the heart weak and intermittent. In about fourteen hours sensibility returned. Acute gastritis ensued, with rapid collapse, and proved fatal in twenty-nine hours from the time the chloroform was taken. (*Am. Journ. Med. Sci.*, January, 1870, p. 276.)

Treatment.—In poisoning from *liquid* chloroform, the stomach pump and emetic should be resorted to. If evidence of suspension of the action of the heart (syncope) exists, there should be free exposure of the face to a current of air, compression of the chest, and artificial respiration, with warm applications, to the chest with active friction and stimuli externally and by the rectum. The poles of a galvanic battery applied to the chest and side of the neck with sponges dipped in hot water should be used. Spirit of ammonia has been found useful when injected hypodermically, and strychnia in the same way, to act upon the respiration. This must be given in minute doses, and great care must be given to the gastritis, and disturbance of the liver, which are apt to follow in the convalescence of the patient.

Ethers ; in their Medico-Legal Relations.

Ethers as a class are poisons, and, if taken into the stomach in very large quantities, will produce death. Still they can be employed for a long period without dangerous action on the heart and respiration. The habitual use of ether ruins the digestion, and causes chronic disturbance of the nervous system (see cases, subsequently reported), and this has been confirmed by A. Martin Ewald, of Berlin.

In dogs, whose brains are exposed, the vigorous inhalation of ether soon renders that organ completely insensible to the electrical current. (Hitzig.)

After introducing ether into a dog's stomach, Claude Bernard observed an immediate secretion of a large quantity of pancreatic juice. There was vascular congestion of the intestine, and its secretions became more abundant, while absorption was accelerated. The chyle vessels were strongly injected, which must be explained by the abundance of pancreatic juice present in the bowel (Binz), the fine subdivision of the fat thus produced, and the consequently increased facility with which it could be absorbed.

If the blood be examined (Binz) after twenty drops of ether have been taken, the colorless corpuscles in it are found to be twice as numerous as usual. It is probable that here also ether has a direct action on the abdominal glands, and especially the spleen.

Ether Intoxication.

"A few years ago there was published in the *Reporter** the 'confessions of an ether inhaler,' a member of our own profession, for whom it subsequently became our sad duty to sign a certificate of insanity.

We are reminded of this by a paper in the London *Medical Record*, by Dr. Ewald, of Berlin, on a somewhat similar case. It is that of a man aged thirty-two, who was lately admitted into the Charité Hospital, under Professor Frerichs, suffering from general debility and trembling of the muscles. On inquiry, it was found that he was notorious in Berlin for intoxicating himself with ether, his abuse of which had reduced him to his present miserable condition. He was originally temperate, and had been a university student, passing all his examinations with credit; he was, however, of a mysti-

* Med. & Surg. Reporter.

cal turn of mind. Unfortunately, a little more than nine years ago, there fell into his hands a medico-popular treatise, in which the use and effects of ether, used medicinally, were described, and a glowing account was given of its effect in quickening the creative power of the mind. He procured about two or two and a half ounces of sulphuric ether, and inhaled it from a handkerchief; the result being to produce insensibility for about a quarter of an hour, during which time he imagined that he lived for an indefinite time, and traveled over whole worlds. This condition, however, he was not again able to induce in so high a degree. Becoming gradually more and more addicted to his habit, he no longer confined himself to indulging himself in his own room, but, with his etherized handkerchief before his face, he wandered through the streets, purchasing small quantities of ether at the druggists' shops, until at last he became so great a nuisance to them that many of them closed their doors against him. He was also turned out of his lodgings, on account of the annoyance produced by the smell of his breath, and became a houseless wanderer, reduced in means and in health. In the hospital there was no indication that his mind was affected; his memory was not impaired; his style of speaking was fluent. On one occasion an attempt was made to produce complete anæsthesia. For this purpose more than seven ounces were required; the ether being given by an inhaler, and loss being prevented by closing in the apparatus with cotton-wool. No sooner, however, was the inhalation stopped, than the state of insensibility passed off. He was then allowed to take the ether in his own way, by inhaling it from a handkerchief. Given in this way, it produced a stage of excitement, during which he danced about the room, talked nonsense, and appeared much pleased, but there was no true narcotism. It was not thought justifiable to subject him to other experiments with ether, as it was desirable to break through his habit. It is interesting, that his susceptibility to the action of cannabis indica was not impaired. This drug was given as a substitute for ether, and on the first occasion, too large a dose having been given, the result was the production of phantasms, such as are induced by the smoking of hasheesh."

The late Dr. Morgan, of Dublin, states that ether is employed in certain portions of Ireland as a substitute for whiskey.

A case has come under the writer's notice in which a patient began the use of sulphuric ether in teaspoonful doses, as a nervine ordered by a physician, and ultimately increased the dose to one pint per day. When informed of its injurious character, she had lost her appetite, and suffered gastric disturbance; she gradually diminished the quantity, and was able to give it up after a month or two. The only effect it had upon her was to give her apparent strength to go on with her teaching of music. Large quantities of ether have been taken internally, and, so far as we have been able to learn, no death has yet occurred from its use in this way.

APPENDIX.

THE DISCOVERY OF THE ART OF ARTIFICIAL ANÆSTHESIA.

In point of time, December 11, 1844, Wells, a dentist of Hartford, Connecticut, made the first successful application of nitrous oxide gas to relieve the pain of the extraction of a tooth, although the fact was known and published long before by Sir H. Davy, who proved in his own person that the inhalation of the gas would relieve intense pain in the teeth. Dr. Jackson, of Boston, afterwards suggested to Dr. Morton, a dentist, the application of sulphuric ether, which had also been known and employed for amusement in the medical lecture rooms. Dr. Morton, after numerous and careful trials on his own person and others, succeeded (September, 1846*) in proving this agent, if carried to a certain stage, a true anæsthetic to abolish sensation in long and painful operations. Dr. Jackson, who gave a hint to the discoverer, was not entitled to the credit he received from the French and other governments, but only he, who by labor, great application, and perseverance, was successful at last in proving to the world that sulphuric ether was a true, potent, and pure anæsthetic, safe and applicable in almost every instance. Dr. Morton was as much the inventor of modern anæsthesia as Jenner was of vaccination, or Morse of the electro-magnetic telegraph. Morton's great mistake was in procuring a patent. Dr. Long, of Georgia, has put forth a claim which has been stated very fully by Dr. Marion Sims, of New York. It is based on the personal evidence of friends and neighbors, but was never published to the world until December, 1849.

In 1847, Prof. Simpson discovered chloroform to be a good substitute for sulphuric ether, by experimenting on himself and friends. His first public test was by rendering insensible a patient of Dr. Miller.

---

* For a full account of this discovery see History of the Discovery of Modern Anæsthesia, by Prof. H. G. Bigelow, in "A Century of American Medicine:" H. C. Lea: Published, 1876. Also, Discovery of Anæsthesia, by Dr. J. M. Sims, Virginia Med. Mon., May, 1877. History of Modern Anæsthetics, by Sir James Simpson, of Edinburgh: James Campbell & Co., Boston, Mass.

INDEX.

AFTER-TREATMENT of anæsthetized patients, 20
Alcohol as an anæsthetic, 17
  as a local anæsthetic, 182
  methylic, 18
Amyl, nitrite of, 92
  to antidote ether and chloroform, 94
Amylene, 75
Anæsthesia, artificial, discovery of, 208
  from rapid breathing, 171
  local, 172
  of the head (butylchloral), 195
Anæsthetic, chloral as an, 126
  mixtures, 18
Anæsthetics, action of, on the blood, 143
  in labor, 85
  list of, 16
  medico-legal aspect of, 195
  mode of action of, 152
  of the ancients, 13
Asphyxia, 40
  from nitrous oxide gas, 137

BICHLORIDE of methylene, 73
  deaths from, 74
Blood, action of anæsthetics upon, 143
Brandy prior to the anæsthetic, 17
Bromide of ethyl, 76
Bromoform, 79
Butylchloral, 195

CARBOLIC acid as a local anæsthetic, 183
Chloral hydrate, 112
  as an anæsthetic, 126
  hypodermically, 127

Chloral hydrate—
  internal use of, 194
  in tetanus, 123
  poisoning by, 194
Chloroform, administration of, 83
  and morphia, 96
  antidote for, 92
  bibliography of, 155
  causes of fatality of, 105
  criminal use of, 197
  dangers of, 84
  in renal disease, 110
  deaths from, 67, 84, 97
  during labor, 86
  ether, and alcohol (mixture of), 18
  externally, use of, 185
  general conclusions concerning, 106
  in ovariotomy, 65
  internally, use of, 184
  mixed with the spirit of wine, 66
  narcosis, method of resuscitation (Nélaton), 87
  physiological action of, 92
  poisonous action of, 203
  preparations of, 187
  to antidote strychnia, 185
  treatment of poisoning by, 204
  versus ether, 111
  versus nitrite of amyl, 94
Croton chloral, 195

ETHER, administration of, 21
  alleged dangers of use of, 61
  bibliography of, 155
  comparative merits of chloroform and, 111
  danger from use of, 40
  deaths from use of, 41

Ether—
 experiments with, 32
 fainting, syncope, etc., from, 41
 favorable conclusions concerning, 62
 in bronchitis, 44
 internally, use of, 191
 intoxication, 206
 medico-legal consideration of, 204
 mixed with chloroform, 65
 physiological action of, 22
 precautions in use of, 22
 preparations of, 192
 pulse writing, after inhalation of, 45
 sulphuric, 40
 syncope after use of, 51
  following use of, case, 47
 test for full anæsthesia from, 22
 versus chloroform, 44
 vomiting prevented by bromide of potassium, 22
 warning symptoms of, 40
Eucalyptus extract, for local anæsthesia, 182

HYDROBROMIC ether, 76
 action on the pulse, 78
 as an anæsthetic, 78

ICE and salt, for local anæsthesia, 183
Inhaler, Allis' chloroform, 83
 ether, 27
 Angrove's ether, 36
 Carter's ether, 24
 Cheatham's ether, 25
 Clover's (ether and nitrous oxide gas), 161
 Codman & Shurtleff's (ether and nitrous oxide gas), 167
 Hawksley's ether, 24
 Lente's ether, 26
 Morgan's ether, 34
 Richardson's ether (B. W., of Dublin). 35

LOCAL anæsthesia, 172

MANDRAGORA wine, 13
 Methylene, bichloride of, 73
Methylic alcohol, 18
 administration of, 19
 ether, 72
Mixed narcosis, 96
Mixtures, chloroform and alcohol, 18
 and ether, 18
  (Atlee's), 65
Morphia as a local anæsthetic, 183
Mortality statistics of ether, 41

NITRITE of amyl, 92
 to antidote chloroform or ether, 94
Nitrous oxide gas, 129
 and ether, 161
 bibliography of, 155
 constriction of the glottis, 137
 deaths from, 156
 liquefied, 134
 manufacture of, 130
 physiological action of, 139
 post-mortem appearances following death from, 159

OVARIOTOMY, bichloride of methylene in, 75
 chloroform and ether in, 65
Oxide of ethyl, 21

RENAL disease, dangerous to administer chloroform, 110
Rhigolène, 173

STATISTICS of mortality from chloroform, 109
 from ether, 41
Strychnia, to antidote chloral, 127
Symptoms, warning, from ether, 51
Syncope from ether, 47
 from nitrous oxide, 137
 from chloroform, 101

TABLE of anæsthetics (Richardson), 41
Tetanus, chloral hydrate hypodermically for, 195

THE END.

By the same Author.

A CLINICAL MANUAL

OF

DISEASES OF THE EAR.

INCLUDING THE

Anatomy, Physiology, Pathology, and Treatment.

By LAURENCE TURNBULL, M.D.,

Aural Surgeon Jefferson Medical College Hospital; Physician to the Department of the Eye and Ear, Howard Hospital, Philadelphia.

8vo. 500 pages. 106 Illustrations. Full Index, etc. Price $5.

TESTIMONIALS.

From D. HAYES AGNEW, Professor of Surgery, Univ. of Pennsylvania.

Your work on Diseases of the Ear will, in my judgment, not suffer in comparison with any book published on this subject.

From Dr. JOHN F. MEIGS, the able Author of the best work on Diseases of Children in the English language.

Now that I have looked over your work with some care, I am ready, not only to thank you, but to thank you very much, for so good an account of the present knowledge possessed by our profession in regard to these diseases, and also for your own contributions in the treatment of these troublesome affections.

From Professor S. D. GROSS, the Nestor of American Surgery.

I think your book will add another laurel to the triumphs of American medical literature.

From Dr. H. KNAPP, of New York, a distinguished teacher and authority in Ophthalmology and Otology in the United States.

Dr. Turnbull's work is an exhaustive compilation of everything that is practically worth knowing on the subject; while, at the same time, the author's own experience and judgment, everywhere deliberately expressed, serves as a guide in matters which are still *sub judice*.

From the "American Journal of the Medical Sciences."

The plan of the work is comprehensive, and, besides the anatomy and pathology of the ear found in all aural text-books, includes chapters on the "Physiology of Hearing," "Acoustics," and "Deaf-Mutism." The last gives an interesting account of the different systems of teaching deaf-mutes, and the principal institutions devoted to that object. . . . . The book gives evidence of research; its bibliography is copious, and it presents a full summary of the subject of which it treats. . . . . Indeed, it might almost be called an aural encyclopædia.

From the "Leavenworth Medical Herald."

This book is unquestionably a work of the highest excellence, rich in information, and, perhaps, fuller in details than any text-book on the subject with which we are acquainted. The author has treated the subject of the ear with judgment and ability.

From the "Monatsschrift für Ohrenheilkunde, Berlin."

After perusal, the purpose of the author is to impart to his countrymen, who have not paid much attention to "Otology," the results of the studies of other specialists, and he has furnished them an ample exposition of the present state of this branch of medicine. From this point of view, Turnbull's handbook deserves our praise. Our author gives ample quotations from the works of others, but does not, however, withhold his own judgment and experience, which is interesting. Dr. Turnbull proves himself thoroughly acquainted with the literature of the subject, and employs it very properly.

From the "Boston Medical and Surgical Journal."

Sound, clear, and eminently practical in all its parts.

From the "Dublin Journal of Medical Science."

It is worthy of note that the two best works on Otology of the present day—viz., Turnbull's and Roosa's—both emanate from the American press.

From the "Detroit Review of Medicine."

A book of great value to all, both specialist and general practitioner.

From the "Atlanta Medical and Surgical Journal."

Dr. Turnbull's book will be of great service to all who purpose to keep pace with the progress in this department of our profession. Every physician should have it.

From the "Transactions of the American Otological Society."

In connection with the tables of classification, a schedule of the method of investigation in various diseases of the ear is given, which is of decided practical value to the student. . . . There is, in addition, a bibliographical table, including 440 works relating to Otology, and a full index.

From the "St. Louis Medical and Surgical Journal."

On the whole, the work is a valuable one, and such as we can recommend.

From the "Cincinnati Lancet and Observer."

Take it altogether, we think our readers cannot do better than to place a copy of "Turnbull's Manual of the Diseases of the Ear" in their library for reference.

From the "Canada Lancet."

The work deserves well of the profession, and will, no doubt, sooner or later, find a place in every reading man's library.

From the "Philadelphia Medical and Surgical Reporter."

The book, as a whole, is the very best work on aural complaints, for the general practitioner, with which we are acquainted.

For sale by Booksellers generally, or will be sent by mail, postage paid, on receipt of the price.

J. B. LIPPINCOTT & CO., Publishers,
PHILADELPHIA.

www.ingramcontent.com/pod-product-compliance
Lightning Source LLC
Chambersburg PA
CBHW020859230426
43666CB00008B/1247